Red Bike Boys

A History of Leicester's

Telegram Service

1870 – 1982

Andy Marlow & Michael Petty

Red Bike Boys

A History of Leicester's

Telegram Service

1870 – 1982

Andy Marlow & Michael Petty

Red Bike Boys

A History of Leicester's

Telegram Service

1870 – 1982

Andy Marlow & Michael Petty

RED BIKE BOYS

A HISTORY OF LEICESTER'S

TELEGRAM SERVICE

1870 – 1982

ANDY MARLOW & MICHAEL PETTY

Published by Blackwells Court Leicester

© 2003   Andy Marlow & Michael Petty
A catalogue record for this book is available from the British Library.

ISBN : 095453090X

CONDITIONS OF SALE

All rights reserved. No part of this publication may be reproduced, stored in a retrieval system, or transmitted, in any form or by any means, electronic, mechanical, photocopying, recording or otherwise, without the prior permission of the publishers.

This book is sold subject to the condition that it shall not, by way of trade or otherwise, be lent, re-sold, hired out or otherwise circulated without the publisher's prior consent in any form of binding or cover other than that in which it is published and without a similar condition including this condition being imposed on the subsequent purchaser.

Printed and bound in Great Britain by
Nation Printing Skills Centre
Grafton Place St Johns Street Leicester LE1 3WL
The NPSC is a business division of Leicester College

FRONT COVER PHOTOGRAPH
Louis George Lightfoot (Joe) 1883

CONTENTS
PAGE

ACKNOWLEDGEMENTS		vii
INTRODUCTION		1
CHAPTER 1	TELEGRAPHS THE EARLY YEARS	3
CHAPTER 2	THE NEW CENTURY	19
CHAPTER 3	THE GREAT WAR	28
	WW1 ROLL OF HONOUR	31
CHAPTER 4	THE ROARING 20's	35
CHAPTER 5	THE GREAT DEPRESSION	42
CHAPTER 6	1940's THE WAR YEARS	58
	WWII ROLL OF HONOUR	70
CHAPTER 7	POST WAR	72
CHAPTER 8	1950's THE CITY GROWS	81
CHAPTER 9	WEATHERING THE LATE 50's	110
CHAPTER 10	SWINGING 60's	140
CHAPTER 11	1970's ON THE MOVE	152
CHAPTER 12	THE FINAL CURTAIN	174
POSTSCRIPT		177
GLOSSARY		179
THE TELEGRAPH DEPARTMENT		180
SPECIAL FEATURES		189
APPENDICES		201

ACKNOWLEDGEMENTS

In the five years it has taken to produce this history of the Telegram Service in Leicester many people have taken the time and trouble to provide us with help, personal recollections and in some cases items from family albums and memorabilia. To name them all from ex-colleagues to the Town Hall would take up another book. A special thank you is due to the staff at the Leicestershire Records Office including two with a connection to the Royal Mail who provided extra thinking power when ours was running low, also the Editor of the Leicester Mercury for allowing us to use items from the now long gone Leicester Evening Mail and the Leicester Mercury. The help given by Royal Mail staff in Leicester and at the Postal Records Office in London was invaluable. Finally the help given by Michael's wife Anne in providing many cups of coffee every week for us both and still finding the time to proof read and correct the text was dedication beyond the call of duty!

PHOTOGRAPH ACKNOWLEGEMENTS

FRONT COVER	Douglas Preston (Deceased)
SPECIAL PAGE 1 & PHOTO 32	Colin Burbage
SPECIAL PAGE 2	Christine Walker (Hinde)
SPECIAL PAGE 3	Lord Mayor's Secretary
SPECIAL PAGE 4 & PHOTO 4	Leicester Evening Mail
SPECIAL PAGE 5	Oadby & Wigston Mail
SPECIAL PAGE 6	Paul Bond
PHOTO 1 & 10	Stanley Garratt
PHOTO 2	George Goddard
PHOTO 3	Mary Welbourne (Marshall)
PHOTO 5 & 62	Sheila Kukk (Richardson)
PHOTO 6, 7 & 9	Claire Avery (Wakefield)
PHOTO 8	Pauline Packwood (Ball)
PHOTO 11	Cecil Greenwood
PHOTO 12	Christine Smalley
PHOTO 13	Terry Eagle
PHOTO 14, 33, 38 & 39	*John* Tilley
PHOTO 15	Christine Stephenson (McNally)
PHOTO 16, 42, 59, 60, 61, 64, 65, 66 & 67	Leicester Mercury
PHOTO 17 & 22	Fred Draycott
PHOTO 18	Cedric Greenwood
PHOTO 19	*Henry* Fendell
PHOTO 20	Stan Jones
PHOTO 21	*Lew* Stone
PHOTO 23	Betty Flavill
PHOTO 24 & 26	Margaret Bryan (Broughton)
PHOTO 25	Leicestershire Record Office
PHOTO 27	*Joe* Catlin
PHOTO 28	Ken Hunt
PHOTO 29	Nigel Calver
PHOTO 30	Post Office Archives

PHOTO 31	*Mick* Sylvester
PHOTO 34	*Mick* Swinfield
PHOTO 35 & 36	*Tom* Tester
PHOTO 37, 40, 41 & 63	Brian Monk (Deceased)
PHOTO 43	Beryl Stephens
PHOTO 44 & 45	*Nev* Goodman
PHOTO 46, 47, 48, 49, 50 & 51	*Mick* Petty
PHOTO 5 2	*Bill* Liquorish
PHOTO 53, 54, 55 & 56	Phil Hendy
PHOTO 57 & 58	*John* Simpson

A name given in italics is the name the person is known as.

INTRODUCTION

'Red Bike Boys' is the story of the Inland Telegraph Service in Leicester. This is told using information gleaned from many sources, Post Office records in Leicester and London, The Leicestershire Records Office and from 'The Lads' themselves. The name stems from the colour of the cycles, motor cycles and mopeds used by the boys over the years. One term used by the boys to other Post Office workers was "Have you got Red Oil in your veins?" This sorted out the ex-messengers from the others, or to put it another way volunteers (the lads) from conscripts (the rest!)
The 'Red Oil' comes from way back when cycle lamps were lit by oil.

In the personal recollections some of the names have been omitted for various reasons, many of the 'old boys'
reading this will have heard those immortal words "You are not too big (or old) to get a smack!"

This is the history of the Telegraph Service in the Leicester area. If we have left out any important details or personnel it is due to the scarcity of information in some of the periods from 1864 until 1982.
In the early years records were compiled with full forenames but after the First World War only initials were used. Records for the latter part of the 1900's do not show Telegraph Messenger badge numbers, as many of the boys just stayed for a few weeks and only their names were listed. Record keeping following the Great War was not to the same standard as before, handwriting had changed considerably, gone was the clear, concise copperplate in ledgers and in it's place was a style which has often been hard to decipher.

Some of the tales related cover more than one angle on the same theme, we have not tried to put them together as one version because it would be unfair to those who were kind enough to spend the time delving into their memories of years ago. A large "Thank You" is owed to them all.

The cartoons are the work of Brian 'Dondi' Monk. Brian drew them for us a week before he died. He will be remembered as one of life's natural comics. We suppose Brian will still be trying to work the angles in that large delivery office in the sky!

Amounts shown are in £ s d throughout the book as being more historically appealing, for readers who wish to compare prices with the decimal equivalent, a conversion chart is provided on page 213 in the appendices.

During the compilation of this book we were able to help with information about a Boy Messenger from 1883 resulting in his descendants finding a whole new branch of their family in the South East of England. The Grandson kindly lent us the photograph of his Grandfather, which appears on the cover of this book.

We hope you enjoy reading this book and it will shed a little light on a part of everyday life, gone forever.

Andy Marlow & Michael Petty
May 2002

CHAPTER 1

TELEGRAPHS - THE EARLY YEARS

The Telegraph was invented by Samuel Findley Breese Morse (1791 - 1872) in 1832 on a voyage from France to the U.S.A. By 1835 he had his first working model and on the 4th May 1844 he sent the first test message from Washington to Baltimore (a distance of 50 Miles.)

In Great Britain William Cooke and Professor Charles Wheatstone invented a train control system using five wires connected to five needles, which was installed between London and West Drayton (18½ miles) in May 1843. This was the world's first public telegraph line and was used in 1845 to apprehend a murder suspect. John Tawell was spotted boarding a train at Slough but it was too late to stop him, the news was telegraphed ahead to London and he was arrested near to Paddington Station. He was later tried, convicted and hanged.

The first commercial telegraph in Great Britain came into existence when the Electric Telegraph Company was formed by an Act of Parliament in June 1846. It held the monopoly of telegraphy until 1850 when another Act of Parliament opened the way for competition from other companies such as; the Magnetic Telegraph Company and the British and Irish Magnetic Telegraph Company. More private telegraph companies continued to open throughout the 1850's and 1860's.

By March 1864 the Electric and International Telegraph Company had opened offices at 1, Millstone Lane and at the Campbell Street Station of the Midland Railway Company, also in that year a rival company The United Kingdom Electric Telegraph Company opened an office at 2, Hotel Street, Leicester.

In the early days all telegrams were written out by hand, which must have been quite a task given the number of telegrams sent annually. Nationally in 1869 6,830,872 telegrams were sent from 2,932 offices by clerks operating 4,045 machines. Each machine was capable of transmitting seventy words per minute, the average cost of a telegram was 2/2d.

In 1869 an Act of Parliament was passed to enable the General Post Office (G.P.O.) to take over all the private Telegraph Companies and thus create a monopoly for itself.

LEICESTER G.P.O. TELEGRAPHS

When the G.P.O. Leicester Telegraph Department began on 5th February 1870 it's first officers in charge were Mr. Thomas C. Morris (Superintendent) and Joseph Goddard (Clerk,) both men had previously seen service with private companies. By 1872 boys were employed either as Minimum Wage Messengers on 5/- per week or as Fixed Docket Messengers paid at a rate of 8d per dozen telegrams.

In 1874 the first horse drawn tram service started in Leicester and it appears that messengers were soon permitted to use the tramcars for their journeys. In those days the Borough of Leicester boundaries did not extend much further than those of the middle ages. To the south the Toll Bar (Victoria Park) the north, Belgrave Gate (Great Northern Station) the west, Braunstone Gate - Narborough Road and to the east, the Toll Bar (Pembroke Street.)

The population of Leicester in 1871 was 95,220 (this was up 27,000 from the 1861 figure) living in 20,553 dwellings.

Very little is known about individual Telegraph Messengers during the first decade of the Telegraph Service 1870-1880 it seems very few of them remained to take up adult duties with the Post Office although one or two attained senior positions in the service.

The first Telegraph revision took place in 1875, the number of boys employed at this time was sixteen, there were also sixteen Telegraphists.

Nationally, when telegraph boys were not on delivery they spent their time in rest rooms. The controllers in London were concerned that the boys were often unruly and could get into trouble, consequently Inspectors were introduced to control discipline and one was appointed in Leicester about 1875. Tasks to keep the boys occupied were started, cutting string into lengths, trimming lead seals, tearing up waste paper, tidying up the office and addressograph work soon kept them all busy.

The Telegraph Office was situated in the left hand corridor on the ground floor of the Granby Street building and it was open twenty four hours a day Monday to Saturday, On Sundays, Good Friday and Christmas Day the office was open from 7.00 am to 10.00 am and 7.00 p.m. to 9.00 p.m. Between 9.00 p.m. and 7.00 am messages could be given in at the side door. The minimum charge was 1/- for twenty words plus a charge of 3d for each additional five words, this was to anywhere in the country. The addresses of the sender and recipient were not charged for. The fee paid covered delivery by a messenger on foot up to one mile from the telegraph receiving office. Outside this limit a further charge was made at 3d per mile on foot, if it was quite a distance from the office and a cab, fly (both horse drawn vehicles) or horse express was necessary then the charge was 1/- per mile. If the sender was not prepared to pay the extra fee, then they could have the telegram delivered the following day by the foot delivery postman for no extra charge. A prepaid reply service was available, the sender could pay the fee at the time of sending the original telegram.

In 1877 the minimum age for candidates was raised from thirteen to fourteen, why the change was made has not been recorded but it was rescinded in 1890. Recruits also had to appear before a magistrate to swear an oath before they could start working for the General Post Office, this was before the Official Secrets Act came into being. The minimum height was four feet eight inches in boots, that lasted until 1911 when the requirement was the same, but without boots. All recruits were issued with a rule book which they had to keep in their delivery pouch. This had to be produced when demanded by a senior officer. Some of the rules were straight forward, to be clean and tidy with uniform kept clean, hair to be brushed and kept short, curls at the back and fringes at the front were not allowed. Other rules covered things not to be done when on duty and in uniform, smoking, gambling, entering public houses unless delivering a telegram and for small active boys the strict rule that they usually tried to ignore, sliding down hand rails of staircases and practical joking. Boys were required to salute the Postmaster and other supervising officers. The working day was ten hours, sixty hours per week until it was changed in 1891 to fifty four hours per week.

During 1883 telegram irregularities were reported and the Superintendent was dismissed, the Clerk was reduced to a Sorting Clerk and Telegraphist (S.C.&T,) but after a few weeks he was re-instated to his former position. The whole staff were given a General Caution by order of the Surveyor of The Post Office. Possibly as a result of these happenings, Ralph Burdett a former soldier and Town Postman since 1875 was appointed Assistant Inspector of Telegraph Messengers in 1883. It seems that all the early supervisors were former military men who could, no doubt instil some discipline into the young boys under their control. The Inspector of Telegraph Messengers at this time was a Mr. Paulson. Mr. James Gibbins arrived from Sheffield to replace the Superintendent dismissed by the Surveyor he was paid a salary of £160 per annum. His second in charge the Telegraph Clerk, was paid £130 per annum and a 1st Class Telegraphist received 40s per week. At the lower end of the scale a Telegraph Messenger on the minimum wage was paid 5/- per week. In 1880 an additional Telegraph Office opened at the Corn Exchange in the Market Place followed in 1881 by one at the Cattle Market on Aylestone Road and by 1884 one was also opened at the Midland railway station in Campbell Street, which led to the number of Indoor Messengers being increased.

THE 1886 SPLIT AND GROWTH

During 1886 several changes took place. The opening hours on Sundays and public holidays were extended, the evenings had an extra five hours added, the Telegraph Counter was open from 5.00 p.m. until midnight. The cost of sending a telegram was reduced to, 6d for the first twelve words, additional words were charged at ½d. The new charges were not as generous as they appeared. The names and addresses of the sender and recipient were now subject to a charge. If the recipient was further than one mile from the telegraph office an extra charge of 6d per mile was added, if a mounted messenger was used then this fee increased to 1/-. Postal and Telegraph forces separated and did not re-unite until 1946. The Sorting Clerk and Telegraphist forces merged to form a new grade S.C.&T. (Sorting Clerk & Telegraphist.) In the summer months of 1886 eight extra Messengers were employed.

In 1887 a new General Post Office was built further along Granby Street with the telegraph entrance situated in Bishop

Street. To convey telegrams and telegram forms a pneumatic tube was installed between the Telegraph Instrument Room on the top floor and the counter on the ground floor. With all the extra machinery being introduced a Telegraph Engineer was employed to maintain it.

The 1887 building was enlarged several times until replaced by new premises further along Bishop Street. The new office opened for business in 1935.

The Inspector of Telegraph Messengers was reported to have absconded in 1887 and the position declared vacant. In the same year there was a transfer of Superintendents, Mr.J. Gibbins returned to Sheffield and Mr. James Dayson came to Leicester in exchange. During 1888 the vacant post of Inspector of Telegraph Messengers was filled by Mr. William Neale who was only twenty-two years of age making him the youngest Inspector in the history of the Leicester Post Office. Whether the boys took advantage of Mr. Neale's relative youth is not clear, but in 1889 he was admonished by the Surveyor for not reporting the theft of several capes in his care, for which a messenger was dismissed.

In 1890 the telegraph messenger force was again increased when the starting age returned to thirteen. Recruiting was a problem as the official medical, which had replaced the private medical certificate was very strict.

By August 1891 an un-established Postman was recruited as an Adult Night Messenger, he delivered telegrams which were received between 9.00 p.m. and 6.00 a.m. as boys under sixteen were not allowed to work those hours. He also had to sweep the Instrument Room floor during his shift.

In 1891 a new post of Assistant Superintendent (T) was created to make a stepping stone from Overseer (controlling Clerk) to Superintendent. Mr J. Goddard was promoted to this position and was assisted by three Clerks, Mr J. Frisby, Mr C. Lucas and Mr R.H. Lippitt.

TELEPHONE SERVICE

By the 1890's the fledgling telephone services were still out of reach for most people because they were very expensive to install. Leicester's own Central Exchange at the Head Post Office had only eleven subscribers at that time. As early as 1891 wooden telephone boxes were installed inside some Town Sub Post Offices (T.S.O.s) these were referred to as call offices. Sub Postmasters were paid £2 per annum to look after them. The Post Office was trying to promote this new service by installing those boxes. Belgrave office had a box installed by 10/1/1891 West Bridge from 12/1/1891 Belgrave Gate followed on 25/10/1893 Humberstone Road from 8/11/1893 Highcross Street 15/11/1893 and finally Welford Road on 24/8/1900. Telegrams were still the main way of getting urgent messages through.

MILITARY DRILL

In November 1891 the G.P.O. introduced military based drill all over the United Kingdom. It was thought to be the best way to introduce discipline and pride in the uniform. Drill halls or parade grounds were hired in Leicester boys had two one-hour sessions per week before their duty. Marching and saluting were taught, an odd aspect was gloves had to be left off during drill. At first the boys performed drill using sticks, later the War Office lent the G.P.O. carbines for the boys to use.
They were marched from Granby Street Office to the Drill Hall in the Corn Exchange and back at each session. At a later date the Drill Hall in the Magazine was used instead.

1891 BOYS AND THE ARMY

Two schemes started in 1891. Due to limited vacancies for Postmen only one fifth of the Boy Messengers at eighteen and a half could progress to that position. The remaining four fifths were encouraged to join the Army for five years, which was the only way the boys could eventually secure a position as a Postman. This time although counting as Post Office service, was not pensionable. Those who did not join up had to leave. The scheme only lasted until 1893 because of parental opposition. The 'Soldiers Scheme' found employment in the Post Office for ex-soldiers as it was thought they were used to discipline and would make good Postmen.

1892 REVISION & T.S.Os

The Telegraph Revision in 1892 gave the following staff levels and pay rates as follows; Mr. J.M. Dayson Superintendent £190 per annum, Mr. J. Goddard Assistant Superintendent £160 per annum, Mr. T.W. Lapham Engineer pay rate unknown.
3 Clerks £130 per annum,
11 Telegraphists 1st Class (M) 40/- per week,
29 Telegraphists 2nd Class (M) 12/- per week,
2 Telegraphists 1st Class (F) 28/- per week,
10 Telegraphists 2nd Class (F) 10/- per week

In addition to these were Mr. W. Neale Inspector of Telegraph Messengers and 48 Telegraph Messengers, 107 in total adding up to a large department.

1892 TELEGRAPHS & THE T.S.Os

In 1892 several 'Single Needle' offices (the morse type of system) were established. Each office had a rate of pay linked to the level of traffic generated and claims were either met monthly or quarterly. The reason for the difference is not recorded, nor can it be understood by looking at the staff or generated. Welford Road was listed from 18/5/1892 at 1d per message with minimum pay set at 2/6d per week until 1/10/1893 when the minimum pay was dropped. Charnwood Street Office opened on 5/10/1892 and a minimum of 7/6d per week was paid for delivery of telegrams, this office also covered Billesdon. Clarendon Park Office opened on 5/10/1892 also on 7/6d per week minimum for delivery the rate was 1d per message within the FREE delivery limit of one mile from a telegraph receiving office. Outside this area a system of payment was linked to the distance travelled. For the sender a similar system operated in that the first mile was FREE, then the greater the delivery distance, the more a telegram cost. If transport was necessary then further cost was added, this might have been the hire of a horse, which was shown on some of the published rate tables. The delivery rates payable to the T.S.O's are shown below.

DISTANCE ALLOWANCES

1d up to 1 mile.
2d up to 1¼ miles.
4d up to 1½ miles.
6d up to 2 miles.
9d up to 3 miles.

Aylestone Park opened after 1892 for telegram delivery at 1d per message in the FREE area and 6d per mile outside the FREE area. This office also delivered to the new Cattle market on Aylestone Road and to Wigston. The minimum rate was 7/6d per week. Highcross Street opened on 15/11/1893 on a minimum of 2/6d per week, a small office compared to the others. Humberstone Road another small office opened on 8/11/1893 on a minimum of 2/6d per week. London Road opened on a minimum of 5/- per week, this office later moved into Highfield Street. West Bridge opened from 1/1/1894 on 1d a message and

2/6d per week minimum. New Evington started on 29/7/1896 on a minimum of 2/6d per week, this office also delivered Thurmaston. To the north of the town was Belgrave Office it opened for telegrams at the same time as the others mentioned. It was during this time the area between the Great Northern Railway Station and the village of Belgrave was filled with factories and housing. Charles Bennion built a large factory for his company, British United Shoe Machinery Company (B.U.S.M.C.) covering several acres and houses were built to accommodate the workers. Before this development, Belgrave was quite isolated from Leicester Town by open fields.

MORE CHANGES AND THE LADIES ARRIVE

Ralph Burdett resigned in 1892 as Assistant Inspector of Telegraph Messengers. Another ex-soldier Stephen Plant took his place in September 1892. In addition to his wage he received an extra allowance of 3/- per week. In 1893 the number of messengers was increased yet again, this may have been due to the Borough Council receiving Royal Assent on 3rd July 1891 for a Bill to extend the Borough boundaries to include, Aylestone, Knighton, Belgrave and West Humberstone.

In the 1892 revision several female posts were introduced with the successful candidates starting in January 1893.
During Christmas of 1893 it was recorded that telegram boys went round the town carol singing.

WEEDING OUT

First suggested in 1877 'weeding out' was a process of dismissing boys at the age of sixteen who were thought to be unsuitable for retention. Various reasons were given, a physical defect, educational deficiency or being of questionable character. In 1893 it was thought that at age sixteen these boys would still have a chance of learning a trade rather than getting corrupted once out on the street. To help the boys, attempts were made to find them employment with the Railway companies or similar employers. Telegraph boys' pay was kept low as it was considered that the 'privilege' of eventually being employed as a Postman was sufficient enough reward.

ALLOWANCES

A list of allowances dated 31/12/1894 provides some unusual facts; one un-established Night Messenger was paid 18/- per week to deliver telegrams during the night in the town area. 2/- per week for providing assistance in the Telegraph Delivery Office on Sunday Nights. The Corporation of Leicester was paid £20 per year for the use of the Corn Exchange and the services of a Drill Instructor two mornings a week for the messengers drill, this was cancelled on 31/12/1895. An allowance of 1/6d was paid to the Caretaker of the Volunteer Drill Hall. Leicester Corporation Tramways Department was paid £20 per year to convey Telegraph messengers on delivery. The rate used by the tramways was 1/- per dozen fares. Using the Corporation horse trams saved the G.P.O. from setting up arrangements with other private hire firms to use their horses or horse drawn vehicles. The boys were issued with brass tokens by the booking out officer to give to the conductor in exchange for a ticket.

T.S.O.CHANGES

In 1894 three telegraph messengers were appointed at Clarendon Park T.S.O. in Queens Road, Leicester. They replaced the allowance paid to the Sub Postmaster for delivering telegrams. A record of the boys' time there can still be seen today, they are the 'T' numbers carved into the brickwork on the wall of the Sub Post Office, which is on the right hand side of the entry, leading to the rear of the T.S.O. By 1895 Charnwood Street T.S.O. had three boys. The boys came out from the Head Office on a two- week rotation for a wage of 5/- per week.

TRAFFIC INCREASES

In 1894 the number of telegrams sent in Great Britain reached 71,465,380 a massive increase of 65 million since the G.P.O. had taken over running the service in 1870. The number of instruments in use now totalled 26,764 these improved machines were able to transmit 600 words per minute. With the efficiency of the service improving all the time, the average cost of a telegram had been reduced to 7¾d.

PAY & CHANGES

William Neale the Inspector of Telegraph Messengers had a sustained period of sick absence and was awarded a Gratuity on 21st December 1895. He was succeeded by William Norris an ex-army Sergeant Major who had joined in 1894 as an Adult Night Messenger and later a Town Postman. In 1897 he was promoted to Inspector of Telegraph Messengers.

Mr. J.M. Dayson retired as Telegraph Superintendent in December and was replaced the following month by Mr. R. Featherston.

By 1896 Senior Messengers called Corporals were paid 7/- per week, two senior boys F. Brown and S. Underwood who were called Sergeants received 8/- per week. There were part time Check Messengers and Learners on 5/- per week. The duties of a Check Messenger appear to have a role linked to the early telephone service, collecting the operator's connection slips. Another change in 1896 was the need to produce a birth certificate when applying for employment.

AMALGAMATION

The Postal and Telegraph Staffs were re-amalgamated on 30/3/1896. After the amalgamation the male telegraphists were called S.C.&.T. (Tels) (Sorting Clerk & Telegraphist) they were not known again by the title Telegraphist until 1946. Also at this time the grading of both indoor and outdoor posts into first or second Class ceased for all ranks.

BICYCLES

In 1896 the Post Office nationally bought 100 bicycles because of the extension of the FREE delivery area for telegrams from one to three miles. Telegraph cycles were painted red and had a larger fixed rear wheel. Postman's cycles had two free wheels of the same size and both were fitted with brakes.

RURAL DELIVERY OFFICES

The Telegram delivery rate was paid for by the mile, the further out from the base the greater the cost. Some offices were so busy that the Sub Postmaster gave up the allowance and a messenger or messengers were employed to deliver the telegrams. When Leicester Town expanded it's boundaries in 1891 it changed some of the surrounding areas delivered by the Head Office staff. Outside these boundaries boys were located in what are today small villages, nearby larger places which had messengers can possibly be explained by the presence of coal mines or other large industries. From 19/9/1896 Coalville had two messengers who were paid 5/- per week. Ibstock from 1899 to 1903 had two messengers and a cycle. Ashby De La Zouch with its Standard Soap Works, Gas Works, tramway and other industry and Groby with Groby Quarries, both had one messenger each. South Wigston had the Leicestershire Regiment Barracks, a large biscuit factory and a small quarry, there was also an important railway exchange sidings at Wigston Triangle they had two messengers until 1902 then only one. As well as a large number of factories Syston also had railway exchange sidings and two messengers were located there. Telephones were very expensive to install in the cities and they were a rarity in country areas. The G.P.O. ran land lines to rural Sub Post Offices that is probably why there were messengers in unexpected places. Gaddesby had one Billesdon had two. Both villages had a number of large country houses nearby where people of importance lived. The Lord Lieutenant at that time lived near to Billesdon. Kibworth had two messengers until 1902 then only one. Narborough had one messenger, perhaps the nearby quarry at Enderby was the source of their telegraph traffic.

PROBLEMS

Maintaining discipline in a large group of teenage boys was difficult, with only one Inspector and one Assistant Inspector it was almost impossible. It is not surprising that there were incidents, in the 1890's several boys were dismissed for theft, dishonesty, gambling and destroying telegrams.

1897

The recruitment process was rigorous in 1897 with the Inspector visiting the home of the intended messenger or his relations if he was to live with them, this was because of the rule

about living within walking distance of the office. Even when a boy was successful and possibly because of tight discipline an estimated 40% of sixteen year olds left the service nationally.
In 1897 the 'Alternate Scheme' was brought in with messengers sharing the Postman vacancies equally with ex-servicemen.

1898 TELEGRAPH MESSENGERS INSTITUTE

By 1898 a Telegraph Messengers' Institute was open in Leicester, this was an early version of The Boys Clubs, which started up years later in England in many cities and towns. The Institute provided tuition in mathematics and english, to encourage the boys to improve their education. Eventually the institute provided physical training in the form of gymnastics, swimming, tennis, football, cricket and cycling. The messengers were charged 1/- per year.

In 1898 discipline was tightened up at the morning inspection. Several boys came to work 'improperly dressed' not wearing the full uniform for which they were given half an hour extra duty, without pay. As records do not show this punishment being handed out for some time afterwards, they must have attended in full uniform, the lesson had been learnt!

During 1898 Mr. Featherston Superintendent Telegraphs was promoted to Chief Clerk. Walter Bolton from Derby took up the vacant post. Mr. J.Goddard retired as Assistant Superintendent, to be replaced by Mr. J.Griffths. A second Assistant Superintendent post was created that year and filled by Mr. A.W. Champion.

FEMALE TELEGRAPHISTS

The number of women telegraphists increased to the stage where the Post Office created a post of Assistant Supervisor (F.)

On 18/4/1898 Miss Elizabeth Mary Oakey was promoted at the tender age of twenty-two on a salary of £85 per annum. In common with other supervising female posts such as the telephone service and hospitals, she was referred to as Miss Oakey and was expected to remain single for the duration of her career. She started as one of the original Female Telegraphists back in 1893

1899 FREE RECEIPTS

Occasionally money handed to the messenger had not found it's way back to the office. In 1899 as an attempt to resolve this situation free receipts were, issued by messengers to members of the public when money was handed over in payment for telegrams sent via the delivery messenger.

GREAT CENTRAL RAILWAY

A Telegraph Office was established at the newly opened Great Central Railway Station in Great Central Street in 1899.

STAFFING LEVELS

In 1899 ten extra docket messengers were employed taking the total to sixty-two (fifty-six Docket & six Fixed Wage.) In addition to these there were five indoor messengers. Also that year there was another telegraph revision owing to the growth of telegraph traffic. The new level of staff was;
1 Superintendent £220 per annum,
2 Assistant Superintendents £170 per annum,
4 Clerks £140 per annum,
38 S.C.&.T.(M) 12/- per week,
28 Telegraphists (F) 10/- per week.

CHAPTER 2

THE NEW CENTURY

PROBLEMS OF THE 1900's

There were over sixty Messengers by 1900. One boy was cautioned in that year for climbing through a skylight and three others for unruly conduct. In 1902 a boy was dismissed for playing with a loaded pistol on duty and injuring a fellow messenger. Misdemeanours were dealt with harshly and even constant misdelivery of telegrams was considered a Serious Offence and could lead to service being terminated (dismissed.) One punishment for breaking the rules was to be given extra duty without pay. If a messenger was seen scooting on one pedal down Post Office Place instead of walking with his cycle, he could receive up to two hours extra duty without pay. Boys on duty caught not wearing their official hat would also have to work an extra hours duty without pay. Running in the corridors, whistling when in the building, loitering in the toilets to evade being sent out were all things that were said to 'Bring the service into disrepute.' Harsh days, especially if a boy was brought in front of one of the ex-military supervisors for punishment. Even the weekly drill was under scrutiny and from time to time a Director of Telegraph Messenger Drills would visit from Headquarters to check that all was in order. Prizes were awarded to the best offices.

In 1900 irregularities were found in the messenger wage sheets and the Tramway Token records were also found to be incorrect. This resulted in the two Assistant Inspectors being demoted to Postman rank.

Mr. W.W. Bolton, Telegraph Superintendent transferred to Derby as Superintendent Telegraphs on 1/7/1900, his post was taken up by Mr. F.G. Richardson.

STILL RISING

The number of telegrams sent in Great Britain was still rising. They were now counted in tens of millions. Despite a continuing increase in traffic the G.P.O. continued to lose money. As telegrams were seen as a vital public service, the government continued to write off the losses.

1901 HAPPENINGS

John Kent Harrison replaced the two demoted Assistant Inspectors in 1901 this was on a weekly allowance of 3/-. In this year three messengers were appointed to Belgrave T.S.O. as the area was beginning to see a rapid growth in both population and housing. Telegraph Messengers were also paid for performing music during rifle drill at the Magazine.

Two new rural Telegraph Offices opened on 4/- minimum per week, Fleckney on 27/3/1901 and Burton Overy on 8/5/1901.

LEICESTER'S FIRST BICYCLES

Great excitement was created in 1901 with the news that eighteen cycles were to be supplied to the Leicester telegram boys. Cycles No 1632 to 1649 came into service on 6th May 1901. In the district, Ibstock received a cycle on 31/12/1899 for telegram delivery. Kibworth Harcourt received one on 14/5/1901 but this was withdrawn on 5/6/1902. Coalville 12/6/1901 Syston 13/7/1901 South Wigston 16/8/1901 and Groby 31/8/1902 all received one cycle each.

Resulting from this new innovation was a large increase in recorded accidents to Telegraph Messengers, which was probably no coincidence as many boys got to grips with a bicycle for the first time. The boys also received an allowance for cleaning the bikes. One odd fact remains a puzzle, the records show that on 10/5/1901 Coalville had an allowance of 1/- per week to clean the official cycle, this must be the one which was allocated to Ibstock, as the one listed to Coalville did not arrive until a month later.

THE BOER WAR (1899 - 1902)

During this period there was a great deal of difficulty in recruiting messengers because of the great demand for boy labour. This was caused by the high number of men volunteering for the armed forces fighting in South Africa. As far as it is known, no ex-messengers lost their lives in either of the two Boer Wars in South Africa.

1902 HAPPENINGS

In 1902 the Telegraph Messengers Institute provided band instruments for the boys, which no doubt they enjoyed learning to play. Added to the list of things they could do was cycling, which was, a little like taking coals to Newcastle with their normal daily work routine.

In addition to delivering telegrams boys acted as guards for Postmen delivering parcels in the town, by handcart.

Coalville office had three messengers in 1902 who, delivered up to three miles, they were paid 5/- per week.

The Telegraph Superintendent had two Assistant Superintendents and six Clerks. A second Female Assistant Supervisor was appointed in 1902. She was Miss Elinor Annie Leak who in 1910, was promoted to Supervisor (Telephones) and transferred to the Central Telephone Exchange.

MAP WITH LOCAL OFFICES

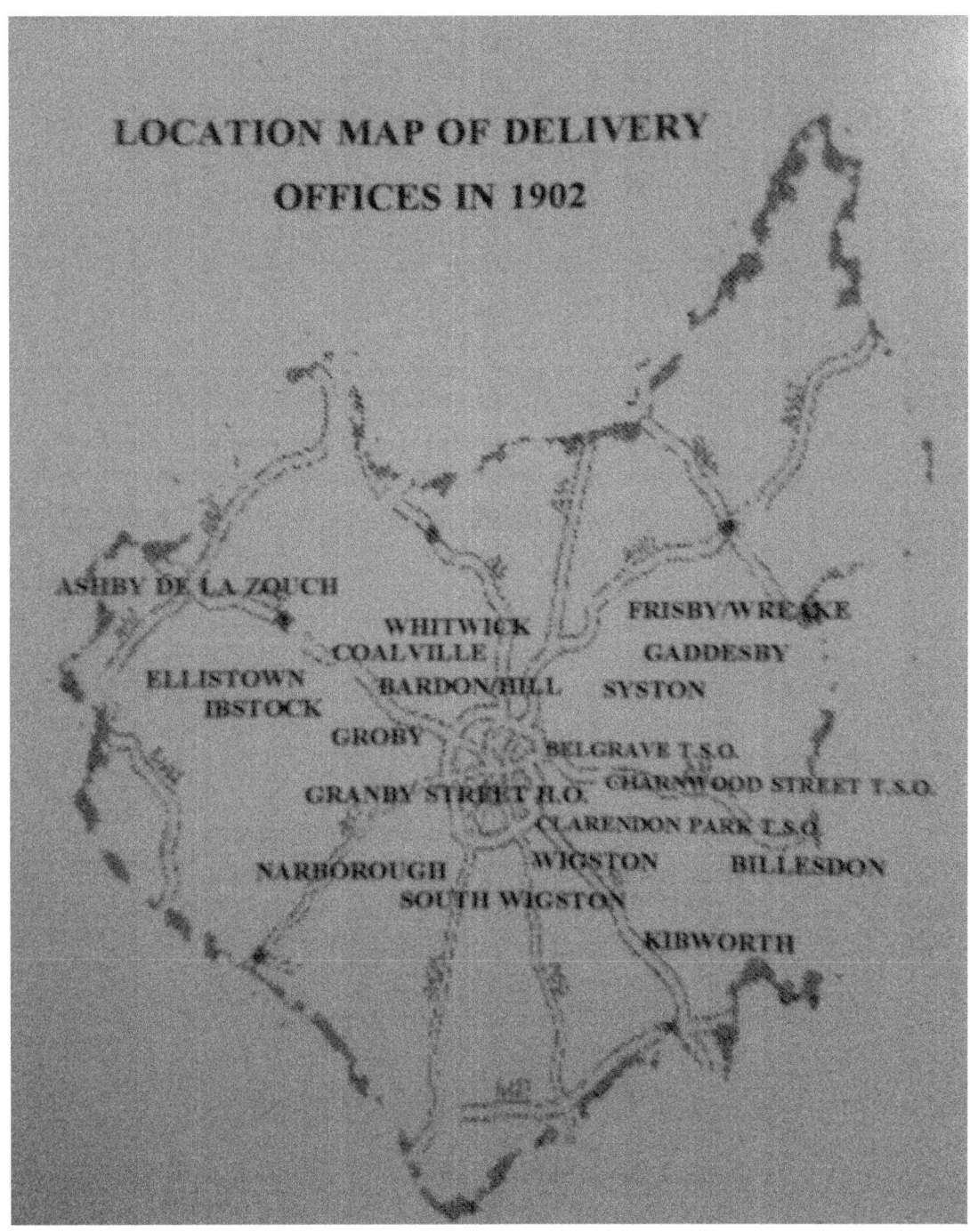

RURAL T.S.O.s

Four more rural T.S.O.s opened for telegraph business in 1902. They were all paid at 4/- per week. Frisby on the Wreake 13/8/1902 Ellistown 3/9/1902 Bardon Hill 1/10/1902 and Anstey. The date for this office is not recorded.

1903

Three boys were cautioned following an accident in 1903 whilst playing with a lift.

On the 7th December 1903 a new post was created for a Town Postman to act as Assistant Inspector of Telegraph Messengers.

1904 A YEAR OF ACTIVITY

Thomas Charles Marshall was promoted to the new post on 17/3/1904. He was an Army veteran who had served in the Boer War and was known to the boys as 'Snuffy' (possibly due to the then popular habit of taking snuff.) He was such a character that even in the 1950's Snuffy Marshall was still mentioned. The Inspector in 1904 was Mr. W.E. Norris and he was provided with a cycle for patrol duties. The messengers at Clarendon Park T.S.O. were also provided with cycles. The number of messengers stationed at Charnwood Street was reduced at this time. Belgrave Gate T.S.O. opened for telegraph business on 29/3/1904 at a minimum of 5/- per week. A messenger was given a fine of 2/6d approximately half a weeks wages for knocking a lady over whilst riding his cycle. The condition of the lady following the accident is not known.

DAILY ROUTINES IN 1904

The life of a messenger in 1904 is worth reflecting upon. There were over sixty boys working throughout the day in shifts. The morning inspection, marching to the Magazine for rifle drill and attending the Telegraph Messengers Institute all took up a large part of the working day. The institute had its own band, sports activities and educational classes.

Mr. W.E. Norris and Mr. T.C. Marshall both took a keen interest in the boys and the Telegraph Messengers Institute. In 1905 the Post Office Surveyor gave a formal vote of thanks to Mr. Marshall for his work with the institute, which was an impressive accolade to come from Postal Headquarters.

1904 STAFFING LEVELS

The Telegraph Department consisted of ;
Mr. F.G. Richardson Superintendent

2 Assistant Superintendents	35 Female SC&T.
1 Engineer	11 Telephone Operators.
6 Clerks	45 Male SC&T.

Mr. W.E. Norris Inspector of Boy Messengers, Mr. J.K. Harrison & Mr. T.C. Marshall the Assistant Inspectors of Boy Messengers and there were sixty-three Telegraph Messengers. On 17/9/1904 Mr. Harrison resigned to be replaced by Mr. Thomas Parker Watts.

1905

1905 brought the downfall of one of the Assistant Inspectors of Boy Messengers who, following an assault on one of the boys was fined, cautioned and reduced to the rank of Postman.
The supervisors must have had quite a task trying to keep over sixty boys in order. On this occasion it obviously proved too much with severe consequences. Incidentally this gentleman continued for many years as a Postman until he retired in 1933. Mr Bob Chalmers took over the post of Assistant Inspector of

Telegraph Messengers he was later promoted to Head Postman in 1914 the new title for the post.

1908

From the 1st of January 1908 Adult messengers were used to provide assistance in Telegraph Delivery on nights during the week at the rate of 13/3d per week. Sunday night was covered at a cost of 2/3d.

On the 1st February 1908 Mr. A.W. Champion who began as a Telegraph Messenger in 1870 succeeded Mr. F.G.Richardson in charge of the Telegraph Department, however the post was at this time downgraded from Superintendent to Assistant Superintendent (1st class.) Mr. R.H. Lippitt was promoted to Assistant Superintendent (2nd Class) in 1908 replacing Mr. Champion.

MEMORIES of HARRY HUBBARD circa 1908

In 1903 the method of payment for messengers was changed from per journey, to per message, older boys who were stronger cyclists and more experienced could deliver at a quicker rate than the younger boys. The Booking Out Officers tried to change the duties so that the amounts each boy had to deliver evened out. Some of the boys could earn 8/- per week if they had several deliveries close to the office.

In 1908 Telegraph Messengers were re-named Boy Messengers.

Staff changes occurred in 1910 when Mr. G.H. Voss died in service. He had been promoted to Clerk in 1902. Mr H.W.C.Morris was promoted to the vacant post of Overseer. The rank of Clerk had been changed to Overseer (Telegraphs.) in 1905.

Miss Helena Maud Sweetman was appointed Assistant Supervisor (Tels) on 26/4/1910 on a salary of £100 per annum. She replaced Miss Leak who transferred to the Telephone Service. Miss Sweetman remained until 23/10/1921 when she took early retirement.

In Leicester the G.P.O. acquired the National Telephone Company Exchange in Rutland Street this later became the Granby Exchange until it was replaced by Wharf Street in 1960.

1911

The Telegraph Institute's educational arrangements were changed in 1911 when attendance at schools was made compulsory. Before 1911 boys had been encouraged to attend with the Post Office paying half the fee. When attendance became compulsory for four hours a week, the whole fee was paid.

The weekly attendance helped to prepare the boys for the Civil Service Examination at the age of sixteen. Passes in the examination resulted in boys who gained high marks becoming Sorting Clerk & Telegraphists lesser marks, a Postman. Failure meant eventual resignation from 'the service' and the loss of a much sought after job

1912 THE TELEPHONE SERVICE

On 1st January 1912 the G.P.O. took over all the private telephone companies except for one area, Kingston upon Hull Corporation successfully bid for a licence to run telephones in their own area. Their telephone boxes were easy to find as they were painted white and are still the same colour today. G.P.O. cast iron telephone boxes were painted Post Office Red.

1912 STAFFING CHANGES

A new grade was created in 1912 that of Girl Probationer who usually started at the age of fourteen. This grade had previously been titled Learner. At the age of eighteen they either stayed in the Telegraph Department or transferred over to the Telephone side of the G.P.O.

The Adult Night Messengers were increased to two in 1912 and the rate was 6/9d each, the Sunday rate went up 1d to 2/4d. Both these duties ceased on 1/12/1922.

On 8th March 1912 Mr. William Norris retired as Inspector of Boy Messengers having stayed on two years past the usual retiring age of sixty. Mr. Thomas Marshall previously his deputy took over the post.

1913

The peak for telegrams in Great Britain was reached in 1913 when eighty two million telegrams were sent.

In 1913 Messenger Postmen were introduced as a stepping stone between Boy Messenger and Postman, boys usually transferred at the age of sixteen after taking their Civil Service Examination. Another option made available at this time was to transfer to the newly formed Engineering Section.

Mr. Samuel Vanes another ex-Boer War veteran was promoted in 1913 to Head Postman to join Mr. Bob Chalmers the Acting Assistant Inspector of Boy Messengers under the control of Mr. Thomas Marshall the Inspector in Charge.

By 1914 two Head Postman performed the booking out duties working under the control of an Inspector of Boy Messengers this arrangement lasted until 1926.

CHAPTER 3

THE GREAT WAR

On 4th August 1914 the First World War began, which considerably increased telegraph activities. Several staff who were due to retire during those years, continued to work to help in the war effort. Mr. R.H. Lippitt stayed on working as a S.C.&T. until 1921 due to the acute shortage of staff at the end of the war. Not only did they give up retirement, their pension was reduced by the amount of pay received for the work they undertook, dedication indeed.

The Roll of Honour for the Great War is to be found at the end of this chapter.

Ten minutes physical exercise was introduced in 1915, this was carried out on days the boys were not at military drill.

Between 1916 and 1918 Girl Messengers were used because of a shortage of boys, many had resigned to join the Army on reaching the age of sixteen. This was the only time girls were used to deliver telegrams. The 1916 establishment was;

1 Assistant Superintendent (1st Class)
2 Assistant Superintendents (2nd Class)
5 Overseers   37 SC&T (M)   29 SC&T (F)
1 Telephone Superintendent   27 Telephone Operators (F)
1 Inspector of Boy Messengers
2 Assistant Inspectors of Boy Messengers
53 Boy Messengers.

It can be seen that since the previous decade, the number of telephone operators had more than doubled, whilst the SC&Ts

and messengers had declined. As the War progressed, news started to come through of casualties, which of course included many ex-messengers. When news of somebody being reported missing was received, their jobs were held open for six months, after which they were presumed dead and a gratuity was awarded to their next of kin.

MEMORIES of ARTHUR ATKINS circa 1916

There were some eighty boys, telegrams were delivered either on foot or on a fixed wheel cycle at a rate of three for 2d. The lowest weekly wage was 9/-. The cycles were heavy, with no gears to help climbing the hills which were on most roads leading away from the centre of the town. If a boy misbehaved, the usual punishment was to be given 'up the hill' telegrams, that was anywhere up London Road hill. On Friday mornings each messenger's telegrams delivered during the week were added up, if it fell below 162 he was given the extra number of telegrams to deliver to bring it up to the required total.
Until 1920 messenger boys delivered telegrams up until 10.00 pm. Telegrams were delivered through the night using Adult Night Messengers. There was strict discipline, with morning inspections for smartness the hair had to be short and tidy, the uniform clean and buttoned up correctly, the boots had to be polished and the badges shining. Attendance at night school twice a week was compulsory and unpaid! There was also rifle drill at the magazine and later a Delivery Boys Drum and Fife Band came into existence.

This was disbanded around 1931.

1917

Mr. A.W. Champion the Assistant Superintendent (1st Class) in charge of the Telegraph Department retired in 1917 and was succeeded by Mr. David Ross from Edinburgh.

1918

In 1918 the Telegraph Office opened in 1880 in the Corn Exchange closed for business.

1919

After the Great War the telegraph service gradually returned to normal operations leading to a re-organisation on 1st July 1919.

The post held by Mr. David Ross was up-graded to Superintendent (Telegraphs) on an annual salary of £280. Mr Edwin Crafter was his deputy as Assistant Superintendent on a salary of £210 per annum. There were also six Overseers on £165 per annum and two Assistant Supervisors (F) on £110 per annum.

THE GREAT WAR
1914 – 1918
ROLL OF HONOUR

Alfred George Atkins (18)
Rifleman 8th Battalion London Regiment
(Post Office Rifles)
Died Sunday 21 - 5 – 1916

Thomas George Atter (35)
Rifleman 8th Battalion London Regiment
(Post Office Rifles)
Died Saturday 7 - 10 – 1916

George Herbert Baguley (19)
Private 1st / 5th Battalion Leicestershire Regiment
Died Wednesday 13 - 10 – 1915

George Sidney Button (19)
Private 1st / 4th Battalion Leicestershire Regiment
Died Wednesday 13 - 10 – 1915

William Edwin Chetwyn (41)
Corporal 2nd / 8th Battalion London Regiment
(Post Office Rifles)
Died Tuesday 30 - 10 – 1917

Ernest Dowell (34)
Private 2nd Battalion Leicestershire Regiment
Died Tuesday 17 - 8 – 1915

Arthur Foreman (19)
Private 1st / 4th Battalion Leicestershire Regiment
Died Wednesday 13 - 10 – 1915

THE GREAT WAR ROLL OF HONOUR CONTINUED

Edwin Arthur Gardiner (38)
Rifleman 1st / 8th Battalion London Regiment
(Post Office Rifles)
Died Sunday 21 - 5 - 1916
~~~~~~~~~~
Gunner 353rd Siege Battery
Royal Garrison Artillery
Died Friday 19 - 10 – 1917
~~~~~~~~~~
George Charles Hardy (21)
Rifleman 1st / 8th Battalion London Regiment
(Post Office Rifles)
Died Saturday 7 - 10 – 1916

George Cecil Frost Hodgson (23)
Private Leicestershire Regiment
Died Saturday 6 - 10 – 1917
~~~~~~~~~~
Percy Arthur Hubbard (22)
Lance Corporal 2nd / 8th Battalion
London Regiment
(Post Office Rifles)
Died Saturday 20 - 10 – 1917
~~~~~~~~~~
Samuel William Hubbard (28)
Private 8th Battalion Leicestershire Regiment
Died Wednesday 11 - 4 – 1917
~~~~~~~~~~
Thomas Kirkland (32)
Corporal 1st Battalion Leicestershire Regiment
Died Thursday 19 - 9 – 1918

THE GREAT WAR ROLL OF HONOUR CONTINUED

Lewis Lewis (18)
Private 7th Battalion London Regiment
Died Thursday 8 - 8 – 1918
~~~~~~~~~~

William Thomas Russell Munton (22)
Rifleman "C" Company 2nd / 8th Battalion
London Regiment (Post Office Rifles)
Died Wednesday 11 - 7 – 1917
~~~~~~~~~~

James Palmer (32)
Signaller 286th Battalion Royal Field Artillery
Died Friday 27 - 9 – 1918

Ernest William Peer (29)
Lance Corporal 8th Battalion
London Regiment (Post Office Rifles)
Died Sunday 15 - 7 – 1917
~~~~~~~~~~

Ben Powers (32)
Lance Corporal 18th Battalion
London Regiment (London Irish Rifles)
Died Thursday 5 - 9 – 1918
~~~~~~~~~~

Alfred George Southern (27)
Private 8th Battalion Leicestershire Regiment
Died Saturday 15 - 7 – 1916
~~~~~~~~~~

Frederick Isaac Whiston (30)
Private 7th Battalion Leicestershire Regiment
Died Saturday 6 - 10 – 1917

THE GREAT WAR ROLL OF HONOUR CONTINUED

William Arthur Wood (29)
Rifleman 8th Battalion London Regiment
(Post Office Rifles)
Died Monday 27 - 8 – 1917
~~~~~~~~~~

Edward Ernest Wright (38)
Driver H.T. Army Service Corps
Died Tuesday 6 - 3 – 1917
~~~~~~~~~~

23 ex-messengers lost their lives
in the service of their country.
21 were buried in Flanders.
2 were buried in Leicester,
1 at Belgrave Cemetery and
1 at Welford Road Cemetery.

CHAPTER 4

THE ROARING 20's

A further revision came into force on 18/1/1920. The Messenger Postman Grade ceased from this date. The two Head Postmen received an allowance of 6/- per week to supervise the boy messengers, working a two-week rotation of an early and a late shift under the control of an Inspector of Boy Messengers. On 29/9/1920 the Adult Night Messenger duty was abolished and converted to the Postman's grade. Mr. E. Orton was the post holder at this time. From this date the Telegraph Office was closed at night for the delivery of telegrams.

1921

In 1921 the practice of the boys performing drill from 1st March to 30 November annually was stopped on grounds of economy, nationally £3,600 was saved by abandoning drill. The allowance of 1/6d paid to the caretaker of the Territorial Drill Hall, which had been used by the messengers for drill purposes since 1/1/1896 ceased on 3/9/1921. Messengers from this time remember being shown carbines, which were still held in the early 1920's. At the same time their ten-minute physical exercise sessions ceased.

By 1921 the Civil Service Certificate examinations for sixteen years old Boy Messengers were being held twice a year, in May and November.

1922

The number of messengers decreased after the First World War. There were thirty-four boys in 1922. There were also a total of nine Indoor Messengers located in offices around the city in the Sectional Engineers Office, District Managers Office and the Surveyors Office. In addition the boys stationed in three T.S.O.s at Belgrave, Charnwood Street and Clarendon Park were withdrawn to the Head Office on 4/3/1922. In 1922 an instruction was issued stating, the post of Inspector of Boy Messengers was to be downgraded to Head Postman on the retirement of the present holder Mr. T.C. Marshall.

GETTING ON

When applying to become a Boy Messenger it was necessary to attend an interview panel usually consisting of three men including the Superintendent Telegraphs and the Inspector of Boy Messengers. They would assess whether the boy was a suitable candidate, he would stand against the wall to check his height and he would be expected to provide two independent character referees. The Inspector would later visit the home of the prospective employee and also see the people acting as referees to check each candidate's background. Nothing was left to chance, it was considered a 'prestigious' job in those days and there was never a shortage of candidates wishing to join the service, even in times of full employment. Another part of the selection process no doubt remembered by many boys, was the medical examination by the Treasury doctor who dealt with all civil service personnel. The Treasury Doctor Dr. Binns whose surgery was located at 32-34 Humberstone Road (now the site of the Cardinal International Exchange) was appointed to see Post Office Staff from 1/1/1922 and was still practising in the 1960's. Reasons to reject candidates besides health problems found during the examination, included being under the height limit of 4' 8" and/or flat feet.

Full details of the conditions of employment can be found on pages 207 to 209.

1923

In 1923 Mr. E. W. Crafter succeeded Mr. D. Ross as Telegraph Superintendent with Mr. A. W. Walker being appointed Assistant Superintendent.

There were nine Boy Messengers in various rural offices by 1923, a figure, which steadily decreased during the decade. An interesting aside is that in 1923 the Girl Probationer force was reduced from eighteen to ten with the reduction being covered by Boy Messengers.

LIFE AS A MESSENGER IN THE 1920's

It might be interesting to stop and reflect on how life was for a Boy Messenger during the early 1920's. The earliest shift started at 6.00 am and these boys would work until 3.00 pm, other boys would sign on duty at hourly intervals until the last shift which started at 12 noon, this shift would finish at 9.00 pm. For each time block, up to six boys would attend. There was one half day each week working from 10.00 am until 1.00 pm this changed each subsequent week, with the day off progressing e.g. Monday week one, Tuesday week two etc. A total of forty-eight hours were worked each week. Starting pay was 6/-, which was raised to 19/- by annual increments at the boy's birthday. Sunday attendance was compulsory but attracted extra money. Messengers were given two weeks holiday a year with pay. The Supervisor sat at a high desk known as the pulpit, from where he was able to see all around the office, looking down on the boys in his charge. The boys would sit on a wooden bench in front of him, watching as telegrams came down the pneumatic tube and were placed in order on the desk. When it was time for a despatch, the boy's number e.g. T16 would be called out and he would be handed his telegram run to sort into delivery order. He checked his route on the huge map situated on the office wall and off he went.

The serial numbers of the telegrams to be delivered were all logged onto the boys docket sheet, the time of departure, the estimated time of return and the actual time he returned. If there was a great difference in the estimated time and the actual return time, explanations were called for. The officers in charge were usually quite adept at estimating the return time to within five minutes, often to the boys' dismay. In addition to the serial number, each envelope was stamped on the right hand top corner with a sequential delivery number by the booking out officer. The Instrument Room serial number enabled complaints or enquiries to be investigated easily. Should there be a problem such as non-receipt, or with the wording of the original message, a repeat copy could be quickly made available from the original held in the telegraph instrument room.

As each boy went out on his delivery, the remaining ones moved along the bench in line to wait their turn. Occasionally high spirits would get out of hand and the boys might get too noisy for the supervisors liking, sometimes it could develop into an exchange of blows, usually out of sight of the pulpit. Bob Chalmers favourite saying "No boys no noise" as he cleared the room, must have caused great amusement to the perpetrators.

There was a large fireplace in the part of the room set aside for the messengers, and ovens where the food brought in was heated up. This was in the days before a canteen was provided for employees. Several kettles hung in the fireplace ready for tea to be mashed.

Messengers were allowed ten minutes tea break morning and afternoon, there was no fixed time for a meal relief this was dependant on the flow of telegrams. The telegrams in the centre of town would be delivered on foot, cycles being used for further a-field, taller boys had large frame bikes with a double crossbar. Two Postmen were employed to maintain the cycles, no doubt repairing or replacing wheels buckled by the tram tracks! On the messenger's duties was cycle cleaning, this could be supplemented with extra cleaning time when work was scarce. On Sunday duties, a boy would be stationed at the Granby Telephone Exchange situated in Rutland Street next to the Fire Station, in case the engineers needed to be called out. Messengers were also hired out to salesmen for the day to show them around the city. Sir Arthur Wheeler was a well-known local stockbroker his office was on the corner of Every Street and Horsefair Street. He sponsored many Post Office events e.g. Sports days and also donated several trophies including a swimming cup for the boys.

Sir Arthur Wheeler's office was in the building, which is now occupied by Barclays Bank P.L.C.

WHO SAID IT WAS EASY?

In Granby Street Head Post Office the telegram delivery room was situated on the ground floor, the boys used an entrance off Blackwells Court to enter the building. The Telegraph Instrument Room was on the top floor with the Central Telephone Exchange on the floor below.
There was a morning inspection for the boys. The Inspector walked along the line checking belts and buttons were clean and polished and hats were on straight. Like soldiers in the British Army, boys wore putties strapped around their legs. These were later withdrawn as they were found to be causing varicose veins. Army boots were supplied to messengers and

the boys had to polish them to the same high standard expected in the forces. Many boys were able to ask parents or grandparents on how to get the perfect shine. Anyone failing to come up to scratch, would be sent home to rectify the matter, then required to make up the lost time later in the day.

Occasionally a boy might return past the estimated time for his run, perhaps because of getting a puncture, getting lost on route, or more scurrilous reasons like dropping in at home or the old favourite 'Popping' a term known to all telegram boys throughout the ages. This involved, meeting up with another boy and delivering their telegrams together. It usually meant furious peddling to make up the lost time back to the office and woe betide you, if spotted by an Inspector out on patrol, or if a member of the public had rung in to complain! The boys were careful not to leave or return to the office in pairs and to have a plausible excuse to hand if needed.

1925

The Telegraph Office in the new Cattle Market on Aylestone Road closed in 1925, it had opened for business back in 1881.

1926

The Union of Post Office Workers (U.P.W.) re-organised following the First World War, from 1926 the Boy Messengers had two representatives who attended the monthly meetings. This continued until at least the Second World War.

Another change came in 1926 with the retirement of long serving (since1904) Inspector of Boy Messengers Mr. Thomas Marshall. The post was downgraded from an Inspector to

Assistant Inspector. Mr. Samuel Vanes the senior Head Postman was promoted to Assistant Inspector of Boy Messengers he was assisted by two Head Postman.

STAFFING REDUCTIONS AT THE END OF 1920's

The telegraph traffic continued to decline as the 1920's drew to a close, due to a combination of an ever expanding telephone service and the increased efficiency of the letter post, both of which were considerably cheaper alternatives to the telegram.

By 1928 the Telegraph Force had dropped to;
1 Superintendent
1 Assistant Superintendent
3 Overseers (half the number of 1919)
1 Assistant Supervisor (F) previously two,
24 S.C.&.T.(M)   19 S.C.&T. (F)
down from the 1921 figures of 37 male and 28 female S.C.&.T.s.

CHAPTER 5

THE GREAT DEPRESSION
FURTHER LOSSES IN THE 1930's

As the 1930's dawned, the Telegraph Service was in decline. Indeed the service made a loss of over £1 million in Great Britain in 1930-31. In Leicester itself only three new Boy Messengers were recruited in 1931, with six Girl Probationers performing redundant Boy Messenger duties, this was cited as being due to a reduction in telegraph traffic in 1930.

Another change that occurred in 1931 was the retirement of Mr. Samuel Vanes, Assistant Inspector of Boy Messengers. He was replaced by, Head Postman Mr. Frank Rhodes. In the early 1930's there was high unemployment nationally and a job with the General Post Office was much sought after. To gain employment as a Boy Messenger at this time was considered a real honour because it was a secure job, with good prospects of advancement and also a Civil Service Pension. There could be as many as twelve boys applying for each vacancy. In order to qualify for a position it was necessary to live within the city boundary, some even lived with relations to get round this rule. If not selected at the initial interview (boys who displayed some sporting prowess usually took precedence) they could be placed in a 'queue' for the next available vacancy. If a vacancy did not occur before a boy reached fourteen and a half he would be removed from the list, as this was the upper age limit for recruitment of Boy Messengers.

DAILY DUTIES AND DODGES OF 1930's

By 1932 there were forty Messengers on a starting wage of

9/6d per week. Frank Rhodes, (affectionately known to the boys out of earshot as 'Dusty') and his deputy Jimmy Lumb had control of the boys. The boys always addressed the officers as Mr or Sir. They would sit in the pulpit, a raised desk two or three steps up enabling them to see all around. When first joining the service, boys would have to undergo an initiation ceremony, which usually involved a ducking in the mess room. Another ritual was to cut off the large red button from the top of a new boy's cap. Indeed some of the Senior Messengers (over sixteen) who could by then be over six feet tall were known to throw new, smaller recruits across the table to each other.

To familiarise themselves with the job, new boys were first given telegrams to deliver on foot around the city centre, to places like the Wholesale Fruit & Vegetable Market in Halford Street. Each boy had a form known as a docket with his name and badge number at the top on which the supervisor entered the serial number of all the telegrams to be delivered. There could be up to twelve telegrams on each run.

FASHION CONSCIOUS?

A few of the boys whilst being measured for their uniform, would twist the tape measure round their fingers to make the trouser leg measurement up to four inches longer, when the trouser bottoms were pinned up with the side cycle clips the excess material hung down over the boot, allowing it to soak up the oily mess from the chain. All part of the custom of being a Boy Messenger apparently! Some of the ways of wearing the uniform seemed to have come from the Royal Navy. The jacket was worn with only the top button fastened, allowing it to open in a 'V' shape. The trouser seams were ironed Navy style from side to side. Another curious rule which had a naval origin, was to allow a straw hat to be worn in summer but only if the person wore a lanyard to complete the uniform!

ROUTES AND ROUTINES

Two Senior Messengers would report for duty at 6.00 am at Campbell Street Sorting Office, collect any Overnight Telegrams and Express Letters, which were usually for delivery to the wholesale Fruit and Fish Market in Halford Street. They would return to Granby Street office for breakfast at 7.00 a.m. after delivering what they could. Then two other Senior Messengers took over the deliveries. Only Senior Messengers carried out these early duties. Once the early deliveries were completed the boys would work in the Instrument Room until the Delivery Room opened at 8.00 am.

The supervising officer would carry out a daily uniform inspection before duties commenced. Each boy's delivery pouch was checked for the necessary supply of cards. T16B Yellow slip (no answer returning later form) T35H Pink (slip left, Telegram put in your letter box or if no box left under the door etc.) P198H Buff slip left for Express Packet items (unable to deliver; sent out again by Postman or can be collected from.........on producing this card) a small pad of telegram reply forms and a sharp (indelible) pencil. It may be of interest to note that once an Express item had been tried three times, it would be endorsed with the words, unable to deliver service rendered, it would then be treated as a normal packet for delivery by a Postman.

Each boy's delivery pouch was checked by the supervising officer for undelivered telegrams at the start and finish of their duties.

'Dusty' Rhodes carried out a cycle inspection every morning. Armed with a spanner and accompanied by a senior messenger holding a clipboard, he would check that all the bikes were in good working order. Two evenings a week it was compulsory to attend night school at Alderman Newton Boy's School in Peacock Lane, this was always linked to a boy's early finishing days. There was an option of a third night although this was never very popular as most the boys preferred to go to the pictures together in their free time.

OIL AND INK

When not required on delivery work there were other duties the boys had to perform. First there was the messy job of cleaning and filling the oil lamps for the cycles in winter, a job usually allotted to those who were being a nuisance. Then another messy but popular duty was working the instrument room Addressograph machine, this was done by hand. The machine used a series of stamped metal plates to print the telegraphic addresses for confirmation and regular business telegrams onto the telegram envelopes which were sent out from the instrument room, cutting down the work of the telegraphists, not having to type out the addresses for regular users.

THE INSTRUMENT ROOM

The Instrument Room consisted of three aisles of teleprinters, which connected with most of the major cities in the United Kingdom. This type of teleprinter with a full keyboard was brought into service in the mid 1930's replacing the single needle type. When outgoing messages were sent, the machine reproduced the message onto a gummed strip, which was then stuck onto a telegraph form and collected by a messenger to be filed. The incoming messages were also printed onto a gummed paper strip, which was stuck by the operator onto a telegram form and then placed into a telegram envelope after the serial number and delivery address had been typed on to it. If special delivery instructions were received to deliver at a particular place or time, those instructions were typed onto a green, gummed slip, which was stuck to the top left hand corner of the envelope. The envelopes were then sent down the pneumatic tube to the Delivery Room.

The boys found that if they placed their hand over the bell end of the tube immediately after placing the carrier inside it, they could build up the pressure, which when released caused it to explode into the receiving cage in the Instrument Room, making the nearest operator jump out of their skin. A practice that was tried whenever the opportunity presented itself!

Another stunt that caused the engineer a great deal of trouble was when a table tennis ball mysteriously found its way up the tube and jammed the system. The poor man spent a long time trying to find just where the ball was lodged before he was able to remove it. Fortunately this was, not attempted too often by the boys as when the system was out of use the climb up several flights of stairs to collect the telegrams was a suitable deterrent.

Two boys worked in the Instrument room along with two Girl Probationers, occasionally this led to situations resulting in the boys being ejected and sent back to the delivery room. They would be banned from the instrument room with the words "Don't ever return" echoing in their ears!

The next page has a diagram of a pneumatic tube system, which is basically the same as the type used at Granby Street and Bishop Street Offices.

The tubes used by the G.P.O. differed in that they were open ended with the telegrams placed inside, held in place by a metal clip.

PNEUMATIC TUBE

The Pneumatic tube system installed in both the Granby Street and Bishop Street Offices worked in the way described below. Castells Book of Knowledge C 1926

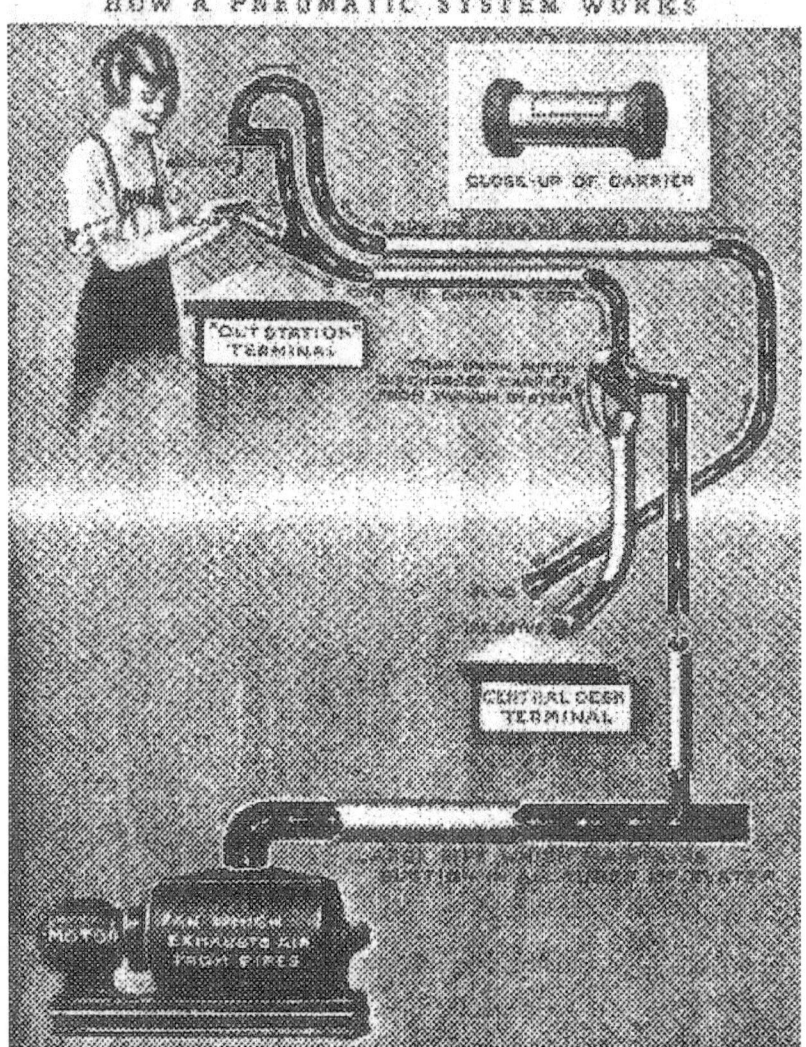

The picture shows how the carriers travel to and fro in the tubes of the office. When the carrier is inserted at either end of the system it speeds forward until it strikes a trap door, which opens outwards. The door snaps open long enough to let out the carrier, but not long enough to let in much air. A suction fan is constantly exhausting the air from the pipes.

An Indoor Messenger collected telegrams from the counter as the public handed them in, which could prove a slow and boring task, some misdemeanour usually ensured removal from this job. A job, which would however become desirable on cold and wet days!

THE CIVIL SERVICE EXAMINATION

In the Boy Messengers Civil Service Examination a boy needed to attain 360 marks to become an S.C.&T, if he scored 240 he could become a Postman. Under, 240 meant a FAIL and the candidate was required to leave on reaching the age of eighteen. This gave them two years to find another job! Often candidates who did fail resigned shortly after receiving their results. There was no opportunity to re-sit this examination, although several boys returned as Postmen following World War II and then took the open examination.

IDLE HANDS ETC

Whilst waiting your turn to go out on delivery there was a library available, operated by Mr. Frank Rhodes, from which books could be borrowed.

A popular prank involved the long wooden bench the boys sat on between deliveries. While waiting to be booked out, a sudden shout of "Off the end" and everyone would move along pushing the unfortunate boy on the end onto the floor. However if he anticipated quickly enough and moved, there was often a whole pile of bodies sprawled on the floor.

WATERING DOWN HIGH SPRINTS

If a boy offered too much cheek, or made too much noise, a swift remedy was administered by the supervisor, Mr Frank Rhodes "That's enough boy top docket." This meant placing your docket 'out of turn' at the top of the pile as next in line to go out, even if you had just returned from a run. This usually warned the others to keep their heads down. Further punishment for persistent offenders was to be given long distance runs like Birstall. The phrase was "Go and see the Poplars" meaning anywhere north of Red Hill or "Up the hill" London Road, the longest steep climb going out of the city, no easy task on a heavy fixed gear G.P.O bike.

CRIME AND PUNISHMENT

Boys being boys, attempts were made to 'put one over' on the Officer in charge. Popping was a great favourite, although not without dangers, perhaps having an accident off route or being seen by the Assistant inspector on patrol (now armed with motorcycle and sidecar.) Smoking or not wearing a hat on duty, were considered to be serious offences. Another rule often disregarded, was not riding cycles until reaching the main road at Granby Street. This included scooting on one pedal down Blackwells Court, which if caught and a plea of not riding given, would be regarded as 'insubordination' One messenger came out of the doorway in Blackwells Court so fast he crashed through the window of Moccasins shoe shop directly opposite. Happily he escaped injury but no doubt he had some explaining to do!

THE STRONG ARM OF THE LAW

Another lucky escape occurred when a messenger skidded on

tram lines (an occupational hazard) in Welford Place and a coal wagon ran over his legs, amazingly he only suffered bruising, although the cycle was not so fortunate. A risky source of amusement could be had with the policeman standing on point duty at the Gallowtree Gate junction where four very busy streets converged. Boys would try to arrive at the crossroads at the same time, from opposite directions this gave the officer who stood on his box with his back to Gallowtree Gate a headache. Who should have right of way? It was made harder, because the boy who came up behind him from the Clock Tower direction, usually called out or rang his bell to get the policeman's attention and as he turned to look and beckon the boy on, the others all did the same. Depending who was on duty, some policemen when spotting a telegram boy approaching would always let him across, whilst others would make a point of holding him up. Any crass comments would often result in an attempt to cuff the offender round the head as he passed. Failures to connect did not result in getting away with it, only delayed the inevitable. If a policeman of rank was watching, the punishment could not be carried out as usual, the substitute punishment was to either lift the left arm up horizontally, just as the boy was about to cycle past catching him across the face, or just holding him on the spot when there was no other traffic there. Some cheekier boys were known to hold onto the officer's outstretched arm to balance, saving them having to put their foot down to the ground. This love hate relationship often didn't stop police officers coming into the mess room for an illegal smoke and a cup of tea. One favourite policeman was known as 'Boily Bill,' but not to his face.

OFF DUTY PASTIMES

Swimming was a favourite pastime for the boys' they were given free tickets to the Public Baths. Stuart Sandom who was killed in World War II was an excellent swimmer and won the Wheeler Swimming Cup on several occasions.

CYCLES

In the 1930's an experimental cycle was tried out, a three speed with Derailleur gears. This design was never put into service. The 1929 design of G.P.O. Cycle built by the Co-operative Wholesale Society in Manchester (Federation Cycles) was so robust that it was in production until 1992 with only slight modifications. Motorcycles were introduced in January 1933 for telegram delivery in London and Leeds, but not in Leicester. The reason given was that the Leicester traffic was too dense and it would be unsafe. Leicester boys must have felt hard done by, to be left to struggle on for many more years on cycles. One of the attractions of these large heavy bikes was the loud bell attached, which when sounded, passing some attractive girl(s) usually got the desired attention. Despite the fact that it was estimated that boys could ride over fifty miles a day during their duties, it was a common occurrence for them to meet on Sundays and go on cycling trips together.

REVERSING THE DECLINE

In 1935 an attempt was made to reverse the declining number of telegrams sent annually in Great Britain (35,250,000 in 1934 down by more than half from 1913) due to the, ever expanding telephone network. A decision was taken to reduce the cost of a telegram to 6d for nine words and every extra word at 1d this took effect from 31st May 1935. This certainly worked as the number of telegrams sent nationally that year increased by 29.4% and almost 50% by the outbreak of war in 1939. The sight of a telegram boy was always looked upon as a sign of ill fortune until the advent of the pools company telegram announcing a winner, then people looked more kindly on the telegram boy. Another important innovation during 1935 was the introduction of the Greetings Telegram, which was larger than other types of telegram and cost 9d for nine words. Nine million were sent annually in Great Britain but from midnight on 30/4/1943 they were suspended due to the war.

TELEGRAM WEEK JUNE 1935

In Leicester the Lady Mayoress Mrs Grimsley inaugurated Telegram Week by sending a telegram to H.R.H. The Prince of Wales (later to become King Edward VIII.) The silver pen used to sign the telegram was later presented to her.

On Monday 4th June 1935 a publicity stunt was arranged to advertise both the Express Parcel Post Service and a film about horses due to be shown at the Trocadero Cinema on Uppingham Road. The trainer of the horse accompanied by senior messenger (T6) W.S. Sandom (known as Stuart) walked the horse from London Road Station to the cinema. As this was so unusual, it made the headlines in the local newspapers. The reporters asked Stuart what experience he'd had with horses and he replied, "He only knew how to control the donkeys at Skegness." Frank Rhodes when asked if his boys were used to horses said, "They're used to anything. If we had lions and tigers to deliver, we'd manage it."

NEW BUILDING & OLD TRICKS

Whilst the new office was being built at the rear of the Granby Street Office, the boys were given temporary accommodation in part of a room at the very front of the Granby Street building next to Blackwells Court. A board partition divided the boys from the accounts branch next door. The boys' behaviour in the early evening often got out of hand. When the officer in charge left the room, rolled up waterproof capes were thrown at one another and on one occasion, several went over the top of the partition into the other part of the room. Inkwells were knocked over and ledgers left on the desks were spoilt. The next day the evidence was clear to see who was responsible, with the inevitable results.

In July 1935 the newly built Head Post Office was opened in Bishop Street at the rear of the Granby Street Office, which was then demolished. At this time forty messenger boys moved into their new home. One of the attractions for the boys was the presence of a large window in the mess room, which looked over the cycle parking area. When it was opened horizontally a container of water could be balanced on its outer edge, then at the sound of anyone approaching, the cord could be pulled to close the window, tipping water onto whoever was passing underneath. Of course boys soon learned to be very wary if the window was open. Unfortunately on one occasion, the visiting Postal Patrol Officer was unaware of the trap and received a soaking. Needless to say repercussions were swift and the window trick subsided for some time afterwards. Punishment for offences such as this could be a fine but usually resulted in being given extra hours duty without pay known as 'donkey.'

THE PAST, PRESENT & FUTURE

Boys who started together often shared a common background and in future years it could help or hinder them. Some of the boys who went on to become Supervisors would help those in trouble when the time was right. Many were very grateful when caught off route or using (misusing) Post Office equipment, for a lenient telling off from an old ex-messenger friend. One boy stayed as a Postman while his friend became Chief Inspector but the lower rank was the one with the upper hand, he was never lost for words when in a tight situation, some even said the ranks were the wrong way round. The Chief tried for years to get the better of the Postman but never succeeded. Even when the war came the Chief (at that time an Inspector) went on parade for the first time and the Corporal in charge of the new intake was, yes you guessed, the Postman.

Tom Blakemore one of the last members of the Messengers Fife & Drum Band (which was disbanded around 1931) donated his fife and case to the local Postal Museum. This is located in a Travelling Post Office Sorting Carriage at the Great Central Railway Loughborough, Leicestershire. Several pieces of messenger memorabilia are on display in this museum.

An amusing incident occurred when a boy's cycle lamp went out whilst on delivery. He continued on his way in the dark, carefully keeping a watch out for Policemen. As he delivered the telegram to a house in Manor Road, he asked the occupier if he had a spare bulb because he didn't want to get caught by any 'coppers.' The gentleman produced a lamp and said "Take this, and take it into the Police Station when you get back and tell them it belongs to the Chief Constable." Exit one very red-faced boy!

1930's messengers were expected to attend for duty ten minutes early and to sign the attendance book immediately. They were inspected, paraded, drilled and exercised all before their delivery work.

Occasionally a messenger, after being the victim of a dousing with water would have to go out on delivery, leaving his tunic to dry in the oven. Sometimes a hat full of water was put into the oven 'to be cooked.' The instigator hoping it would shrink before the owner noticed it was missing and rescued it.

Sport played a large part in the messengers' lives. Table tennis was very popular, often played on the large mess table and several boys excelled at this, as well as at football, cricket and swimming.

Duties for Junior Messengers involved boys working early shifts on Mondays, Wednesdays and Fridays, to accommodate attendance at night school, with the older boys (sixteen plus) working early shift on Tuesdays, Thursdays and Saturdays. Sunday duty involved two hours in the morning and two in the afternoon at time and a half pay 4d per hour. Overtime was paid at 3d per hour and Bank Holidays at double time' which was 5d.

STAFF CHANGES

Mr. E. W. Crafter retired in 1935 as Assistant Superintendent (T.) Mr. J.H. Judson was appointed as his successor. He only served until 1936 and was succeeded by Mr. M.J. Darch who transferred from Newport Monmouthshire.

1938 ONWARDS

There was a Telegraph Revision in 1938 due to the increase of the Telegraph Delivery force. Mr. F. Rhodes Head Postman in charge was promoted to Assistant Inspector on the 27th March. There were now thirty-nine Boy Messengers on a starting pay of 12/6d per week including one Indoor Messenger at the

Sorting Office in Campbell Street, three at the Telephone Managers Office (T.M.O.) at 66, London Road and two at Bishop Street Head Post Office. There were also two Boy Messengers stationed at Coalville, one each at Ashby De La Zouch, Wigston and Syston. These all came under the control of Leicester. Lower graded Head Post Offices with their own Head Postmasters were located at Loughborough, Melton Mowbray, Oakham (with Uppingham under its control,) Market Harborough and Hinckley.

RED BIKE BOYS TIE

There was such good camaraderie in the late 1930s the Boy Messengers asked the firm of Turner Jaques in Granby Street Leicester to produce a tie for them. This firm was known for its stock of school and regimental ties and badges. The tie, which was made, had a blue background and thin red and white diagonal stripes. So far as is known, no example of the tie exists today.

During the 1930's the recruitment of ex-servicemen was gradually curtailed, it was realised that although ex-servicemen were used to discipline they were at a loss when on their own. Having to take orders was fine until there was no one on hand to give direction. Recruitment of non-service personnel was increased during the 1930's.

EVENING CLASSES

The venue for evening classes changed frequently, the reason for this is not known. By the late 1930's classes were held at King Richard III School on King Richards Road.

In the 1930's several changes were made to the uniform and accessories. In 1935 armlets bearing a Kings crown with the words, O.H.M.S. beneath were worn on the left upper arm. These were withdrawn in 1939 saving £700 nationally. Afterwards they were only issued to casual messengers. A larger pouch was bought into use with two compartments, one for telegrams the other for the forms the boys had to keep with them. Then in 1936 the tunic changed, out went the high neck collar to be replaced by a roll neck type. The shoulder cords and buttons were also removed. It was up to the boys to provide their own white shirts and a black tie, which had to be tied in a sailors knot. In May 1936 boys were offered the option of shoes or boots for the first time.

Between 1937 and 1939 a large number of Boy Messengers resigned many to join the Armed Forces, as the Second World War loomed large. On 3rd September 1939 the country was again plunged into conflict and soon the Telegraph Service in Leicester as with all over the country was at full stretch.

RAMP AND RUIN

In 1939 a messenger who was late for work broke the rules by leaving his own cycle near the top of the ramp leading to the Bishop Street basement. A Supervisor told another boy to walk the cycle down to the basement and put it in the private cycle racks. The ramp was very steep, with a tight left hand bend half way down, the basement entrance was at the bottom of the ramp on the right hand side. Every cyclist knew, riding down was too dangerous, even if the brakes were in first class order, as the incline was ribbed, steep and slippery even when dry. The boy decided he could ride down and the inevitable happened, he crashed into the wall at the bend wrecking the other messenger's cycle. Both boys were disciplined for different reasons following this unfortunate incident. Afterwards an official notice was placed at the top of the ramp forbidding the riding of cycles down into the basement.

CHAPTER 6

1940's THE WAR YEARS

As the war continued it put heavy pressure on both the Telegraph and Telephone Services of the G.P.O. To help offset this, more staff was quickly recruited in both departments. In 1940 Jimmy Lumb the deputy to Frank Rhodes, was retired on health grounds. Dick Stocks (who was awarded the O.B.E. in 1938) succeeded as second in charge of Boy Messengers. By 1941 the number of boys had risen to fifty-three. Glenfield, Oadby, Birstall and Thurmaston were still rural offices and as Wednesday afternoons was their half day closing, any telegrams for these areas were delivered from Leicester. During the war cycle mudguards were changed from red to white allowing for greater visibility in the blackout. Small dimmed lights were fitted to the front and back of the cycle and the belt lamp had a shield fitted over the top of the glass. When sirens sounded to warn of air raids, houses were suddenly blacked out and as there were no street lights it made it very difficult to negotiate the city streets, if a boy happened to be out on delivery at the time. Despite these problems the boys seem to have avoided any unfortunate mishaps.

THE LEARNING CURVE

At 7.30 a.m. the boys, who had been arriving for duty since 6.00 a.m. were lined up military style in ranks for inspection. There was a lot of competition between the boys as to who could look the smartest with sharp creases in their trousers etc. Rumour has it, that on slack mornings the inspecting officer would search particularly hard for enough faults to send a boy home, thus giving himself some extra cover for later in the day. The time the boy spent away from the office would be added to the end of his shift therefore saving on overtime payments. As every telegram boy knows, the first day on duty is eventful, filling out numerous forms, from the Official Secrets Act to a receipt for an official cycle lock. Later in the day came some form of initiation ceremony, being grabbed by the older boys and receiving a ducking or worse.

On the first day a boy would go out with a senior messenger following this instruction from the Officer in Charge "You will have to learn where Every Street in Leicester is by the end of the day." Quite a daunting task for a newcomer! He would be shown the 'ropes,' which short cuts to take, the locations of the main businesses in the city, and such useful information as following the tram lines if he was lost as they all eventually led back to the Clock Tower. Failing that he was told, "Sit down in the road and cry and someone is bound to come and help you."

At the end of a boy's first day at work the Inspector would ask if he had learnt where Every Street in Leicester was, if he replied "No Sir" the Inspector would instruct one of the other boys to show him on the map. Every Street is the short street, which runs from Bishop Street to Horsefair Street and had just one delivery point at that time. Suitably relieved now having this 'awesome' knowledge the boy was sent home. This tradition and many initiation ceremonies passed down through the generations of telegram boys were played on the new boys joining the service. They all had to pay their 'dues' to be accepted into the 'club.' This comradeship extended in many ways. Boys who told tales to the supervisors were most unpopular and those suspected, or known to do this were dealt with accordingly. One boy had his trousers glued to him and was then sent on delivery. The Officer in Charge tended to turn a 'blind eye' to this type of retribution and the boy usually quickly resigned. On the other hand occasionally a boy could be verbally abused and sometimes set upon by youths while he was out on delivery. On returning to the office, sometimes with a bloody nose, explaining his experience, it was not unknown for the Officer in Charge to despatch three Senior Messengers to take the offenders to task. If Police enquiries followed, all knowledge was denied. It was all right to be knocked about by your own, but not by outsiders!

ROUTES & REWARDS

The city was divided into eight delivery areas, which followed the eight tram routes. TRAMLINES were the bane of a messengers' life. Hitting the points could often buckle a wheel, which made it impossible to ride the bike. If returning to the office with a damaged cycle a 'paper' would be issued by the Officer in Charge, beginning with the words 'Please explain why.' The written explanation of the misdemeanour would then pass to a higher authority for judgement to be passed. During the war 'Life and Death' telegrams had to be delivered informing relatives their loved one (son, daughter, husband etc) had been killed or was missing presumed dead. This could be quite upsetting for the boys as the reaction on receiving bad news ranged from, cool acceptance to hysteria.

As a mark of respect Policemen and Boy Messengers would always salute a passing Funeral Cortege. Boys kept their pillbox hats on and would dismount if time permitted.

There were no traffic lights at this time and Policemen were on point duty in the city centre, The Clock Tower, Rutland Street and Horsefair Street.

One of the perks of being 'sent up the hill' as a punishment for being cheeky was if delivering to one of the big houses in Stoneygate sometimes to receive a 6d tip or a glass of lemonade from the maid which was unobtainable for most families during the war.

Sunday duty was compulsory once a fortnight. Three hours in the morning and three in the afternoon from 4.00 p.m. - 7.00 p.m. The rates of overtime pay were different depending on age, 4d per hour at 14 6d per hour at 15 7d per hour at 16 8d per hour at 17

A boy was not allowed to swop duty with someone on a higher pay rate than himself.

During the war everyone was in a Youth Group. Air Training Corps, Army Cadets, Sea Cadets or the Post Office Home Guard Unit. There was a rota for Night Fire Watching duty on the roofs of Bishop Street Head Office, Campbell Street Sorting Office and Free Lane Telephone Exchange.

HOURS, HOLIDAYS & DAYS OFF

The boys worked a forty-eight hour week which included one half day. If he was lucky enough to be given a tip, which could be anything from, a ½d up to 6d a time by the end of the week he sometimes had the 1/- he needed to get into the pictures. Most boys' weekly ambition!

Wages were 12/6d per week and there were two weeks paid holiday per year. The summer leave period ran from April to October and was signed for in order of seniority. A junior boy could finish up with October for his summer holiday! Working over two hours twenty minutes on a Bank Holiday gained a day in lieu, which was taken during the winter leave period. It was possible to accumulate five or six days like this.

If absent from duty up to four days uncertified sick leave could be allowed per year, these were known as 'Whitley Days' and were paid but this type of official absence could be withdrawn if it was judged that the boy had 'abused the privilege.'

Producing a doctor's note when a boy was absent meant that it became certified sick leave and a boy's wages were paid. If the sick leave became protracted, one of the two Treasury Medical Officers would make a home visit to confirm the reason for a boys continuing absence.

MORE STRIFE & DODGES

One incident recalled is of several messengers hanging a boy by his feet over the parapet of Bishop Street Head Office roof, in order to show him a closer view of the St. Georges Day Scout parade passing by the office three floors below! Another prank involved a notice being stuck on the window of Birrells Sweet Shop at 74, Granby Street one night during the war, stating that Easter Eggs were available for sale. As people passed by in the morning, they saw it and a queue formed which in a short time, ran from Alfred Place up to Northampton Street, as usual the telegram boys were the chief suspects.

STRIPES & BIKES

When the boys turned eighteen and went on to adult duties an S.C.&T. or Postman, others moved up the 'pecking order.' At sixteen a boy was given one stripe, worn on the right arm. At a later date a further stripe was added to the first. The three senior boys of the messenger force wore three Sergeants stripes, any one of them could be called upon to stand in for the booking out officer should he be called away. Senior boys were eligible for 'privilege' jobs including taking the horse racing results from Leicester Racecourse at Oadby back to the Instrument Room. On Saturday evenings when greyhound racing was held at Leicester Stadium on Parker Drive a senior messenger was on duty to collect the racing results and return to the office with them.

Once several boys on the latest finishing shift of 8.00 p.m. decided to end the day with a massed bike ride around the city after they had completed their final runs. There was a strict rule that no messengers were allowed to ride side by side (this was to prevent popping,) but must be at least eight yards apart, and ride at an estimated speed of 8 m.p.h. So carefully observing these rules, boys started appearing out of the various streets off London Road riding down Granby Street and round the Clock Tower several times, before finally returning to leave their cycles in Blackwells Court and heading for home.

MILK, BUNS & TWINE

Boys will be boys, so they enjoyed playing tricks on the newcomers to their ranks. Favourites included tying a small boy into a parcel bag and hanging him on the coat rack in the delivery room. Sending a boy on a fool's errand to buy 5d worth of pigeon's milk from the local dairy, where the lady, who was used to the scam, gave out a bun instead! A more serious errand was being sent to Winn's Turkey Cafe in Granby Street with some rationing coupons to fetch some 'pregnant tarts.' Needless to say the unfortunate boy was sent on his way empty handed, followed swiftly by a complaint from the manageress. Yet another thankless errand was for the hapless new boy, to be sent to Billson & Grant to see sisal twine (a type of string used to tie letter bundles in the Post Office.) The counter man would go along with the deception. "Sorry lad he's not here today, come back tomorrow." This harmless fun could be found in all types of trades, go and fetch a bucket of steam, go to the stores for a long wait (weight) were suffered by innocent boys in industry and often a red face resulted when the penny dropped!!

MINI REVISION

The increasing flow of telegrams in 1942 resulted in a mini revision. Mr. M.J. Darch was upgraded to Superintendent (T) and the number of staff was further increased.

SHORTAGES AND TRANSFERS

During the war several boys transferred to the Post Office Engineers, as there was a shortage of staff due to older men being called up for war service.

MAN TRAPS & OWN GOALS

The majority of the staff was now female, most of the younger men having enlisted in the forces. Some of the male counter clerks at Bishop Street Head Office fell victim to the boys' mischief. A bucket of water filled with dirty cloths was placed on top of a slightly opened door to catch some unsuspecting S.C.&T. on his way to the toilets. He would then face a wet return to his counter position. Luckily the bucket always seemed to miss the unfortunate recipient.

One incident occurred around Bonfire Night. (No bonfires or fireworks were allowed during the war.) A guy was made using some old overalls belonging to a cleaner, which were stuffed with straw, completed with gloves, scarf and boots. It was then shoved head first into the gas oven (which was turned off,) and left there for the night. Of course during the night the cleaners thought they smelt gas, saw the 'body,' assumed the worst and called the Police, who soon discovered the identity of the corpse! The next morning all the boys were called in for an interview with the police, needless to say no one knew who the culprits were.

SPECIAL DAYS

One of the Bank Holidays worked was Christmas Day when due to the sheer volume of telegrams, boys were sent out in vans with Postman Drivers.

A SAD DAY

On a serious note, one of the boys was involved in a real tragedy on 22nd December 1944. Billy Raymond Pickering was cycling from his home to work, along Welford Road. As he reached Carlton Street, a lorry overtook a tram and somehow Billy came off his bike between the lorry and the kerb and was killed. A verdict of Accidental Death was recorded as no one saw exactly what happened. The loss of one of their colleagues was deeply felt by the lads and at his funeral about fifty boys travelled in several mail vans to the church. They lined up in two rows, in full uniform to provide a guard of honour whilst the hearse went by. The telegraph delivery duties were covered until midday by Postmen to enable the boys to attend the funeral.

THE SECRET ROOM

One of the boys' duties was up in the Instrument Room on the top floor of Bishop Street Head Office where around thirty teleprinters sent telegrams all over the country. During the war, a second secret instrument room was located in the basement. As access was restricted, only six boys were allowed inside. Telegrams of a sensitive war nature were sent and received from this room. It was in the instrument room that the boys came into contact with the Girl Probationers who wore green overalls as their uniform. Some of the boys began courting these girls or Telephonists from Free Lane Automatic Telephone Exchange and several couples eventually got married.

DAILY DO'S & DON'TS

Running to houses to save time was frowned upon. A boy was expected to walk in a dignified manner at all times. He was allowed ten minutes in the morning and afternoon for a cup of tea and forty minutes for lunch. During slack times table tennis competitions were held, when required Mr. Rhodes tapped the window between the Delivery Room and the Mess Room and called out T2 etc. Other boys borrowed something from the library of donated books held by Mr. Rhodes, Zane Grey Westerns and Bulldog Drummond thrillers were firm favourites of the boys. An indication of mutual respect between messengers and their supervisors (despite the constant battle of wits that ensued between them) was proved when Frank Rhodes wrote to 'his boys' whilst they were serving in the forces overseas. The boys were called up for war service on reaching the age of eighteen. When home on leave they made sure that they went into the Telegraph Delivery Room to see Mr Rhodes.

Even after fifty years some of Frank 'Dusty' Rhodes boys remember him as a gruff disciplinarian but with a heart of gold!

It is surprising with the Blackout and Air raids during the war, there were no casualties amongst the boys, other than the traffic accident mentioned earlier.

WARTIME SWEETS & SWEATS

During the war most items were on ration, including sweets,

but boy messengers could knock on Joblins sweet shop door at 19, Granby Street when it was closed and buy cut price sweets, as they were regular customers.

When a telegram was delivered the messenger boy would ask if there was any reply. If there was, he would fill out a reply form from the pad in his pouch, calculate the cost and hope that the customer had the right money, as a messenger never carried any change himself. Back at the office the completed telegram form was handed in for checking by the counter clerk, sometimes the boys sums let them down and they were out of pocket, rarely did they make a profit. Messengers also delivered Registered Express letters for which a receipt was necessary.

By 1942 apart from the forty-five boys at Bishop Street, there were two Indoor Messengers located at the T.M.O. 66, London Road, one in the Registry and another in the Drawing Office. The Postal Branch Campbell Street Sorting Office, the Telegraph Branch at Bishop Street and Free Lane Telephone Exchange had one Indoor Messenger each.

The location of the evening classes had moved once again, this time they were held at the City of Leicester Boys School in Humberstone Gate. Girl Probationers also attended them. Extra knowledge could be gained from a Skeggs Home Correspondence course, which was paid for by the boy himself.

SERVICE CALLS

Post Office cycles used special size tyres, which caused problems when punctures occurred. In the event of a breakdown or an accident, the messenger had to telephone the delivery office by using a free service call. Invariably he would be asked the question. "Have you delivered all your telegrams?" If he had done, it was followed by the words you dreaded to hear "Walk back to the office then!"

STAFFING CHANGES

At the end of 1943 Head Postman Dick Stocks retired. He was replaced by, Lou Worts. The following year 1944 Mr. Montague Darch retired as Telegraph Superintendent, his deputy Bill Neal succeeded him.

TELEX

During the 1940's a new type of machine came into service. The service and machines were called Telex. They were installed all over Great Britain, used by operators located in businesses and government departments. The machines were able to connect one to another bypassing the telegraph offices. They were popular with businesses as they were quicker and cost less to operate than going through the G.P.O. direct. This was another 'nail in the coffin' of the service.

WARS END IN EUROPE

The War in Europe ended in 1945 and with it came happier times, many street parties were held around the city. The telegram boys were given lemonade unobtainable during the war years. The service was very busy with War Office messages giving news about prisoners of war, units that were being demobilised and others destined for service in the war continuing against the Japanese Empire.

CYCLE RELIABILITY TRIALS

In late 1945 Leicester City Council decided to promote a Cycle Reliability Trial open to all delivery boys working in the city. As well as the G.P.O. Leicester Co-operative Society, Worthingtons Stores, Maypole Stores, Home & Colonial and many butcher's shops had boys delivering on cycles. At the beginning of the trail boys were sent off at intervals on a pre-determined route, which was different every year. At certain points along the route they were checked for road sense, use of correct hand signals and speed between check points. Of course the telegram boys who delivered to all parts of the city had the upper hand over the other delivery boys, who only knew certain local areas, and consequently the telegram boys won the trophy each year of its existence. The competition ran from 1945 and was thought to have ended in 1949.

The Telegraph Service had now been in existence for seventy-five years and had gone through many changes in its time. Generations of boys had passed through the messenger ranks, some going on to achieve high positions within the service whilst others left and were successful in other careers.

The Roll of Honour For World War II is on the following pages

The two names below are not on the War Memorial in the entrance to Bishop Street Post Office in Leicester as both boys had resigned in 1939 before war was declared to join the armed forces.

Denis Issiah Pallett (19*)
Sergeant 61 Squadron Royal Air Force
Died Saturday 26 - 10 – 1940

Edward Bert Beach (22*)
Corporal No 45 R.M. Commando
Royal Marines
Died Monday 12 - 6 – 1944

The age of the boy is given if known. If the date of birth is not in Post Office records or their age is not shown on the War Graves Commission Lists, the probable age is given *.

There is one very strange coincidence. T6 was the badge number issued to three of the ex-messengers listed. Not only did they follow each other in Post Office Service as messengers but they also died in the same order during the hostilities. The number at the end of their entry relates to the issue of T6 in Post Office Service.

Of the eight ex-messengers who lost their lives in the conflict, only one has a resting place in Leicester. Stuart Sandom is buried at Welford Road Cemetery.

There was one other ex-messenger who died during the war, he was listed on the City Civilian Casualty list as a
Fire Warden. His details are as follows;
Ernest Venables Bown (70)
Died Tuesday 18-4-1944

CHAPTER 7

POST WAR

WINNING WAYS

POST WAR CHANGES

There were a lot of changes in the years immediately following the war. In the re-organisation of 1946, the S.C.&T. Grade (Postal) and (Telegraph) was abolished and in its place a new grade of Postal & Telegraph Officer (P.&T.O.) was established for the counter and writing staff. The telegraph side reverted to their old title last used in the 1880's of Telegraphist. Many of the staff carried the rank of S.C.&T. (R) = Redundant for many years. In 1946 the number of telegram boys was forty-six.

END OF THE 1940'S

A second telegram boy was killed in 1946. He was the Syston area delivery boy Eric Swann. Eric was off duty at the time and was in collision with a lorry in the village. A boy messenger was sent out from Leicester to Syston to cover the duty until a new boy could be recruited.
It is remarkable that in over 112 years of the service, only two boys out of probably 2,000 were known to have lost their lives while serving as telegram boys.
 1946 was a very busy time, men were being de-mobbed from the forces following the end of the war and telegrams were being sent with the good news.

WINTER WOES

The winter of 1946/1947 was one of the worst for many years with flooding, and after Christmas very heavy snow. It was so bad at times, the cycles were taken off the road and messengers had to deliver their telegrams either on foot or by tram if they were running. Only the main roads were cleared, the side roads remained impassable for weeks.

RE-GRADING & NEW FACES

To head the Instrument Room staff, a Supervisor (M) had been appointed in 1947, he was Choice Chapman, previously Overseer (T) and Harold Ball was the Assistant Supervisor, both were ex-messengers. There were also several Female Assistant Supervisors who were appointed during the war years due to the heavy increase in telegraph traffic.
In 1947 eight Boy Messengers were recruited as Junior Telegraphists, several went on to work as P.&T.O.'s.

On 1st October 1947 the Boy Messenger grade was abolished. Boys were then called Young Postmen or Postman (C) C = composite, this could mean a combination of postal delivery work with the delivery of telegrams from the age of fifteen. A new pay structure was also introduced. They were now part of the Postal side of the G.P.O. Previously they were part of the Telegraph Department and the T numbers proudly worn since the early days of the service were replaced with a 9** prefix e.g .901. From this time the numbers of boys employed, which had risen through the 1940's due to the war, started to decline. This had been the last great era of the telegram service things would never be quite the same again.

In 1947 Mr. Howard William Neal retired as Superintendent Telegraphs, he was the last person to hold this rank. Following his retirement the post was downgraded and Mr. Reginald Yarnell Assistant Superintendent was appointed in his place.

Later that year the long serving and much respected Frank Rhodes retired. He had been in charge of the telegram boys for sixteen years, affectionately known by many generations of boys as "Dusty". His replacement was Mr. Harold Peel.

As there was no sport allowed during the war, one of the first activities under the auspices of Harold Peel was the reforming of messengers' football and cricket teams. These teams were known as Telegraph United and played in the local Saturday afternoon youth leagues. Sometimes the boys duties had to be rearranged to enable them to take part, an obvious advantage if you liked to finish early on a Saturday! This could be why none of the boys as far as we know ever became full time professionals.

There were no canteen facilities so the boys prepared their own meals, or brought sandwiches to eat in their mess room, which was off the delivery room. The enamelled topped tables could be used for shove halfpenny. Playing table tennis was taken more seriously, indeed the boys later joined an evening league. Matches were played in Youth Clubs usually located in Church Halls.

POACHER TURNED GAMEKEEPER

In 1947 the newly formed Postman Higher Grade (P.H.G.) replaced the redundant Head Postman. Telegraph Delivery now had two P.H.G.'s working two shifts. Early 6.00 a.m. - 2.00 p.m. and Late 12 noon - 8.00 p.m. these were under the control of Harold Peel Assistant Inspector. The boys also worked this hour range, with one half day of 7.00 a.m. - 10.00 a.m. or 10.00 a.m. -1.00 p.m. The late shift on Saturdays finished at 8.00 p.m. Some of the P.H.G.s were former telegram boys who were returning to their old 'stamping grounds.' It must have been a strange experience admonishing boys, for getting up to the very same types of mischief they had got into themselves, several years before. At least they knew from personal experience the dodges and the excuses that had been tried before.

NATIONAL SERVICE

In 1948 National Service began when all men aged eighteen were required to join the armed forces for a minimum period of two years. As with all other occupations this affected the telegram boys and certainly opened up a whole new world for the boys who usually went into National Service straight from the messenger ranks instead of to adult duties as Postmen.

BANK HOLIDAY SATURDAYS

The Saturday starting the August Bank Holiday fortnight was a nightmare, with so many people wanting to let the folks left at home know they had arrived safely. Telephones in the home were still few and far between for the average working family, so a telegram was the quickest way to get a message home. Boys could be sent out with up to ninety telegrams tucked into as many as three pouches. On top of this the wedding telegrams still had to be delivered. These were larger and came with strict instructions DO NOT BEND OR GET DIRTY. Not easy to achieve! It could take up to thirty minutes to sort out the delivery route, then anything up to three hours to deliver them. During hot summer days this was a daunting task.

TROUBLE & STRIFE

Despite the demanding schedules, boys did have some time to

kill and one way to amuse themselves was for several boys to stand in a group at the bottom of Blackwells Court pointing upwards, first one, then another, at the tall buildings in Granby Street opposite. This was guaranteed to get passers by looking up to see what was going on. Before long there could be quite a crowd gathered, trams were even known to stop to see what all the fuss was about, bringing traffic to a standstill. Of course there was nothing to see, but the public didn't know that and the boys had been entertained, at no cost to themselves, which was the whole point of the exercise. Other pursuits were visiting Joblins to sweet talk the girl assistant into letting them buy one cigarette from a pack of five a real bonus for lads who were always hard up. Another place to visit was Jeromes the Photographer where a boy had his picture taken in uniform to save for posterity. Hats were the pillbox design with a peak and were to be worn whilst on delivery at all times, it had a chinstrap to prevent it blowing off in high winds. Boys who disliked wearing these hats would, when safely out of range of the office take them off and attach them to the pouch belt being careful to look out for any patrol officers. The hats were often targeted when out on delivery from youths who tried to snatch them. Back at the office even work mates tried to ruin any un-guarded hats.

WILY WONDERS

One dodge practised by the boys after returning from a run was to hang around in the toilets, this would delay his docket being put back into the pile, hopefully giving him more time in the office. Incoming boys always checked the toilets on their way back to the delivery room to make sure a boy in front of him was not hiding trying to miss his turn. A way of getting an 'easy ride' from the office, was to hold on one handed to the rear of a Mechanical Horse. These were three wheeled vehicles fitted with an articulated trailer. They were part of vehicle fleet of the London Midland & Scottish (L.M.S.) Railway Parcels Service. Because they were slow moving, getting a grip on the trailer was quite easy. Many boys found it very handy when faced with a run somewhere 'up the hill.'

SPECIAL JOBS

One of the boys' jobs was to use the Addressograph machine in the basement at Bishop Street Head Office. Regular telegram users such as engineering firms and the Wholesale Fish & Fruit Markets used Telegraphic Addresses. This was an abbreviated form of the address, which cut the cost of sending the telegram via the G.P.O. The recipient firm was charged for each telegram and an annual fee for the Telegraphic Address Service. The firm's Telegraphic address was often the brand name of the product e.g. St Dalmas Leicester, this was the name for a firm Dalmas Limited of Junior Street Leicester which produced adhesive plasters. None of the boys liked delivering telegrams to this firm as the whole area around the factory was covered in a fine white powder which would get everywhere including his mouth and all over his clothes, the sickly cloying taste gave the boys a legitimate reason to 'spit.' Another use for the addressograph plates was to produce the Confirmation Copy envelopes. Customers sent telegrams for firms, which when received by the Instrument Room were 'phoned through to the addressee. The next morning a confirmation copy of the message was sent out in the post.

The C.S.E. which was taken at age sixteen for progression to S.C.&T. or Postman Grade ceased in 1948. It may have been influenced by the raising of the school leaving age to fifteen in September 1947. Future entry into the P.&.T.O. and Telegraph Grades was by way of a Limited Examination for G.P.O. staff, and an Open Examination for those employed elsewhere.

By 1949 there were forty-eight Postmen (C). The city was expanding rapidly, putting increasing pressure on this small army of 'pedal pushers.' Boys were still wearing pillbox hats and stripes on their arms. The job of a telegram boy was much sought after, as there was a pension on reaching retirement.

EARLY SOCIALISING

In 1949 there was a weekly Youth Club held in the Gladstone Buildings in Bishop Street, which was next to the Head Post Office building and was used as the Telephone Training School. The Head Postmaster Mr. A.E. Hall and his wife hosted a Christmas party for the boys in January of 1950 and as far as it is known, this is the only time a Christmas Party was held.

HALF DAY CLOSING

When Rural Sub Post Offices had their half day closing on Wednesday or Saturday afternoons they did not accept telegrams for delivery, so messengers would go out from Leicester to Anstey, Blaby and Broughton Astley to name a few. Going out in the sticks as it was known could be fun on a motorcycle but an entirely different thing on a cycle. Being despatched to Groby on a cycle, after falling foul of the Officer in Charge, soon made a boy regret his clever ad lib or cheek while trying to impress or amuse his colleagues. Delivering to Kibworth could be a problem, if the telegram did not have the last part of the address on it, was it Beauchamp or Harcourt? Often the person stopped on the main road (A6) to ask the whereabouts of Willow Cottage etc was unable to help. Either they had never heard of the address or were just visiting a friend or relation and had no local knowledge. Several precious minutes could be spent in blind panic as the clock ticked on and the boy was no nearer finding the address. The race back to the office to recover lost time was all in vain. There was always some clever 'know it all' who would say, "You should have asked me. I've been there before." Or the officer in charge would say, tongue in cheek, "You took your time, did you meet a girl on the way?"

THE TELEGRAPH MONEY ORDER (T.M.O.)

Telegraph Money Orders (T.M.O.) were a popular method for transferring cash easily and quickly round the country. The sender paid cash in at a Post Office Counter and a fee was added. The (T.M.O.) advice was sent to the nearest delivery office with a short message from the sender and the value of the Money Order. On receiving the T.M.O. advice, the Instrument Room transferred it to the Delivery Room, and a messenger boy took the advice to the Counter Overseer who then filled in the money order. When it was ready, the order was sealed in the envelope with the sender's message, the Overseer then telephoned for the item to be collected for delivery. The service was often used to transmit emergency funds to people who needed to get home quickly by rail if a life or death situation had arisen. Another common use for T.M.O.s was payment for goods that were needed urgently by a business that did not have an account with the supplier. As with Postal Orders, on receipt the bearer took the order to a Post Office Counter to encash it.

78 R.P.M AND ALL THAT!

In their spare time boys would sometimes visit Daltons Record Store in Granby Street, where it was possible to listen to the latest 78 R.P.M. records, that was by standing in a listening booth which was a hood fixed to the wall at head height. It was mostly Big Band music that was popular at the time. The store also sold wireless sets, record players and eventually televisions before it closed in 1960.

LOCK OUT NO LOCK IN!

Returning from a run a new recruit was grabbed and forced into a wooden locker by two older boys who then slammed the door shut. The lockers were very narrow with air holes in the door so it posed no danger to the boy squashed inside. After a while they thought it prudent to let him out, easier said than done, they found the door was jammed tight. After several attempts to release him they threw themselves on the mercy of the P.H.G. who tried to prise open the door using a belt buckle, which did just that, buckled. As the P.H.G. decided to inform the Overseer the door sprung open and the young man inside calmly stepped out apparently none the worse for wear. Open mouthed they watched him, how had he managed this Harry Houdini trick? The P.H.G. decided it was in everyone's interest that the matter was quietly forgotten, or was it?

CHAPTER 8

1950'S THE CITY GROWS

THE NEW CITY ESTATES

In the years following the Second World War, Leicester City Council carried on with the programme to demolish slum housing and build new council estates, which had started in the 1930's but was interrupted by the war. The beginnings of large housing estates started with the Sutton estate off Catherine Street, Braunstone, Northfields, Tailby Avenue and Garden City at Humberstone. The next estate planned was New Parks. Roads had been laid before the outbreak of war but only used as parking areas for military vehicles in transit during the war. Now the house building started in earnest with the peak being reached in the mid 1950's when private estates were also starting to be developed. Telegrams for what were once outlying villages, such as Birstall, Glenfield and Thurmaston were now delivered from Bishop Street Head Office.

Discipline was still fairly strict as the century drew towards the halfway point (1950.) Morning inspections still prevailed although more relaxed than they had been before the war. They were gradually phased out in the early part of the 1950's.

CHANGES TO EDUCATION

With the C.S.E. ceasing in 1949 the messengers were required to attend on day release, Leicester College of Art & Technology in the Newarke, later to become Leicester Polytechnic, now Leicester De Montfort University.

THE SERVICE IN DECLINE

On 20th November 1950 Greetings Telegrams re-started after their wartime suspension. Despite the popularity of these telegrams, total numbers of all telegrams sent were in decline. Telegram boys and Instrument Room staff were gradually being reduced in number. The G.P.O. started to promote the Telephone service, which had begun to rapidly expand, at the expense of the telegram.

EXTENDED NATIONAL SERVICE

Following the introduction of National Service in 1948 several boys realised, if they applied for special leave from the G.P.O. they could sign on for an extra year and then be classed as a regular soldier, sailor or airman. They then received the same pay and leave entitlements as a regular recruit. The G.P.O. gave them one year of unpaid leave, which still counted as unbroken service towards their pension. After service overseas or in other parts of the United Kingdom many boys returned only to resign after a short period, some did not even return and were classed as 'abandoning the service.' A few even found service life so good, they signed on for a full term as regulars. Even though most recall their days as a telegram boy with fond memories, warts and all, returning as a Postman was not considered a good option.

ROYAL NAVAL RESERVE

An after duty activity for the older boys was to join the Royal Naval Reserve at their branch on London Road. One of the

P&T.O.'s was an officer in the Leicester branch and many of the boys wanted to learn to be telegraphists or wireless operators. Some had the idea that they would be able to take it up when they were due for National Service, however very few did. They went into the Army or Air Force, only a few were able to get into the Navy, much to their disappointment.

CHANGING HATS

It was possible during the 1950's to sit a Civil Service Examination to become a Clerical Officer and if successful move into other Government Departments. Several ex-messengers after passing the examination were promoted and moved to the Ministry of Supply or the Ministry of Transport. Other ex-messengers resigned to join the Fire Service or the Police Force. This came in handy when an ex-telegram boy slipped up and after a misdemeanour came face to face with his superior officer, if he happened to be someone with whom he had broken the rules as a telegram boy, the punishment could sometimes be tempered because of indiscretions they had shared in their youth. An advantage of moving from one branch of the civil service to another was that the service time and pension were continued.

During the 1950's the Telephone side of the business was rapidly expanding and boys were encouraged to transfer over as their service time was unbroken and there were wider job prospects. The Youth in Training scheme did not recruit boys under the age of sixteen so they joined first as telegram boys until they reached the lower age limit and then transferred over.

In the early 1950's a Communications Exhibition was held at the Granby Halls and three messengers were selected to help demonstrate the use of the equipment.

A NIGHT AT THE THEATRE

Up to twenty boys would go together to a variety show at the Palace Theatre in Belgrave Gate on a Friday evening. As a joke they would cheer louder and louder for the worst act on the bill. How many dreadful acts thought they were well liked in Leicester? I wonder!!

PEDAL POWER OUT - HORSEPOWER IN

With increasing distances to be covered by the boys on cycles, the introduction of motorcycles was very welcome. Very tiring and long journeys still had to be made by cycle if the motorcycles (of which there were only four with one in reserve) were out on delivery, or the boy had upset the booking out officer! Nothing had changed in that respect. The new motorcycles were 125 cc B.S.A. Bantams green in colour, as supplied ex-works by the manufacturer. They were fitted with leg shields and a rack for packets over the rear mudguard by the G.P.O. workshops. The bikes were repainted Post Office Red some time after the summer of 1951. In April of 1950 motorcycle training was given to some of the senior messengers and the bikes were first used for delivery in June. The boys only used them for part of their shift at first, the early boys handed the bikes over to the late shift at midday. It was quite a come down to go back on a cycle after riding a motorbike. Several boys left the G.P.O. as trained motorcyclists! One boy joined the Police Force and eventually became a Police Motor Cyclist and it was with some relief when a messenger, following a minor traffic infringement, was approached by this Officer, seeing his friendly face and following a warning, was told "Get the kettle on, I'll be in soon."

UNUSUAL COLLECTIONS

Bishop Street Head Office counter staff and the telegraphists often left behind at home their spectacles, sandwiches or other items that they should have taken to work with them. A telephone call to the Booking Out Officer soon had a boy sent to collect the forgotten article. A more unusual job for the boys was to go to the home of a Booking Out Officer to feed his parrot!

CRIME? AND PUNISHMENT

Worker pronounced Wuker by the boys was a term used to describe punishment from the Booking Out Officer for committing some mundane offence (in their eyes.) A boy could be despatched to some distant point of the city such as Birstall on a cycle. Riding along believing in his total innocence, muttering all the way, knowing it was not even his turn to go out. By the time he reached the top of Red Hill the hatred he felt had been replaced by thoughts of revenge. Donkey was another term for punishment, which entailed working an extra hour duty without pay. Should the boy not accept his punishment, with good grace both Donkey and Wuker could be carried out together.
 By 1956 Donkey was no longer used as a punishment.

1956 REVISION

There was a major revision in 1956. The cost of sending a telegram was doubled overnight from 1/6d to 3/-, this had a devastating effect on the service. The number of telegram boys dropped to twenty four very quickly. The Assistant Inspector in Charge of Messengers, Mr Harold Peel was withdrawn to the Sorting Office and the Postal and Telegraph services were merged into one organisation. The Officers in Charge of the Delivery Room were two Postman Higher Grade (P.H.G.'s) who rotated on a six day early and late shift with the Sunday morning on overtime. The P.H.G.'s signed for two years on a yearly basis so there was always an experienced officer in charge to train the new man. The P.H.G. who stood down remained as the reserve, as specialist knowledge was needed to cover the work.

SUNDAYS & HOT DOGS

Messengers from the 1st of July 1956 started on 80/- per week at the age of fifteen, this was following a pay rise linked to the 1956 revision.

On Sunday mornings messengers worked from 8.00 a.m. until 12.30 p.m. Telegrams on hand at 8.00 a.m. and any received in the next hour for addresses near to the office were delivered. Any telegrams for addresses in the county or on the outskirts of the city were held back until 10.00 a.m. when the boys were sent out with everything on hand. This was done to ensure adequate cover was maintained given the limited number of boys on duty. Just before the clear out the boys were given permission to go to Eric's Refreshment Stand on Charles Street for a mug of tea and a hot dog. When this stand closed down, the boys went to Eric's other stand on the corner of East Street and Granby Street, which was also used by the men from the Sorting Office on Sunday mornings. After the 10.00 a.m. clear out just a couple of boys remained to deliver any further telegrams, holding the fort until the other messengers returned. Sometimes boys sent out on rural runs had to go so far from the office that by the time they returned the other boys had finished. The messengers on the rural runs volunteered for the longer journeys as it gave them extra time riding a motorbike with little traffic to negotiate and they looked upon it as a bonus. On Sunday afternoon there was only one messenger on duty from 1.00 p.m. until 5.30 p.m. and he was under the control of the Telegraphist in Charge of the Instrument room. At 5.00 p.m. the telegraphist sent the messenger out on his last run with any telegrams that could be delivered and to enable the boy to return his motor cycle to Campbell Street garage by 5.30 p.m. Telegrams that could not be delivered in the messengers duty time and any received in the evening were delivered by a driver from the Sorting Office.

KEEPING OUT THE WEATHER

The old brass link buckle belts were withdrawn and new ones came into use. A large pin type buckle made of steel secured the belt these were Sam Brown Army type, but because the boys cut the shoulder straps off, that design was replaced with a belt without the strap. In Leicester in 1956, the one and only Sam Brown belt fastened with a small polished steel buckle was issued and was still in use up until 1962, unfortunately 'doctored' to a non Sam Brown after three days of constant ridicule. Motorcycle riders were issued with heavy gaberdine waterproofed coats, which required the help of another boy to put on properly. The coat was so full it had to be pulled from the back by another boy into a dovetail while the wearer fastened his belt to hold it in shape. That was the only way it would stay in place in wind and rain whilst riding a motorbike.

Underneath this, individual leggings were worn they were designed to fit over the shoe laces in an attempt to keep the rain out. Because each leg was separate there was no protection for a boy's trouser seat whether the boy rode a motorcycle or a cycle. So after delivering the first telegram he would end up sitting on a wet seat in great discomfort for the duration of the run. Cyclists were issued with new black waterproof capes which covered the rider and the handlebars, all boys were issued with new black waterproof leggings which were better than the previous issues for keeping out the water, but they were very easy to rip on the kick start or cycle pedals. The old issue covered the top of the shoes these leggings did not, therefore in heavy rainfall the water found its way into the shoes. Boys who wore Post Office issued boots instead of shoes kept their feet dry. The heavy gaberdine motorcycle coats once wet soaked up large amounts of water making them a nightmare to dry out. Following heavy rain the mess room was always full of boys' waterproof coats arranged in front of the gas stoves open oven door, dripping water over the floor. It sometimes took days for the coats to dry out, the old style brown leggings also soaked up the wet in a similar fashion.

The next uniform change was when the motorcycle helmets were replaced. Out went the old blue heavy issue they were replaced with white Stadium lightweight helmets with G.P.O. stencilled in red on the front. The issue of motor cycle goggles was also a new innovation, many of the lads thought they now looked like despatch riders and often rode like them, causing more problems for the long suffering booking out officer. Cyclists were issued with several different types of cycle lamp and batteries to try, many were found unsuitable given the harsh treatment a telegram boy could put them through. What was good for a Postman was often useless for the telegraph delivery lads with their rough ground riding habits. If there was a short cut to be taken, then the lads knew it and used it.

SHORT CUTS & BREAKDOWNS

There were many short cuts in use, including the famous Birstall to Thurmaston route across the fields, many a lad came to grief emulating a trials bike rider over the rough terrain. Several limped to Thurmaston with a damaged motor cycle, not daring to report the real accident site, with the thought of the 'sack' being the spur that allowed a puny boy to drag a heavy bike up to a mile.

One of the routes an intrepid cyclist could take was a fast run down the extremely steep and slippery granite sets of Granby Avenue, which runs from Mere Road to Rolleston Street. The idea was to ring his bell like mad and not stop as he crossed the first three streets like lightening on the very steep part of the run, making sure to avoid the cast iron bollards situated in the middle of each junction. After reaching this point the road widened out and started to level off with just two more roads to cross. Boys normally only attempted the full run, risking life and limb when 'popping,' A witness was imperative if he was to be believed. Many boys practised on parts of the run, but often pulled up short to avoid a lorry crossing the intended route or had a last minute panic if the cycle slid on the granite sets. Not a stunt for the faint hearted!

If a boy broke down, he first 'phoned the P.H.G. in charge to inform him where he was and whether or not he had any telegrams left to deliver. The P.H.G. would ring the garage at Campbell Street Sorting Office only if he could relay the boys location, otherwise the boy would have to speak to the Garage Supervisor himself to explain where he was. The call would be made by dialling 100 for the operator and asking for a Service Call (free call.) If of course the boy's voice was recognised by the operator it could cause problems. Some girls would get back at a boy for hassle he had possibly given her or a friend at the Youth Club by refusing to put him through. After pleading for several minutes the girl would connect him, she could not risk getting caught by her supervisor breaking the rules. He would never know if he had been forgiven or not. Sometimes the call would be cut off just as he was giving his location. Boys learned not to upset the telephonists, as revenge for them was easy!

If he had the misfortune to break down outside the city then he could have the additional problem of a 'B' box, which required a coin to call the operator. In these boxes there was a button to press just for the emergency services. Often the boys were broke and had no coins in their pockets so they had to press the emergency button and ask for a Service Call. The Supervisor would give him what for, eventually he would be put through, but not until the Booking Out Officer had his ear bent for letting boys out without money.

The arrival of the mechanic brought fear into even the biggest lad. They treated the bikes like their babies, and woe-betide anyone who damaged their charges. The sight of 'Big Pete' or 'Chick' approaching in the van was a signal to run for it, even though escape was futile. The least a boy could expect was a clip around the ear, being lifted up by the ears was quite normal and a kick in the pants often stopped a boy from breaking a gear lever again.

WET BEHIND THE EARS

Life as a new boy was far from easy and fraught with danger

from the initiation rites, which usually involved water. A regular torture was to be put into a red parcel bag and hung onto the tap halfway down the cycle ramp, which led to the basement at Bishop Street Head Office. The tap was turned on and as the bag filled with water the poor captive hoped that he could escape before the water reached his head, or some senior lad took pity on him and let him out, with the help of others. The hardest part was when he got home that night, trying to explain to his mother how he had become covered in dirt and blue dye, then stopping her from going into the office to complain about the incident. A new recruit, would often be invited by an older boy to see the fishes trapped down a hole in the sink, if he was stupid enough to believe it and look down the hole an accomplice blew down the connecting hole at the other end of the sink and dirty water would hit the unsuspecting recruit in the eye.

It was not unknown for a senior messenger who was often much larger than his victim to stand inside the toilet doorway and grab a passing boy by his coat collar and persuade him to take some of his telegrams. The comment "I'm not going Stoneygate, I'm going to Glenfield" was answered with "You are now." The boy would get back late only to be punished by being sent out again. If the real reason for the delay were given it would only bring him a long period of grief for snitching from the perpetrator, or one of his mates. Either way he was in a no-win situation, hassle from the lads or the booking out officer, or both!

Another old favourite still around, was to be sent into Belvoir Street to the cake shop located under the Grand Hotel to ask for a tin of pigeon's milk and half a dozen pregnant tarts. This usually produced a strong response from the long-suffering manageress who would chase the boy from the shop and later make a 'phone call to the P.H.G. to complain. Because the lads were regular customers the manageress did not want to ban them, this made it easier for the boys to 'wind up' the staff. A main tease was for several lads to go in when the shop was crowded and ask for dead fly cake (Nelson cake.) If the staff tried to stop them from calling it this in front of the other customers the boys would just carry on saying that the currants did look like dead flies. The more the staff protested the more the boys talked in loud voices about the floor sweepings and other things going into the cakes. This sometimes was the last straw for the weary manageress and the boys were shown the door, they usually stayed away for a few days until she had calmed down.

SWINGING THE LEAD

One of the tasks given to the boys to keep them occupied was to make bag ties from cut lengths of stiff twine, these were knotted at one end after a lead seal had been threaded on. The twine was in two lengths, short for letter bags and long for parcel bags. A plait of twenty-five was made and handed in to the booking out officer, some letter length strings were used by them when preparing the despatches in the Accounts Branch. When the telegram traffic was low, boys were sent to work in the Sorting Office. If sent to work in the parcel section the opportunity was taken, to remove made up plaits of seals from the porter's hiding places. The seals were then quietly taken back to Bishop Street and hidden in the boys' lockers. When a boy was given lead seal making as a punishment or as a task before being sent home early, much to the amazement of the officer in charge the seals were produced in double quick time. The only down side of this was if you were spotted by another boy, some of your precious stock had to be handed over, or your secret was blown. Even worse was being caught in the parcel section by a porter 'pinching' his stock of ready made plaits, then the punishment was a serious battering before escaping down one of the mail chutes leaving him to cool off. The letter section was not such a handy source of ready made seals as the P.H.G.s were more adept at hiding their supply and there was always someone around.

LAS VEGAS?

Occasionally during the week and always on a Saturday during slack times the playing cards came out, despite a notice on the delivery room notice board stating that gambling was a dismissable offence. Breaking rules and the thrill of not getting caught was the reason most boys gave for doing anything. No money was in sight only a pencilled note in front of each player on the enamel topped table gave the game away. Lads that had gone over to the Postman's grade and were waiting to do their National Service came in for a game after finishing their delivery. Due to the losses incurred many of the boys were broke by Sunday after getting paid the previous Friday. The only saviour the boys had was the 'POP CLUB' which was run by the booking out officer to raise funds for trips out and to buy records for the Youth Club. "Can I have a loan?" was a frequent request made to the P.H.G. You invariably got one following a lecture about not wasting your money, he presumed your money was lost playing cards but sometimes the money had been stopped out of the weekly wage for a mad moment when G.P.O. property had been broken. If only he knew! The 'Pop Club' standard order for bottles of fizzy pop was dropped in at Hoyes Office in Queens Road and the crates were delivered each Thursday in time for payday. The thirsty work of cycling 'up the hill' made sure that there was always a greater demand than supply. Some flavours were to be avoided but had to be taken to get the overall price right. Occasionally Hoyes put in special flavours, American Ice cream soda was a popular one. To open bottles, the tough, some would say slightly crazy opened theirs with their teeth, others used the openers, but if the P.H.G. was not in his seat then the counter edge was used. The bottle cap was placed on the aluminium edge and hit hard with the heel of the hand, knocking the cap off causing the Overseer to have a fit when he saw the corrugated edge of the counter. Each bottle cost 3d to buy and was sold for 5d which was quite profitable for the 'Pop Club.'

EVENINGS OUT

The main meeting place of the week for the boys was the Youth Club, which met in the Gladstone Buildings in Bishop Street. This was held on a Thursday night at 7.30 p.m. For those on late duty it meant a rush back to the Sorting Office to garage their motorcycle. Trainee Telephonists and girls from Free Lane Exchange provided the female attraction for the boys. A fee was charged to fund games equipment and records played during the evening. The 'Pop Club' sold bottles to boost the funds and when possible the flavours to be avoided were sold to the poor unsuspecting girls, leaving the best flavours for the boys. It was the job of the Youth Club Secretary, to buy the records when funds allowed from Daltons in Granby Street. He usually went each week accompanied by one or more of the boys, but eventually they changed to Cowlings in Belvoir Street where at least six boys could get into a listening booth together without incurring the Store Managers wrath. The selection of records was more to the boys' taste and more than once they were asked to leave because of complaints from the radio and television department on the floor below, as the boys got carried away stamping to the beat of the latest 'Rock 'n' Roll' record. Walking back to the office singing a tune from the selection they had just listened to, the boys got some curious looks and shakes of the head from older people that passed by.

As a group in uniform, messengers often went to the pictures. This was another situation where the boys, of course not only stuck together, but were ejected together, sometimes even before the film had started, having upset the management by chanting, singing, stamping or even beating the dust out of the row of seats in front sending clouds of dust into the air disrupting the projected picture. No amount of protesting their individual innocence stopped the ejection process, which was made easier for the management by the uniforms. One out, all out. No chance of a refund, more money wasted but the boys never learnt!

On one occasion the lads went to the Cameo in High Street and persuaded the booking out officer to go with them. They all bought tickets for the cheapest seats which were right at the front and settled down to watch the film. However one of the group spotted an usherette he had recently dated, after chatting to her they both disappeared out of sight behind the back row. When he had returned to his seat the usherette appeared and the group were asked to move, they all wondered if he had been up to no good and was this to be yet another ejection? But no! As the unhappy band reached the end of the aisle the girl stopped at an empty row of the best seats and shone her touch on them, realising they were intended to sit there the embarrassed booking out officer protested. The boys pushed him along the row and once settled in the very comfortable seat he said nothing more. He made his position clear the following day at work and never went to the pictures with the boys again. Being banned from several cinemas around the city was not too inconvenient as this could be got round when out of uniform unless an individual was recognised by the management. Being banned also extended at one time to Marks and Spencers and Woolworths. During dinnertime breaks the boys visited these stores to chat up the girl assistants to try and get a date. If the boys had no luck in Woolworths they would make their way to the front of the store where the loose sweet counter was and do their best to rattle the long suffering girl assistants as they were weighing out the sweets. If spotted by a floorwalker and ordered to leave they blew kisses to the girls, waved to the floorwalker and shot off out of the door into Gallowtree Gate. Leaving the store this way was no hardship for the boys as they always had one eye on the large clock in the store, the sweet counter was always visited just before they were due back at work, judging when to play this game was a fine art. This togetherness could have its upside, as well as its downside. If ejected from a store or cinema they all left together. If one boy got picked on, the whole group backed him up, 'gently' dissuading the other party from further action.

HAIRCUT SIR?

Like all outside activities, haircuts for the messengers were normally a group project. The boys visited Ron's Hairstylist in Belgrave Gate, if possible several at a time. It was so popular that if a long wait was to be avoided, the extra charge for a booked haircut was preferred. One boy achieved fame with his special crew cut he was photographed, had his picture in the salon brochure, and was seen at the local cinemas in an advertisement for Ron's. When he first came to work with this distinctive haircut some of the senior managers were not amused, this of course made him a hero with the lads. He is still called by his nickname of 'Brushhead' today!

TRAINS AND TRACKS

Half Day closing for businesses was taken in the county on Wednesday afternoons and in the city of Leicester on Thursdays, there were exceptions, some additionally closed Saturday afternoon. As most Sub Post Offices in the rural areas closed on Wednesday afternoons this added to the normal delivery areas for the boys. It could mean a nice trip out into the country in the summer months if on a motorcycle, but if the booking out officer had been upset and was in a mean mood one of the cyclists would be sent instead. This could be a real sweat for the boy and sweet revenge for the booking out officer. Half the problem with rural telegrams was finding the addressee. Sometimes members of the public were very unhelpful with directions, assuming the boy was from their local Post Office, even having been told that the boy did not know the area. Unmade, gated roads and level crossings could make life difficult. The road from the A47 to Gaulby by Billesdon had several gates and at the end the messenger had to ride through a farmyard inches deep in manure and water hoping he did not fall off. The road from Kirby Muxloe to Desford was wide and twisting and gave a motorcyclist the opportunity to speed round the bends. It could be very time-consuming and frustrating if a train was coming, as all road traffic had to stop where the railway cut across the road several times over a relatively short distance. The guard had to get off the train, close the gate to road traffic, see the train through, open the gate, get back into the guards van, travel just a few yards and repeat the whole process over again. For road users there was no way out, once on this road to or from Desford they were committed. On unmade roads the rules stated. Boys should dismount and walk, this was an instruction often ignored. To ask a boy to walk up to two miles with a cycle was hard enough, but with a motor cycle almost impossible. Two routes, which fell into this category, were the areas between Roseneath Avenue and Melton Road Leicester and off Station Road Glenfield. Both were dirt tracks with smallholdings scattered throughout the area.

LITTLE BOYS BEWARE

Danger delivery points for young telegram boys were hosiery factories. When the older machinists were in a teasing mood, the young apprentices kept well out of the way and if an unfortunate telegram boy walked in on a chase, he was considered fair game. One regular delivery point was in Chatham Street on the 1st floor at Bernard & Lakin, a messenger was delivering and happened to walk in as an apprentice mechanic was being chased by the women who intended to remove his trousers and grease his 'wedding tackle.' By the time the messenger had found someone to take the telegram off him he was at the far end of the room well away from the door, seeing what was going on he was trying to make his way back to the door unseen when a shout went up "there's another little boy, get him." He jumped up onto a sewing machine bench and ran from bench to bench making the door in double quick time, he leapt down the stairs three at a time smacking into the corner half way down, reaching the street and his bike in record time. Running towards Granby Street he vaulted onto his bike and peddled furiously back to the office vowing never to go there again and he didn't! On another occasion the same boy again walked in on an initiation ceremony whilst delivering an Express item to Laird Portch in St Margarets Street. The ground floor offices were in darkness and hearing noises from the first floor he went to see if there was someone to leave the item with. He walked half way down the room and saw several women had a young lad in blue overalls on the floor at the far end of the room. The messenger realised it was time to make a hasty retreat but as he turned round two rather large grinning ladies were blocking his way and made a grab for him, he managed to escape their clutching hands and sprinted down the work shop. As he passed the end office a man in a suit stepped out and said "Come through here, its not fair that you get caught." With that he led the boy down the back stairs and into the side street. Remembering he still had the item, the messenger handed it over to the man who told him he was the Managing Director and could recall getting caught himself when he was a lad and suffering a similar fate to the poor soul upstairs. Sometimes there can be worse initiation ceremonies than the 'Red Bike ones!'

HOLD YOUR BREATH AND HOPE FOR THE BEST

Delivery to some of the more exotic addresses was often a short straw job. If there was one for Rollestone House, which was a lodging house in Britannia Street it literally took your breath away. When the telegram boy arrived he would take a large breath, go in and hope to find the manager straight away, if he was unlucky he had to wait for him. On one occasion the manager asked the messenger to take the telegram to the addressee who was in a room near to the front door. In this smallish room there was a large black pot bellied stove which was surrounded by a number of shabbily dressed men who were drying their socks and wellingtons, the heat was intense and the smell was gagging. The hardest part, was having to ask politely which man was the addressee, handing over the telegram the boy crossed his fingers hoping he did not have to wait for a reply. The man said nothing just stared down at the message, another man put a hand on his shoulder and asked what was wrong, holding up the telegram so it could be read, the boy was told he could go. He made a very quick exit into the street heaving as he went and was immediately sick in the gutter. Back at the office looking like death warmed up he shared the tale during a tea break, several of the listeners strangely lost their appetites and had trouble eating their sandwiches. The booking out officer took delight for several days in announcing there was another telegram for Rollestone House and watching the reaction until the joke wore thin!

A rather seedy establishment, was an old building in Foundry Square which was originally a public house known locally as the 'Blinking Owl.' Having to deliver a telegram here was unusual and the boy sent was a little nervous having been told of the reputation of the premises and the occupants. Outside on the pavement the messenger met a young policewoman who asked the boy if he was going in. She was worried because the place was noted to be full of very old ladies of easy virtue and she was afraid to go in on her own. Even though the boy was considerably younger than the constable he agreed to accompany her and wait until she had completed her enquiries. Once the bargain was struck they both went in together and eventually came out together with the boy feeling quite heroic, to be kissed on the cheek and thanked by a police constable was for him a unique experience.

PLEASE DON'T TOUCH

An interesting delivery point were the offices of Goodwin & Barsby in Watling Street. On the way to the first floor office was a half landing with a large window on the ledge of which stood a working model of a stone-crushing machine. One day a messenger stopped to look at the model and was winding one of the gear wheels when he was caught by one of the Directors. Embarrassed at being caught red-handed he explained he was only trying to see how it worked, the Director told him to be careful and went on to explain why it was important to the firm as well as to him because he had helped make it when he was an apprentice. He told the messenger as long as he was careful and didn't do any damage he was quite welcome to see how it operated. The boy went off wiser and surprised that a Director could be so friendly and take the time to explain why the model meant so much to him.

MONDAY MORNING BLUES

Duty Composite 1 was the first to attend at 7.00 a.m. Monday morning started with the most hated job, which was to change the cards in the perpetual calendars. Each held a set of cards with the day, month and year on them. This was very time consuming especially if the container was dropped when the boy was rushing consequently scattering the cards all over the floor.

The next task was updating the hand stamps, no one ever managed to do this without dropping a least one of the boxes containing the metal or rubber dies and having to scramble around the floor to collect the pieces. The hand stamps with metal dies were kept in wooden boxes which if dropped weren't too bad as they were heavy and the pieces didn't spill out too far. On the other hand dropping a tin box with the Parcel Post dies, which were made of rubber was a disaster the pieces bounced far and wide and took ages to find. All the dies had to be put back into their boxes in the correct date order because for the rest of the week the hand stamps were changed at close of business by a Postman from the Sorting Office who worked at the end of the counter stamping packets. If he found a box with the dies muddled he would know who was responsible and not be averse to planting a boot against the offender's backside, no use appealing to their better nature this was one of the unwritten rules of Post Office life, leave things as you found them, or else!

Next was the daily trip to the Wholesale Fruit & Vegetable Market and the Wholesale Fish Market to deliver the Overnight Telegrams. Sometimes at the Wholesale Fruit & Vegetable Market the boys would be given fruit by one of the porters in the market hall. The Fish Market could be dangerous as the floor was very wet and slippery from fish debris and ice. Cast iron spiral staircases led to the offices above where the telegrams had to be delivered, unless a member of the sales staff took it from them. Care had to be taken when climbing the very slippery stairs, which started to sway after the first few steps were taken. Halfway up most boys would be gripping the handrail tightly, trying to reach the first floor as quickly as possible. Because the stairs weren't fixed at the top the higher they climbed the greater the sway. Stepping across the gap onto the landing was a gut wrenching experience and the return trip to the ground floor was no better. Having done the climb once some of the boys with weaker stomachs went to great lengths to avoid ever going up again.

After delivering to the markets on a Monday Comp 1 visited Free Lane Telephone Exchange to clear the box on the operations floor of any overtime dockets from the previous week, which were then taken to the Wages Branch at Bishop Street. The lift at the exchange was operated by a male cleaner one of these was well known to the boys as he worked in the evenings on door security at Bishop Street Head Office. Harry loved to torment the boys and was often joking with them and the Telephonists. Entry to the lift for staff and visitors was via a short flight of stairs which enabled Harry to spot a boy making his way towards the lift, he would then close the gates and go up without him towards the Operators Floor several floors up which resulted in a long hard climb for the boy. Harry would make ribald comments each time he passed the boy staggering up the stairs, much to the amusement of any of the young telephonists travelling in the lift with him. Numerous potential romances were scotched by Harry the cleaner no young lady would admit to knowing the messenger being humiliated in this way even if she'd got a date with him. Once reaching the operational floor, boys often ignored the strict rule of not whistling whilst there. It was done to attract the attention of the telephonists the boys knew from the youth club and to show a total disregard for the rules. It usually abruptly ended with the, much feared Supervisor Miss Beavan catching the boy and giving him a dressing down within earshot of the girls which greatly improved his standing at the Youth Club on Thursdays and was well worth the confrontation!

In the afternoon some time was spent on the Addressograph Machine at the rear of the Instrument Room printing Confirmation and Telegraphic address envelopes. The final task was to turn and fold empty Remittance Bags for the P.H.G. in the Accounts Branch. This last task was the dirtiest job a messenger could get, dust was sucked up into his uniform like water on a sponge and he would look like he had been up a chimney. On Comp 1 life was never dull.

ANOTHER OF HARRY'S GAMES

When 'Free Lane Harry' was door keeping at Bishop Street he took great delight in taking 'phone messages from the girls and altering them before passing them onto the boys, causing numerous complications in their love lives. Whatever Harry said to the exchange girls was taken as gospel when they asked him about a message he had passed on. They never believed he would change the time of a date or slightly alter the meeting place, which always put the boys in the wrong, without a chance to defend themselves. The girls always believed Harry.

This was nothing when compared to his party piece, which was to challenge new boys to a kicking contest with him. If the boy agreed Harry took the first kick and none too gently, trying not to show how much he'd been hurt the boy would take his turn. Harry turned and offered the boy his leg, which the boy would kick as hard as he could only to suffer more pain, Harry would just stand there and laugh and then pull up his trouser leg to reveal an artificial leg made of steel. Exit one very humiliated young man accompanied by gales of laughter from the watching boys, and Harry!

JUST THE TICKET

The canteen for Bishop Street Head Office was located in the Gladstone Buildings next door. This was, reached by a corridor on the 2nd floor of the Head Office, which connected the two buildings. A lasting memory for the boys was of the Manageress, a lady who stood no messing whatsoever and always worked with a cigarette dangling from the corner of her mouth and regularly served the boys while standing directly underneath a large red 'NO SMOKING' sign! The boys were issued with luncheon vouchers for meals Monday to Friday on signature from the Indoor Writing Room. The tickets entitled the holder to a lunch and a sweet. They were blue for fifteen year old messengers, their meals were free. Sixteen to seventeen year old messengers had white tickets and paid half the cost of the meal. One of the older messengers was noted for his enormous appetite. He bought sandwiches from home, ate these first then bought a meal and a sweet, and then, he often bought the sweet ticket off one of the younger boys who was hard up. If of course it was a free ticket, the seller was despatched to fetch the sweet for him. The Telephonists Training School also used this canteen and it was a work of art to talk with the girls and if possible arrange a date. Postal, Counter and Training School Supervisors discouraged fraternisation between the girls and boys, only at the youth club was this allowed. At lunch times notes were often exchanged with the girls and if a request for a date was rejected the boys let fly firing peas from their knives in the direction of the girls, sometimes they got away with it but more often they were caught and were punished by a Supervisor. One Friday things got out of hand, it started with a group of girl trainees making loud caustic remarks about the boys, followed by a lump of fish batter thrown at a boy, the boys retaliated by firing dozens of peas at the girls. It all stopped dead when the Accountant came in who was not noted for his sense of humour. As one of the girls walked past the back of a boy, she dumped a handful of food onto his head. He jumped up and before the girl could escape from the room she was caught and a large handful of peas were stuffed down the back of her dress. Game set and match and honour satisfied you would think, but at that moment the Head of the Telephonist School walked into the dining room straight in front of the pair. The boy was hauled over the coals by the school head and the Accountant. The Accountant later made a report of the incident to the Postal Superintendent. But it all ended well, as the Superintendent was an ex-messenger himself and was quite reasonable at the interview starting with, "If you have to let off steam, don't do it where you can get caught!" The girl was very sorry about the boy being reported and the fact that she had got away with it, so it was resolved with a date at the pictures, but that's another story.

ANOTHER LUNCH TICKET

Getting the messengers duty at Leicester Race Course was a plum job, taking telegrams from the Temporary Instrument Room under the main stand to the press box and returning with the reporters' sheets was an easy task. The Postal staff were given lunch tickets which included a tear off portion for a glass of beer. A Postman Driver who took the messenger and the telegraphists to the course would often try to con the messenger out of this 'beer ticket' by telling him he was too young to drink. It was a great day out, especially if the telegraphists were ex-messengers themselves, they were very easy to get along with. Meeting world famous jockeys and racing reporters added to the kudos of getting this much sought after duty and there was also additional pay for working away from the office.

UNDERSIZE & OVERSIZE

In the mid 1950's two small messengers shared a special red light weight cycle that was referred to by the other boys as the 'Fairy Cycle.' These two worked on opposite shifts so there was no problem. Along came another small boy in April 1956 who topped the G.P.O. minimum height limit of four feet eight inches by just half an inch. On his first day he was sent out by the booking out officer with a senior messenger who quickly told Mr Bullous that the new boy was too small to ride a Post Office Cycle. On investigation he saw for himself that when the boy was on the seat, his feet were well clear of the pedals. Mr Yarnell the Assistant Superintendent soon gave permission for the boy to ride his own cycle until a further lightweight bike was obtained. This must be the only time in Leicester that a telegram boy was to be seen out delivering on a turquoise coloured cycle. After a while the new cycle arrived but another problem arose because it was black and all three boys wanted to ride it. This cycle finished its days being used by an ex-messenger Assistant Inspector as his patrol cycle at the East Delivery Office in St Barnabus Road. At the other end of the scale was one special cycle used by a rather tall boy. It had a double cross bar to give extra height and strength, and was referred to as a 'double clanger.'

GOTCHA!

The Belvoir Billiard Hall in Stamford Street located over Cowlings Record Store, was a favourite haunt of some of the older messengers, they were often there when they should have been out on delivery. Time was gained by either getting a small boy who could be imposed upon to deliver some of their telegrams, or rushing round taking all the short cuts to get back quickly for a game of snooker. In the battle between the boys and the booking out officer, occasionally the lads slipped up. On one occasion a boy was sent with a message from him to the snooker players telling them they were booked out! On reaching the 2nd floor the boy passed on the message and received hostile abuse. His message was not believed until an older boy rushed in shouting "Quick get out, Jack Bullous is coming up Belvoir Street". The boys dropped their cues and charged down the stairs to pick up their bikes, which had been left out of sight at the side of the stairs on the ground floor. Acting cleverly, so they thought, they rode off in the wrong direction down one-way Stamford Street towards Chatham Street. They thought this way they would escape back to the office, only to meet a smiling Mr. Bullous who had doubled back down Belvoir Street after spotting the boy running towards the Billiard Hall. This round went to the booking out officer.

FUN FOR SOME

One friction point for the Instrument Room staff was the Pneumatic Tube. When used correctly it posed no problems but in the hands of the boys' it became a nerve wrecking device. When the booking out officer had to leave a senior messenger in charge, the 'fun' started as soon as he had left the room. Empty tubes were held back until three or four were available, then as each one was placed into the return pipe, a hand was placed over the tube end so eventually they were end to end in the pipe. The pressure built up in the pipe and the tubes were released. Arriving at the Instrument Room end they came out into the collecting basket one after another like exploding bullets, the flap slamming shut again and again making the telegraphist sitting there jump. Occasionally the booking out officer was in the Instrument Room at the time so had a grandstand view of what happened, plus the full force of the complaints. On one occasion for a joke, a boy sent via the tube a selection of topless pictures to the Instrument Room. A popular telegraphist should have been sitting at the other end it was inevitable that when the pictures arrived he had changed position. In his place was a very straight-laced, middle-aged Miss. No prizes for guessing the outcome. The boy was ribbed about it for a very long time afterwards.

CHAPTER 9

WEATHERING THE LATE 50's
'E' MESSAGES AND REVENGE

One of the special services that were offered by the G.P.O. was the 'E' Form Service. Customers were charged 1/- per mile for items to be collected from a Post Office counter and delivered to an address, which could be in another town. There were extra charges for the messengers time, if it involved services other than taking items from A to B. Regular trips were carried out on racing days picking up packets from Sub Post Offices around the city and delivering them to wellknown Bookmakers (Turf Accountants). Some of the packages only travelled short distances, from Welford Road and Hinckley Road T.S.O.s (or King Richards Road on a Saturday when Hinckley Road was closed) to the Silver Arcade. Melton Turn T.S.O. to Windsor Avenue and Belgrave Gate T.S.O. to Rutland Street were runs to other Bookmakers.

It was always difficult to see across the room at the Silver Arcade through the dense clouds of cigar smoke made by three oversized gentlemen 'bookmakers' who seemed to constantly smoke large Havana type cigars. Boys who didn't smoke found getting a signature here left them choking and they left the room with eyes streaming, other boys who smoked thought it was really good and they often tried to get a free cigar but this was never achieved. At the Rutland Street address the bookmakers who worked there were nearly as large as the ones at the Silver Arcade, the difference here was that boys handed over the package and got a signature from anyone who came to the door of the office. The reception the boys got was often very frosty and they were reminded if they used the lift to leave it at the ground floor. Several of the bookmakers had breathing problems and did not like to be kept waiting for the lift to come down several floors. The lift travelled very slowly which suited the buildings occupants. One particular boy was shouted at and he realised when he got out of the lift at the ground floor he could reach through the gates and press the top floor button, which he decided to do sending the lift right up to the top floor. A dangerous act perhaps, but when the other boys were told it seemed an appropriate way to get their own back for the 'shoddy' way they were treated. When a messenger overheard one of the bookies bitterly complaining about the thoughtless person who had forgotten to send the lift back down causing him to stand waiting, the comment was eagerly passed on to the other boys. The 'E' Service could be used in many different ways some of which could bring the boys added reward. Showing a commercial traveller around the city could get the boy not only a meal, which was covered in the rules but often a tip if the traveller had a good day. Another 'E' Service that came up occasionally for the messengers was to take animals from A to B by the most appropriate method usually cats or dogs going to national shows such as Crufts. In these cases the rail fare and money for a meal was into the fee, but for the sender it was money well spent as the valuable pet was escorted from door to door, a trip that could not be covered by insurance in those days. Fees for the service were collected at the counter and postage stamps stuck onto the E form and cancelled. When the service fee was high there was always a dilemma if insufficient high value stamps were available, the back of the form would be completely covered with low value stamps.

DAILY & MADCAP ROUTINES

On the delivery office wall was a map in a glass case which

showed the city split up into sixteen delivery areas. Area one was the City Centre measured in a half-mile radius from the Clock Tower, within this area were the three Railway Stations. The city centre was normally reserved for messengers on cycles they took out 'E' Messages and Express packets as well as telegrams. Collecting Greetings Telegrams from the Instrument Room could be an easy task or a burden. They were collected because they were too large to fit in the pneumatic tube. If a boy was being a nuisance the way to bring him back into line was to tell him he was booked out, then send him to collect the greetings telegrams first. If the lift was busy or out of order the walk to the 3rd floor was quite a journey, using the Head Postmasters lift on the Bishop Street side was forbidden. This lift went from the basement to the 3rd floor opposite the Instrument Room corridor. During the week the lift was also used to take coin bags from the coin counting room on the 2nd floor, down to the rear of the public counter and to protect the highly polished wooden lift panels, special lining boards were fixed into place. At the weekend, to ease their tired legs the boys would use the Head Postmaster's lift hoping not be seen by any counter staff. Coming back down was different, the boys liked to race back, preferring the stairs to the lifts. A technique of using the left hand wall and the rail on the right to swing-jump several steps at once was perfected. Many of the boys were shouted at by startled counter staff coming through the swing doors at the end of the 1st and 2nd floor corridors when confronted by one or more boys jumping down the stairs.

CAN YOU MAKE THE SHADE RING?

A way to lose money was to be caught doing wrong and being fined. Two boys were on their way to the canteen in the

Gladstone Buildings to take a meal break. On the way through the top corridor one said, "Have you rung a light shade?" "No how do you do that?" came the reply. Taking his belt off the first boy swung it at the lampshade and because it was glass it rang when he hit it. The second boy tried, but made the mistake of catching it with the buckle end, the shade came down in pieces and as the first boy fell about laughing saying "You hit it with the other end," at that moment an Overseer walked round the corner. The younger messenger stood holding his belt in his hand looking at the debris on the floor as the Overseer demanded his name and badge number. The end result was a step up the villain's ladder for this boy, but the 17/6d stopped out of his wages for a replacement light shade was something he did not want his mother to find out about and thanks to the 'Pop Club' she never did.

FROM VILLAIN TO HERO

A problem for any young person is to receive a letter asking for an explanation for something, which cannot be remembered. Getting a letter asking what you did with a Telegraph Money Order, for what was at the time, a large sum of money sent panic waves through the receiver. The reply sent to the Telegraph Overseer stated, the T.M.O. had been put in the letterbox, which was fixed to the railings at the front of the yard of a national soft drinks firm's premises and a Slip Left card placed under the door of the office.

A few days later the P.H.G. told the messenger he was to accompany the Assistant Superintendent Mr Yarnell to see the Depot Manager. They were taken there in a G.P.O. van driven by a Postman. On arrival the whole story was repeated, then the three of them went out to see the post box in question. The Manager then said, "The Money order was found blowing around the yard." He asked how the telegram was put in the box, and a slip left card was used to demonstrate what had taken place on the evening when the depot was closed. To everyone's amazement the card was seen to float across the yard inside the fence. There was a viewing slot at the rear of the box and with the wind blowing into the front of the box, it lifted the item straight out at the back. The observers were surprised, stunned into silence and an apology was given along with a crate of Britvic mixers with a request to return the empty crate and bottles later. The Manager said he was impressed with the way the boy had conducted himself. On the way back he found he had changed from the villain to a hero in the eyes of the Assistant Superintendent. The boys were very impressed when they drank the posh free 'POP'.

I DON'T WANT TO KNOW

A craze, which started small and like 'Topsy' grew and grew, was the use of nicknames. It was nothing new, messengers had used them from way back at the turn of the century.

There was a difference this time, instead of just using the nicknames when addressing one another the boys started to draw them on the back of their leather motor cycle jerkins in 'Biro.' It began with one boy and as nothing was said to him, the other boys dared to follow suit. Next it came to doodling on the booking out forms, each boy put his nickname on the top of his form every day and it was inevitable that in time it would be brought to the attention of the Assistant Superintendent. Down came an order from on high to the effect, that he did not want to know who 'Lash, Flash, Natch or Brother' were and he didn't want to see another booking out form endorsed in this way. It was too late to save the leather jerkins and seeing these must have been a constant irritation to Mr Yarnell.

SPECIAL RECIPES

The boys were always on the lookout for new ways to be different and to 'cock a snook' at officialdom so along came the remodelling of the hats. Several boys took out the stiffening material and after bending the peak down forced the top of the hat down at the sides and stitched it firmly into place. There were several variations Coldstream guards style flat peaks were one. None of course met with approval particularly from the Uniform Officer. Gloves and hats, especially those issued to new boys were the number one target for abuse by the older boys. At the first opportunity new hats and gloves, if left unattended were soon put into the hot oven, which was always lit on wet days to dry out the clothes. The hats were filled with water and to this was added anything, which could be found to ruin them. Ink, lead seals even old milk was added before cooking took place. If the frantic owner discovered it boiling merrily away on the top shelf of the oven he reclaimed it and tried to reverse the damage. A variation on this was to put a fire bucket full of noxious liquid on the gas burners to which was added any items of uniform that would fit in. This prank really upset the booking out officer as eventually replacement uniform could be found, but the fire bucket was a different matter!

Officially, going out on delivery without a hat was not allowed so a boy whose own hat had been in the oven would try to 'borrow' another boy's. If he was 'rumbled' by the owner, swift punishment was administered, but this was preferable to getting caught without a hat, by an official. Gloves were carefully guarded because the boys would try to exchange their worn out pair for new ones if possible. There were two types of gloves issued, short dark brown leather for cyclists and long soft leather for motorcyclists, on which later issues had a large reflective arrow on the back. The cycle gloves were targeted when they were new for the oven treatment but it was deemed a 'no go' for motor cycle gloves because they were hard to replace. A boy shrunk one of his cycle gloves to about four inches high, painted STOP across the palm in white paint then mounted it on the rear reflector of his motorcycle. Other boys wanted him to do the same for them, but before this could be put into operation he was caught, given a severe reprimand and the other boys were warned off. That boy became a hero for a while, taking it on and off his bike as he went in and out of the office and the story of the G.P.O. bike with the unusual stop signal went round the city police motor cyclists via an ex-messenger and they all tried to spot him. Unfortunately he came back one day with a long face having lost it and not daring to make another.

UNEXPECTED SCENES & VIEWS

Some days' things happened that could not be invented. A boy was delivering a telegram to a house on Glenfield Road. He knocked on the front door which had a small leaded window fitted with stained glass panes. In the centre was a clear glass pane and as he looked through it he saw on the right hand side at the head of the stairs a nude lady. She called out "Wait a minute please" then immediately walked down the stairs and past the front door and turned towards a row of hanging coats further up the hall, where she took down a raincoat and put it on. The boy was by this time open mouthed watching her. She pulled the coat collar up round her neck and then opened the door just a crack, the boy handed the telegram through the small opening trying hard not to laugh, she read the message and said "No reply thank you" and quickly shut the door. The boy went off laughing so loudly, a passer by looked at him, wondering what was so funny.

GETTING ALL STEAMED UP

On another occasion the same boy had a telegram for a large house in Highfields. When he arrived he put his cycle against the front wall and went up to the front door, which was open. He saw a row of bell pushes and realised the house was split into flats. At the front door he met a very tall West Indian gentleman who asked him what he wanted. The boy gave the name of the lady on the reply paid telegram, "Go straight up the stairs and in the door in front of you" he said, "The girl you want is in there." By this time other people had come out of the ground floor rooms, the boy went up the stairs and knocked on the door, a voice asked "Who is it, what do you want?"

The boy shouted "Reply paid telegram for Miss X." "Come in," said the female voice. The boy went in and found he was in a large bathroom with a very attractive West Indian girl lying in a bubble bath. He handed the telegram to the girl who slowly opened and read it, she looked at the boy who by this time was very red faced not knowing where to look and wishing the floor would open up, she asked him if she could send a reply later to which the boy answered "Yes" and explained where she could send the reply from. When the girl said he could go, he literally flew down the stairs watched by about a dozen people who had gathered laughing at his discomfort. He dashed back to the office dying to tell his tale. Unlike today a sixteen years old boy getting that close to a nubile naked female was unheard of.

'L' PLATES & PROBLEMS

Learning to ride a motorcycle was the dream of most sixteen year old telegram boys. To join the ranks of the lads dashing about the city and county, leaving sparks as they cornered on the leg shield's or foot rests was something special. For one boy, training started with the Driving Instructor arriving from Derby, with a none too steady, worried looking messenger riding in front of his van on a cold frosty morning.

Over a cup of tea the Derby messenger told the other boy how the Instructor had said he was to ride the bike from Derby to Leicester. The boy had protested to the instructor, saying he could not ride a motorbike but it was pointed out to him, he had been seen riding around the Telephone Exchange for some weeks. Derby Telegraph Delivery Office was located within the Telephone Exchange and a perimeter road ran inside the walls around the building, which was why Derby boys were used to riding motorbikes long before they were sixteen. The General Instruction regarding riding a G.P.O. motorcycle was given to both boys and following a break for lunch the Leicester boy went in the van with the instructor to Stoughton Airfield while the Derby messenger rode behind on the bike. On an abandoned bomber dispersal strip, the first shaky lessons were given to the Leicester boy. The next morning the Instructor and the boy came from Derby again and the Leicester boy was told it was his turn to ride and they were off to Coventry. After a while the Leicester boy's confidence on the bike grew and his speed picked up, when he was opposite Jones & Shipman's factory on Narborough Road South he dared to look in his mirror for the first time and noticed the van was not behind him so he stopped. After several minutes the van appeared and a very angry Instructor got out. He had been stopped by the police, because the learner had been seen speeding down Narborough Road hill, they had spotted the Instructor's plates on the van behind the learner so he was stopped and given a caution. When arriving in Coventry a second own goal was scored. As the motorbike and van drove into the Sorting Office yard, a speeding Post Office van cut in front of them and the Instructor let fly with a mouthful of expletives, a female driver got out of the Post Office van and gave him an ear bending about his colourful language, nil points so far! Trips on the following days were made to Derby and Melton Mowbray and at the end of the week, after a test with the Post Office Examiner both boys passed. This went some way to restore the humour of the Derby Instructor.

MECHANICS REVENGE

When a boy had broken down and was waiting to be brought back into the garage, the arrival of the breakdown van was quite traumatic. If the vehicle wash mechanic or one of the more elderly mechanics came it was okay, but on the other hand if Big Pete or Chick arrived on the scene then things were very different. They always dished out some form of punishment geared to the amount of work they were faced with to get the bike back on the road. They were both very large men, very quick on their feet despite their size and could grab a boy by the ears before he could blink. If the messenger was lucky they smiled as they got out of the breakdown van and he knew he would receive some swift but not too painful punishment. If one of them turned up and the boy had not seen a smile then he thought he was dead. Although escape was impossible from these two mechanics it did not stop some of the boys from trying.

One of the downsides of cleaning duties at Campbell Street Garage was, if you had managed to avoid Pete or Chick for days after breaking a part on one of the motorbikes, you stood a good chance of running into one of them, as the motorbike cleaning area was just outside the mechanics rest room. These two mechanics treated the bikes as their babies and woe betide you if you hurt one of their charges. If a new boy did not believe the stories about Pete he soon changed his mind once he saw him lift the engine out of a van in his arms, or see him throw a motor bike across the workshop when he'd lost his temper. Many a complaining Postman Driver with a loose mouth took flight when he realised he was up against either of these two mechanics. Chick was even more feared by the lads, as he had less humour and even greater strength. One boy on cleaning duty was set up by the others, unknown to him a motor cycle carburettor had been tickled to put petrol on the floor, he was then asked to throw the sand from the fire bucket to stop the flow. Un-beknown to the lad it was this bucket outside the mechanic's rest room that Chick saved his breakfast eggs in each day. The sand was thrown onto the floor and with it the eggs, Chick was not amused when he was told and he grabbed the boy by his belt, pulled him into the workshop and up to the ceiling on the engine hoist and left him dangling there, the boy was praying that his belt did not give way and was listening to the threat, "If you come down you will finish up like my eggs". The boy stopped shouting and kept very still until he was spotted by the workshop supervisor who organised his rescue.

BIG MEN, SMALL BIKES

The messengers had a very soft spot for Pete despite being in fear of him at times, they loved to see his party piece which was parking his motor bike inside the Station Street entrance to the workshop. Pete was over six feet tall and rode a very small 98 cc bike from Melton Mowbray each day. As he came into the entrance he would put his feet down, lift the bike up swing it round and drop it onto the stand in one go, Pete always said this was how his brakes lasted so long.

A tall ex-messenger, now a police motorcyclist also had a small bike, a 98 cc Sun. The boys sometimes came up to him on his way to work when he'd stopped at the traffic lights at the Granby Halls. His technique was the same as Pete's for stopping, feet down lift up the bike to keep the wheels moving then drop it down when the time was right and off he went. The only difference was that he had no working brakes on his bike, which why he used the Pete method of stopping, how he managed to get away with it for so long is another Red Bike legend!

FOG & SNOW IT'S WINTER

As time went on some of the hazards to messengers were removed. Following the last tram, which ran in November of 1949 most of the tram lines were taken up. There were just a few short lengths of track remaining in parts of the city. One stretch on Abbey Park Road just before the bridge over the river Soar where the road narrowed was made even more hazardous as it was fixed in granite sets. In some of the old streets granite sets were being covered in tarmac. But of those that weren't Brunswick Street and Catherine Street connected by the railway bridge were the worst. The bridge surface was still made up of granite sets with many missing causing potholes filled with water. No repairs had been carried out on the bridge because it was due for demolition when the railway lines into Belgrave Road Station were removed. Buses travelling over this narrow bridge only added to the danger. Autumn brought another difficulty, all the main roads were tree lined which was very picturesque until the leaves fell which made the road very slippery. Aylestone Road, Narborough Road and Melton Road were treacherous following heavy rain when the lime trees had shed their leaves. Before the Clean Air Act came into being on 5th July 1956 Leicester like many other large cities suffered from the effects of smog. The act did not get rid of the problem overnight it took a long time to resolve. In the late 1950's there were several bad winters with heavy smog, it was sometimes so dense, the only solution was to send messengers out only to the areas they knew, to lessen the chance of getting lost. Sometimes they were even allowed to go out in pairs, the only time that 'popping' was officially allowed. When it was really bad, boys were sent out with a van driver to the area where they lived to deliver telegrams and to help with the letter collections. P.H.G.s and Assistant Inspectors who had been drivers were used to drive the vehicles. Pillar-box collections were reduced to one small area to try and keep the service running. One messenger remembers going out with an Assistant Inspector along Hallam Crescent, walking in front of the vehicle shining his belt lamp to show the way, and to avoid being knocked down. On another occasion he was stopped on Narborough Road by the driver of a No 52 bus and asked if he could lead the way. The boy went very slowly along the road on his motorcycle with one foot on the kerb, the bus following close behind. The driver had opened his front cab window so he could see then sounded his horn to warn the boy when someone wanted to get off the bus. At the top of the hill, at the old tram terminus, the driver was told he was on his own because the boy was turning right into Hallam Crescent. It was not so hard to travel this way, as there were not many vehicles out on the roads in such appalling weather conditions and vehicles were parked in side streets or off the road altogether. During periods of deep snow the boys were taken off the road and very reluctantly went into the sorting office to work. It was preferable to being out in snow but they usually finished up in the parcel section and the porters were not noted for their humour or taking any cheek without giving swift punishment. The only bright spot was the opportunity to remove large amounts of ready made plaits of lead seals, for salting away at Blackwells Court. I wonder how many of the booking out officers realised how the boys managed to produce seals so quickly and so willingly at a later date.

THRILLS AND SPILLS

In the battle between the workshops and the boys, various measures were introduced to stop damage to the motorcycles, and to curb the speed of the riders. Damage to motorbike rear mudguards and the packet carrier mounted above was caused by the boys sitting on the carrier, enabling them to lie flat on the petrol tank trying to reduce wind resistance and hopefully get extra speed out of the bike. To stop this practice the mechanics welded spikes on top of the rack, this was soon overcome by strapping a heavy duty waterproof coat onto it making it far more comfortable to sit on. The Department was not happy to find that the large express packets were getting delivered with puncture holes in them, so the spikes were removed. Round one to the boys! Next they tried fitting a governor in the form of a longer needle in the carburettor. The boys found, that if they carefully wound up the top of the carburettor to the extent of the thread, it was back to normal. Round two to the boys! The mechanics next drilled a small hole in the side of the carburettor and placed a wire through, finishing it off with a small lead seal. The boys found this could be removed, the top wound up and the wire and seal replaced without it being obvious that the seal had been negated. Round three to the boys! This dodge was discovered by a sharp eyed mechanic when a boy had forgotten to remove the evidence before logging off his motor cycle. Eventually these measures were withdrawn though, because it was causing running problems with the engines. Game, set and match to the boys!! Naturally the boys all loved to try and go faster than one another and various claims were made, so a competition was set up which involved coming down Thurcaston Road Hill at the fastest speed possible without using the engine. Boys rode as fast as they could by the end of Birstall Golf Course, as they passed the sign at the top of the hill the bike was put into neutral, racing down the hill past Astill Drive the speed was taken as they reached the railway bridge. The record was around 54 M.P.H. although this fact was disputed by several of the boys.

There was one story (unconfirmed) that a boy was pulled up by the police for exceeding the 30 M.P.H. speed limit on Saffron Lane ON A CYCLE!

SLIDES, SPARKS AND BENT METAL

In the late 1950's the motor cycles were fitted with windscreens which did not last very long, they were often damaged when the motorcycle fell over or was taken through gaps that were not intended for motor cycles. Repairs for the mechanics ranged from broken throttle cables, gear levers and cracked windscreens. One rather solid built lad had a reputation for breaking gear levers and kick start levers, other boys dreaded following his duty as they often found their favourite bike was logged off for one of these faults. A quiet word to him from one of the more volatile mechanics did the trick and peace was restored in the workshop. Damage to bikes and nerves came in many ways. One boy had a lucky escape when he had stopped in Soar Lane Yard to look at the address on his telegram, as he heard a loud noise he looked up to see a large tipper lorry reversing rapidly towards him. Quickly scooting backwards, he sounded his horn but the lorry was making too much noise for the driver to hear him and he reversed onto the bike trapping the boy by the windscreen. Luckily another worker heard the horn and the shouting so stopped the driver of the lorry before any harm came to the boy. After this accident everyone was very careful in Soar Lane Yard. Another close call remembered was riding between two buses that were passing each other on the Narborough Road, near to Imperial Avenue. The boy sped between the buses so closely that the rubber was ripped from the ends of his handlebars. Thanks were given to his guardian angel! Wet granite sets, manhole covers and the odd remaining tram line all helped to keep the workshop busy. Many of the repairs had to be carried out on bent or snapped leg shield bottom brackets. No boy worth his salt would ride round a corner, without sliding on the leg shield bottom bracket, leaving a shower of sparks. One of the favourite places to show off was the Clock Tower, hurtling round, leg shields scraping along the ground on a Saturday afternoon in summer was every boy's delight. One boy however came to grief losing it in a big way in front of the ever-present Police Constable, this boy was charged with reckless driving and came down to earth with a bump. A second boy one Sunday afternoon was given a last minute telegram for Braunstone Estate. It had been raining since he had last been out and scraping round the corner into Bishop Street on his leg shields, trying to impress the queue for the Picture House his front wheel hit the edge of a wet manhole cover, the bike shot across the road, jumping the kerb and hitting the bank wall, which scattered the people standing in the cinema queue. After righting the bike he made a very hasty retreat with insults ringing in his ears just hoping no one would recognise him and report the incident. The mechanics at Campbell Street garage were always complaining that the bottom support fittings on the leg shields were becoming paper thin, but it was an impossible task to stop the boys from wearing them out.

DOMINOES

Six boys were coming back from the garage and held back so

they would all stop together at the traffic lights outside the Grand Hotel on Granby Street. The intention was to rev up at the same time to get the public's attention, then to roar off to Blackwells Court, going in one after the other to stop the Saturday shoppers. Unfortunately things went amiss, the boy on the outside slipped falling into the next boy and DOMINO they all fell down. To make matters worse on the other corner was an ex -telegram boy, now a constable, who delivered several withering comments about the present day telegram boys and finished off with the gentle words. "Get the kettle on, I'll be in, in a minute."

Another failure was the 'John Wayne' method of mounting a cycle or motorbike. Running alongside the mount then jumping on, strictly forbidden. A slip would cause more than a bruised ego! It always seemed a boy was successful when no one was looking, but if he crashed everyone saw him. If he did come to grief, he tried to cover up by pretending there was some mechanical problem with his bike until the interest from people at the bottom of Blackwells Court had gone, then very quietly he would ride off up the road to take out his revenge on the bike!

RAG WEEK

The boys always had mixed feelings about Leicester Rag Week. On one hand there were the college full time students who always looked down on day release students and Rag Week was one way to rub in the difference. The boys and girls always wanted to take part but the G.P.O. Lewis's and Dunlop Rubber always refused to allow their youngsters to participate. It would have meant giving them time off to help prepare the floats for Rag day, (if you did not help with the floats, you could not be in the parade.) What if they pulled a Rag stunt that got their names in the local paper? Not what these employers wanted to condone, so Rag Week was out. On the other hand the boys could always have fun providing they didn't get caught. Pretty students from the University or Art & Tech College were always made very welcome by the older messengers, after they had ventured up Blackwells Court to try and sell copies of the Rag Magazine. On the Saturday (Rag Day) the boys often tried to get revenge on some of the students who had given them grief at college, fire buckets, and on one occasion a fire extinguisher were quietly taken to the bottom of Blackwells Court to wait for the floats to appear. Sometimes the students bombarded the boys with flour and water bombs they had ready on the floats, there were never any real winners on Rag Day, but this did not stop either side from trying.

DAYS OUT AND CARELESS WORDS

The 'POP CLUB' day trips out by coach were other occasions when the boys and ex-telegram boys got together. Girl friends were usually telephonists so they all had plenty in common with one another. Trips were made to the Nottingham Goose Fayre, Belle Vue Fair & Zoo, Battersea Fun Fair and other similar venues. The P.H.G. was usually invited along to keep a fatherly eye on things and often had to smooth things over when high spirits and those out of a bottle took over. The poor girls who went with their older ex-messenger boyfriends really had their hands full, as the boys tried to repeat the reckless stunts that had made them legends amongst the younger boys. Oh to be a fly on the wall in the rest room at Free Lane Telephone Exchange the following Monday Morning! One of the disadvantages for the telephone girls dating telegram boys, especially those working in the rural exchanges e.g. Coalville,

Thurnby, Narborough, was that others listened in to the calls, and supposed secrets would soon be common knowledge. A careless word picked up by the wrong ear and a beautiful romance was stone dead in the blink of an eye.

UNPLEASANT TASKS

Priority Telegrams were one of the least popular types to be received. They often came with a green label attached saying 'life or death' or 'deliver with care' etc. The Instrument room staff or the booking out officer would brief the messenger as to the contents of the telegram. When he reached the address, it was policy to see if the people next door were friends. A lady neighbour was asked to accompany the messenger to help break the news then stay for a while with the person receiving the telegram. Sometimes the recipient would just read the message turn pale and shut the door. Occasionally they just broke down in tears, but worst of all was if they fainted, this could be very alarming to a young messenger. That was why a messenger asked to take priority telegrams was often picked knowing he would not panic and was able to 'hold up the service' as it was said. Extra time was allowed for these deliveries because it was important they were delivered on the first attempt. It often meant making enquiries to find the addressee, then making sure they all right to be left after receiving the news. This upsetting duty made telegram boys able to deal with most situations. Many families in those days, kept bad news away from younger members thinking they would not be able to deal with it.

Good news on the other hand was often received in a very off hand manner. Football pools winners could be so interested in what they had won that the boy did not even get a Thank You! One such case involved a journey in the snow to a large dividend pools winner near Earl Shilton. After travelling in appalling weather conditions across fields to a farm, he had the telegram snatched from his hand and the door slammed in his face. Back at the office he was found sitting in Blackwells Court frozen to the petrol tank, unable to get off his motorcycle. No tip, no thanks and frozen to the core. What a trip!

SPECIAL TELEGRAMS

The Greetings Telegrams got larger and quite popular, so the motorcycles were fitted with panniers to put them in. There was a special small version of a Postman's bag issued for cyclists and motorcyclists but the telegrams were often just stuffed inside a boy's jacket, as the bags were not easy to use. They got caught by the wind and blew about behind the rider. When large wedding receptions were held at Hotels outside the City, boys often went out with so many telegrams stuffed into their coats they looked very odd and received some funny looks.
Saturday afternoon delivery of Wedding telegrams could be difficult. They often came with a specific delivery time to a Country Hotel. To arrive with a pile of telegrams on a wet day was not pleasant, but to walk in, dripping water all over the hotel carpet with 100 people staring at you could be daunting to say the least. One summer Saturday about thirty Wedding Telegrams were taken to a large house on the outskirts of Oadby. The boy arrived, stopping in the driveway to ask a gentleman sitting on the rockery wall who was dressed in a morning suit with a top hat at his side, where the telegrams were to be taken. He said "Give them to me I'm the bride's father." As they were handed over, he asked the boy to sit down, have a drink and something to eat with him. He had in his own words 'escaped,' with his chauffeur into the garden. The chauffeur appeared with two

glasses of champagne and a large plate of food. After a while the boy made his excuse to leave thanking the gentleman and clutching a 10/- note. Feeling very light headed he carried on with his run. When returning to the office he told his tale and everyone volunteered to take any more telegrams to this friendly and rewarding address. Tips on a Saturday were not easy to come by; often Wedding Telegrams were taken from the messenger before he found the best man who usually gave out the tips. At this time a tip of about 1/- was normal.

QUICKEST IS NOT ALWAYS THE FASTEST

Occasionally madness comes in strange forms, some start with a challenge in this case it was who can get to Anstey and back in the quickest time on a cycle! Anstey was normally delivered by motorcycle because of the distance from the Head Office. The first boy, who was a senior motorcycle messenger set off with a telegram, he returned red faced, although almost in a state of collapse his time was magnificent. Several other boys wanted to challenge this but as things happen, telegrams for Anstey dried up. Eventually another telegram came and another senior boy set off to try and break the record and would you believe it, succeeded. The messenger whose record was broken was very disbelieving and wouldn't stop moaning for ages. He could not see how it was possible. Sometime afterwards another boy came in off a motorcycle run. He said he had seen a motorcycle messenger racing up the Groby Road on a cycle, which he thought was strange. The boy told him it was a punishment, so feeling sorry for him, the motorcyclist towed him part of the way to Anstey. When it became clear how the faster run was achieved, all hell let loose! To make matters worse the two involved were until this time good friends, but they fell out for a long time afterwards.

CALL MY BLUFF

Same messenger another day, causing a disturbance on a Wednesday, half day closing. Booking out officer says, "I've got one for Kibworth Beauchamp, if you don't behave you can go on a pushbike!" Boy with temper up "O.K. I'll go on a pushbike, see if I care!" Booking out officer "Here you are, get going!" Boy departs and booking out officer says to the lads left in the room "I didn't think he would do it, cool him off, do him good!" Boy returns a long time later very chastened, looks at the booking out officer mutters "B*****d" Booking out officer grins says "mates" holds out his hand both laugh, friends again but boys do not call this mans bluff. Not on half day closing they don't!

FURTHER EDUCATION

Boys were now going on day release on a Wednesday, later changed to Thursday. The classes were mixed, girl telephonists, telegram boys and boys from Lewis's and the Dunlop Rubber Company. All started off in the mornings at Newarke Street annexe and then moved mid-morning to the main building of Leicester Art & Technical College in The Newarkes finishing up mid-afternoon at the 2nd annexe in Duns Lane. Classes varied from distinctly unpopular (maths, english) to weird (elocution lessons) to the very popular (book binding, art, cabinet making.) The tutors either tried hard to encourage the boys and girls or were browbeaten by the boys and finished up ignoring them. Sometimes the boys and girls got into trouble, not because they disliked what they were doing, but because they were left to get on with something on their own and it went to their heads. One art class tutor let the students go out, down to the area behind the college to sketch the demolition work, and returned unexpectedly, to find they had all gone to the local cafe to drink tea and listen to the juke box. This would have been all right if some clown had not stuck his pad against the wall showing a message which the tutor took exception to. There was one tutor who disliked any day release students and he punished them relentlessly, which led to the boys playing truant in the afternoons. It all came to a head when the boys were sitting in the dark, at the Floral Hall picture house and an off duty tutor was in a seat behind them. After a showdown between the Assistant Superintendent and the College Principal, the boys' plight was recognised and there was a change of tutor, who did like day release students.

IT WON'T FIT

After this incident the boys were relieved to find that after three months of making tenon joints, the new tutor set about teaching them a real skill. He got permission for the boys (including two from the Dunlop Rubber Co) to construct a three man canoe, with the idea that when it was finished they would be able to take it for trips on the canal instead of going to the gym to play tennington. (Tennis played with plastic balls.) Once completed the excited boys found it was too long to get out of the door and turn it in the corridor. The tutor was told college rules would not allow it to be lowered out of the 2nd floor window and as far as it is known, it is still there today, on top of the cupboards where it was left!

JUST KEEP WALKING

After the increase in the price of telegrams in 1956 traffic dropped dramatically, during slack times boys were sent to assist on postal deliveries in the delivery divisions at Campbell Street or Stamford Street offices. At first all went well, then the Inspectors took advantage of the boys by sending them out with half bags of mail. These were made up mostly of door-to-door leaflets, soap coupons and similar items. Boys soon found they had not part of a delivery but several deliveries in one bag, starting out at 8.30 a.m. they were still delivering at 3.30 p.m. with no break and nowhere to take one, or even go to the toilet. Two boys were given half a bag of mail each, starting in Stoughton Road, Leicester they delivered all the roads on each side and continued along Gartree Road until reaching Stoughton Road, Oadby. After several hours walking and delivering, Brocks Hill estate was reached, this was under construction at the time and the properties only had plot numbers to identify them. After struggling for a while to find the addresses the walk was abandoned. By late afternoon they got back to the Sorting office. Fortunately a very understanding Inspector saw the boys and reported what had taken place to the Telegraph Writing Room. Two very tired and footsore boys were sent home. After several complaints from members of the public and some Supervisors who thought the boys were being exploited, the practice was stopped and boys were employed on indoor duties. This is when the fun started in the Sorting Office.

LET SLEEPING DOGS LIE

In the Sorting Office the boys usually worked filling up the sorting board benches in front of Postmen and P.H.G.s. When that work ran out there would always be something else to do in the parcel section. Hard dirty work if you were being watched, but one very small elusive boy always found a way to evade even the sharpest-eyed supervisor. This particular boy found a good place to hide in a wicker parcel skep, which was full of empty bags, with one pulled over his head he could sleep away his time in the Sorting Office. This came to an end when the other boys decided enough was enough and plotted revenge. He went off one day in a nice sunny spot and was soon asleep. The boys left him until it was dinner time, time for action. He was very quietly wheeled up to the telephone box used by the Matron, this was a P.H.G. who took messages and looked after the internal mail. They waited until the Matron was inside the telephone box then placed the skep across the door, one of the boys then rang the Inspector in Charge with a message to pass on. His office was next door to the Matrons desk, he came out of his office calling to the Matron who found the skep blocking his door. As the Matron banged the door hard against the skep, up popped a sleepy messenger giving his best impression of the dormouse in 'Alice in Wonderland.' Retribution followed, but as if by magic all the other boys had quietly slipped away to lunch, leaving the sleepy boy to face the music on his own! Revenge can be very sweet, especially if the Inspector is an ex-messenger himself!

SOME NEVER LEARN

That same boy had a partner in crime they called them the terrible twins, always in trouble. One sport they got others involved in was 'Chariot Racing' in the Bishop Street basement. This involved a boy on a cycle racing round the basement cycle racks against another boy, both were on cycles with a carrier, on which was another boy as 'the parcel.' Needless to say accidents were frequent and the racing was stopped when one unfortunate boy broke his arm. There was no doubt the 'terrible twins' were the catalyst when pranks were being played. One Sunday morning, after they had finished their duties, they borrowed the keys for a 50 c.f. vehicle so they could take a driving lesson in the back of the Sorting Office. It went well until a mix up by one lad between the clutch, brake and accelerator resulted in what was reported as 'dodgems in the sorting office.' One particular booking out officer was plagued by these boys daily. They would wait until he had booked them out, slip through the rest room window and hide in the basement. He knew where they had gone and would shout for them to get out. When his patience snapped he would go to fetch the Counter Overseer, once the boys knew this, they would dash out, up the other staircase from the basement, grab their telegrams, add any new ones to the sheet and depart. They would run down Blackwells Court and start their engines when they had reached Granby Street so they would be undetected. The poor man returned with the Overseer only to find all the boys had gone, along with every telegram, leaving the incoming boys wondering why everyone was so red faced and angry, although they had a good idea!

WATER MESS YOU MADE!

A senior messenger thought he had the measure of one of this pair when he threw water at him one Saturday afternoon in the delivery room. Grabbing a fire bucket from outside the toilets the senior boy ran back in and threw some of the water at the other boy, in trying to avoid the thrown water the younger boy slipped and fell to the floor. The P.H.G. shouted at them to stop but they were both too fired up to listen to reason, they both ran out of the room and a chase ensued down the court and into Granby Street. They ran towards the Midland Bank, shoppers moved quickly out of the way and just as the senior boy drew level to the other boy he dived into the corner shop passageway to escape into Bishop Street. The senior boy knowing he would get away threw the water as hard as he could. Wrong move!

The younger boy ducked and fell over, just as a member of the public walked into the passageway and caught the lot! To cap it all he was a personal friend of the Assistant Postmaster Mr Williams, so a Major Irregularity was issued to the senior boy. Of course the other one got off without any punishment as usual, some have a charmed life!

BRIEF ENCOUNTER

Occasionally telegrams had to be delivered which tickled a young boys fancy. Taking a telegram to the PalaceTheatre in Belgrave Gate where they had started to put on striptease shows made things very interesting. Arriving at the stage door with a reply paid telegram for the star of the show, the boy was told by the doorkeeper to take it up the stairs to her dressing room. On the way up the backstage spiral staircase, he met several scantily clad young ladies who insisted on squeezing by him. Very red faced but enjoying every minute of it, he arrived at the dressing room door to be met by a very well endowed lady in just a pair of decorated briefs, he tried hard to keep his eyes on her face, and had mixed feelings when she asked if a reply could be sent later, and how. He rushed back to the office to relate and re-live the story and for days afterwards all the other boys eagerly looked for another telegram to the theatre, but none came!

MOMA'S PLACE

At the end of the 1950's coffee bars were becoming meeting places for boys and girls. Some of the older messengers had started to go, in the evenings to a coffee bar on Welford Road near to the Welford Road Sub Post Office. The proprietor was a very friendly Polish lady who liked the boys to call her 'Moma.' She treated all the messengers as her boys and frothy coffee was the new in drink for the lads. An added attraction was a jukebox, which was played as often as money allowed. Eventually Moma sold the café and bought a hotel in Loughborough Road, where she installed a coffee bar because she missed the youngsters. The boys went there for a while but it was too far out of town and so they eventually stopped going and Moma became a distant memory after that.

BEST MESSENGER
YOUNG TELEPHONIST AWARD

In the 1950's a prize of £5 and a book was awarded to both the best Telegram Boy and Young Telephonist. How the Department selected the winner for this award is a mystery, perhaps in the case of the messenger it was the boy with the least black marks against his name, which would have made the 'short list' very short indeed knowing the antics of the messengers of 'the day.' Many of the boys were unaware of the award and if they had known about it, it is doubtful that it would have made them behave any differently. The eventual winner would not want to advertise the fact that he had 'won' this award even though his name could appear in the local newspaper.

UNION DUES

During the 1950's some of the boys were members of the Union of Postal Workers (U.P.W.) Many were not interested in joining the Union because of the weekly payment, collected by one of the boys who was also the messengers representative, a thankless task to take on for anyone. Wandering round the office on a Friday after the boys had been paid, book in hand trying to collect the money due and previous weeks overdue payments was like trying to 'plait fog.' All the boys wanted the Union when they were in trouble, but without the bother of paying for the service. The Union wanted the money without the problems, so they were happy to let the 'dues' pile up, week after week. The sole contact the representative had was with the long-suffering Branch Treasurer, there was no attendance at meetings as happened before the Second World War. Much later when Union membership became compulsory the weekly fee was stopped at source by the Wages Branch, which solved the problem 'once and for all.'

O.K. SO IT'S A PARCEL!

It is a male thing that allows even the puniest boy to take on authority if his temper is raised to boiling point. Take one messenger delivering his last telegram on a run one boiling hot Saturday morning at the Welford Place end of Belvoir Street. The boy decided to scoot his cycle along the pavement back to the office, the wrong way down one way Belvoir Street. As he reached Sport's Limited shop, he saw a Police Constable coming towards him, so he immediately jumped off the cycle pedal and remembering a piece of advice regarding one way streets and the law given to him by a senior messenger, promptly lifted the cycle up and started to carry it towards the oncoming officer. As expected the boy was stopped by the constable who asked him what he thought he was doing scooting down a one way street the wrong way? The boy replied, "Carrying this parcel," pointing to his cycle, "back to the office." The constable smiled and said he accepted, that if the cycle was carried it could be considered a parcel. However it was obvious the constable did not fall for this argument and he escorted the boy all the way back to the top of the street. Several members of the public smirked at the sight of the red faced messenger struggling to carry the cycle. By the time the boy had staggered his way to Market Street, he was very hot, tired and feeling pretty stupid for trying to outsmart the constable, who then allowed him to mount his cycle and return to the office the long way round. On the way back he cursed the senior boy who had given him the 'gem' about carrying goods the wrong way, down a one-way street.

HOW DID I GET HERE?

There is a phenomenon that motorists sometimes experience on motorways, driving along and suddenly finding themselves several miles on, without the slightest idea of how they had driven without incident! One telegram boy experienced this on a Saturday afternoon by travelling the complete length of Green Lane Road, only snapping wide-awake as he reached Ambassador Road. Stopping as quickly as he could, he sat shaking, running over in his mind the journey he had made completely oblivious to the major junctions he had gone over, or the traffic on this busy road. He returned to the office very upset and related his story to the other boys, several said they had experienced that themselves on a long motor cycle run. All agreed it was very frightening and not something they wanted to repeat.

CHAPTER 10

SWINGING 60's

By the start of the 1960's the telegram service was in steep decline. A shortage of new recruits had upset the smooth running of the system. In 1958 the last boys due for National Service were called up. These had been deferred for almost nine months and were by this time nearly 19 years of age. National Service which, ended in 1960, had upset the transition from messenger to Postman. Ironically many boys resigned to join up as regulars in the Armed Forces after National Service had finished. Others transferred over to the telephone side of the business, which put an even greater strain on the telegram service. In 1959 a Postman was asked by the staffing office to return to telegraph delivery duties for six weeks, this period lasted on and off for nearly three years. The Midland Regional Director told him that he was the longest serving messenger and had the highest recorded mileage. It was not so hard to do as most weeks he was working six and a half days and always on a motor cycle.

MILESTONES & CHANGES

In 1961 the shorter working week was introduced, cutting hours from forty-eight to forty-five per week. There were by now only twelve messenger duties, which was half the 1956 revision figure.

In December 1961 Charles Keene College opened in Belgrave Gate, on the site of the old Leicester Gas works. The boys on Day release transferred there from the Colleges of Art and

Technology.

In the same month Harold Peel retired, he was the last person to hold the rank of Assistant Inspector of Boy Messengers.

In April 1962 Reginald Yarnell retired, he was the last to hold the post of Assistant Superintendent in Charge of Telegraphs, which ceased as part of the 1956 revision. These two retirements ended the last links with the old days of Telegraph Supervision.

SMOOTH RUNNING, PERHAPS!

The day was Easter Sunday, it was wet and foggy a typical English Bank Holiday. Traffic was fairly heavy for a Bank Holiday or even a Sunday, the P.H.G. was asked to visit the Instrument Room and came back with the news that a large amount of telegrams was on hand for the Melton Mowbray area and Market Harborough. Leicester covered those areas on a Sunday morning. Two volunteers were sought and two senior boys agreed they would be prepared to take the telegrams, leaving the City and Rural areas to the rest of the messengers. Once it was settled the senior boys were sent to Eric's to fortify themselves for the journey with hot dogs and a mug of tea. When they returned to the office the full extent of the task was revealed, fifty telegrams each to deliver. A gulp and a deep breath then out came the maps from the cupboard. The routes were worked out and the furthest point south was Rockingham near to Corby in Northamptonshire and the furthest point north-east was Clipsham near to Grantham in Lincolnshire. The Market Harborough boy returned thirty minutes before the Melton Mowbray boy because several of his telegrams were for the Market Harborough town area, which shortened the distance a little. Three hours plus on the road was a unique ride for both of them, made even more futile by the news when they returned, that both offices had laid on a full delivery staff for the Bank Holiday but had forgotten to inform Telegraph Head Quarters, therefore the telegrams were transmitted to Leicester. The messenger who went to Melton remembers sitting for over ten minutes in the middle of the A1 (Great North Road) trying to cross over through the busy traffic to get onto the Clipsham Road. When he arrived in the village he went, wet and cold into the local pub to get directions to the address on the telegram. There was no street name, just the name of the cottage and village. When he asked directions one villager said, "You Grantham lads are all the same, know nowt!" the messenger told the gentleman he was not from Grantham, or Melton as suggested but from Leicester. Then the man exclaimed, "That's on the other side of the world lad!" There were 124 miles on the speedometer by the time the boy got back to Leicester. The bike ran out of petrol as he turned into Blackwells Court, while pushing the motorcycle back up to Campbell Street Garage the words of the afternoon Telegraphist were still ringing in his ears, "Where the hell have you been? We thought we had lost the pair of you." He kept wondering while walking up Granby Street what had made him fill the tank right up to the top with petrol when he'd collected it that morning? The funny thing was the other boy had done exactly the same even before they had both volunteered and he had ridden 120 miles and had just enough petrol to make it back to the garage!

JUST LIKE A CARRY ON FILM

There were times when the boys put one another through various tortures, which sometimes bordered on the comical, although not perhaps for the victim! One boy was stripped and washed in the sink, he had his neck scrubbed with a G.P.O. scrubbing brush, just to recall the incident makes the writer cringe. On another occasion an unfortunate boy was found by the Booking Out Officer, tied to the large coat rack in a figure 'X' with most of his clothing missing, the boys who had done the dirty deed disappeared like magic to reappear from several directions enquiring, "What's happened?" The most famous incident found a boy lashed face down in an 'X' on the mess room table, with most of his clothing missing and like the famous scene from "Carry on Doctor" a daffodil protruding from a part of his anatomy. Fortunately the Overseer who saw him lying there saw the funny side of it and let the boys off with a warning. As he was an ex-messenger himself, he showed great resolve and kept a straight face while delivering the warning! Oh to be a fly on the wall in the Supervisors rest room, it would have been interesting!!

THE UP'S and DOWN'S OF A 1960's MESSENGER

On Sunday mornings when traffic was light the boys would try out rodeo tricks on their motorbikes. In one such incident three boys came round Pocklingtons Walk corner three abreast into Horsefair Street, leg shields scraping the floor in the time honoured way. Horsefair Street was two-way in those days. A police sergeant and constable who were walking up the street at the time were not impressed. They must have heard the sound of the boys coming long before they arrived, and stepped into the road to stop them, harsh words followed and three shamefaced boys rode off very quietly.

WATER IN AND OUT OF THE WORKS

Boys were always using water to get at one another. Going to the toilet was a trial, some of the boys sneaked into the counter staff toilet to avoid having a bucket of water or sand come over the top of the door onto them when using the boys toilet.

In those days waterproof leggings were the single legged type and on a wet day the rain ran down the tank into the riders lap which was really unpleasant, boys sneaked into the Accounts Branch or the back of Bishop Street Counter to borrow a letter bag, which made a really good water proof for the lap, but there were always complaints by the Postman who emptied the Bishop Street boxes about the number of wet letter bags found behind the counter.

FOGGY DAYS AND POPPING WAY

The days when fog hit the city were pretty nerve racking. Trying to get about and keep reasonable time tested even the best boys to the limit. One boy was delivering in the East Park Road area, following the kerb with his foot where he could he suddenly lost all his bearings and crashed into a hedge. It was not apparent where he was until he spotted the street sign, then realised he had just crossed over the junction of East Park Road and St Saviours Road without stopping, and had finished up in the hedge surrounding Spinney Hill Park. Quite scary!

Two boys were going on a run together in the fog 'popping' which was strictly against the rules. One was due to deliver to Birstall and the other to Stocking Farm. All was well until they reached the end of Ross Walk where they both lost their bearings and missed each other in the gloom. When they eventually returned to the office the air was blue "Where did you get to etc?" One had missed Thurcaston Road altogether and the other had crashed into the bollards at the end of Ross Walk hurting his dignity and breaking one of his bike lamps. On another occasion two boys were 'popping 'on Melton Road, they turned to look behind them and whistle at a group of girls going into Cossington Street, unfortunately one didn't see a car which had stopped in front of him to turn right into Doncaster Road and he collided with it. Thankfully no damage was done and they got away with it.

SPECIAL DUTY

Motor Cycle duty 1 (M.C.1) was only performed by older boys as it started at 06.00 a.m. on a Letter Pressure Delivery which lasted until approximately 09.00 a.m. After a meal break at 09.30 a.m. they changed over to the delivery of telegrams until the end of the duty. As the pressure delivery area built up another smaller delivery area was chosen to prevent the boys being out on a postal delivery after 09.00 a.m. The early start was unpopular, but it was seen as a good way to get the older boys ready for the change over at eighteen to adult duties. It did not always have the desired effect, as around 80% left the Post Office on reaching eighteen years of age, which meant not many boys from the 1960's were around in later years. One round in Glenfield involved delivering to a bungalow with a flock of very lively geese at the end of a long tree lined drive. It was a work of art to creep up to the front door, put the mail in the box and then run like blazes to the gate before being cornered by the geese. Many a boy finished up trembling after a close call with those vicious birds!

FIRST CASUALTIES

Considering the number of boys on the road over the years and the mileage recorded it is surprising that up until the 1960's there were no serious accidents, then three close together. One messenger was injured when a man jumped off the platform of a bus as it was turning at the City boundary on Welford Road. The passenger jumped onto the front wheel of the motorcycle, which consequently rolled the boy over into a construction trench. The injuries were fairly light but an Anti-Tetanus injection administered at the Leicester Royal Infirmary put him at deaths door for a week. The second occurred when a boy rode into a brick wall on Birstall Road and broke both his legs, which did not upset him quite as much as him being unable to go to his weekly Marine Cadet Force meetings at H.M.S.C.T.S. Tiger in Ross Walk Leicester. The third accident happened as a boy was riding down Greengate Lane Birstall on his motorcycle, a car turned in front of him into a house driveway without warning. The boy sustained serious head and facial injuries as he crashed into the side of the car but eventually recovered. The statistics show of course only the recorded accidents, how many went unrecorded was a closely guarded secret, known only to those who kept their mouths shut! The boys who rode motorcycles were entered into the Royal Society for Prevention of Accidents (R.O.S.P.A.) Safe Driving Awards. These were given on an annual basis throughout the Post Office districts. Many Post Office van drivers built up a string of annual awards, some reached more than twenty years without a blameworthy accident. None of the boys ever made it to year two, to be found blameworthy by the accident panel for one accident, disqualified them from an award.

A DAILY ROUTINE IN THE 1960's

A messengers day began after signing on at 08.00 a.m. at Bishop Street Head Office. The boys would walk up to the Campbell Street Garage (usually in pairs) to collect their allotted motorcycles which were left in the garage overnight. The B.S.A. Bantam 125cc motorcycles painted Post Office Red were checked and filled with a petrol oil mixture from special red petrol cans. Each can had the serial number of a bike on it. If a boy was known to be clumsy one of the mechanics would insist on filling the tank for him. Tommy Hands and Sam Daniels were the senior mechanics in charge of the bikes. After filling the tank, the tyre pressures had to be checked before returning to Bishop Street Office for the first run of the day at 08.30 a.m. Boys were not allowed to ride a motorcycle until the age of sixteen, so there were three cycle duties, as well as seven motor cycle duties. The indoor duties started at 07.45 a.m. at Bishop Street and Telephone House (66, London Road) as well as daily collection runs to Free Lane and Wharf Street Telephone Exchanges. Including leave reserves, there were a total of fifteen duties. Discipline, although not at the same level as previous years, was still fairly tight with any misdemeanours usually resulting in a visit to the Overseer in the Telegraph Writing room.

The sporting activity of previous eras had gone by this time. There were no work football or cricket teams, resulting in less socialising together off duty. Perhaps some of the old camaraderie had gone. Spare moments on duty, when not used for making plaits of lead seals, were usually spent playing cards or darts. There was day release at Charles Keene College in Painter Street where such diverse subjects as english, judo and cookery were on the agenda! The meals in Bishop Street Canteen were subsidised, using a voucher system. Interesting special duties involved attending evening football or Rugby football matches and then taking the teleprinter reports back to Free Lane Telephone Exchange for transmission to National Newspapers in Manchester and London. When not taking the reports back he was allowed to watch the match for free. There were still occasional visits to Leicester Racecourse at Oadby. The cut off for telegrams received for delivery was 8.00 p.m. which gave the boys forty five minutes in which to deliver them, as the shift finished at 9.00 p.m. Telegrams for delivery after this time were transferred to the Sorting Office for delivery by a Postman Driver. Many of the boys who joined the G.P.O. at fifteen years of age started on a wage higher than others who were on apprenticeships in outside industry. Although after their eighteenth birthdays the combination of low pay, unsocial hours and full employment opportunities outside, seemed to account for them leaving in large numbers.

CHARIOTS ON FIRE

One hot summer's day (yes there were some) a boy went out into Blackwells Court to start up his motor cycle, he tickled the carburettor (which entailed a small valve being pressed up and down to bring a small amount of petrol out of a hole in the side,) as the fuel hit the red hot engine it ignited and the boy dashed in for help as the flames took hold. The rest of the boys came out with an assortment of sand buckets, fire extinguishers and buckets of water. They all joined in, the bike got some of the extinguishing agents but the helpers got the lion's share. Passers by in Granby Street stopped to see what the commotion was all about and the event was reported, greatly exaggerated, in the Leicester Mercury complete with a picture. Needless to say the bike was a write off.

On another occasion a boy was coming back from a run along Groby Road when he noticed passing motorists were flashing their headlights and pointing at him, as he looked down he saw his bike was on fire. He immediately stopped at the side of the road and dismounted. Fortunately the fire quickly extinguished itself but he had to ring the garage and wait for a mechanic to come out to collect him as the machine was no longer fit to ride.

WHAT DO YOU WANT WITH OVERTIME?

Boys were sent to the Sorting Office to work when telegram traffic was low and were sometimes asked to work overtime. A problem could arise when a boy who had finished working tried to get his overtime docket and record sheet signed by a Supervisor. As with many firms, the young boys were seen as a fair target for leg pulling. There was more than one Assistant Inspector and Inspector who would say, "What does a young lad like you want with docket?" Then promptly tear the docket to shreds and throw it into the nearest waste bin, walking away leaving the boy near to tears. If he had worked two or three days the loss of the supervisors initials was a disaster. It often took precious time to find a sympathetic supervisor who would agree to sign up all the entries on the new docket. Some disagreed with treating the boys this way, but they were in the minority.

FROM RUSH TO PU(S)CH

In September 1967 Mopeds were introduced into service by the Post Office simply because the age-limit to ride motorcycles had been raised from sixteen to seventeen. This meant that around half the staff were not eligible to ride the motorcycles. The first models were 50 c.f. Rayleighs but they were discontinued in December 1969. The Post Office then switched to Puch 50 c.f. Maxi's, which were two stroke machines, using a petrol/oil mixture like the B.S.A. Bantam motorcycles, which had been used since the early 1950's. The restrictions on riding motorcycles were felt even more by the boys, as many of them had their own bikes for use after work. These were well known British bikes such as Ariel, B.S.A. and Norton, all firms that were to disappear within the next few years. The closure of the B.S.A. works and alternate British manufacturers meant the end of the telegram boy on a motorcycle. As the telegram service was rapidly closing down, no foreign source of motorcycles was considered to replace them.

PORK PIE WITH WATER?

When boys went to wedding receptions with telegrams they were sometimes given food to take back to the office, sandwiches, cake etc. One boy was given a large pork pie, but when he returned to the office, he committed the 'cardinal sin' of keeping it to himself. The rule was, share everything, but he did not. The rest of the boys had their revenge at the end of the day. The pie eater went out on his last run and when he returned he took his motorcycle to Campbell Street Garage. As it was Saturday evening, the side gate was locked and the normal route then was to go up the wooden ramp onto the loading dock, through the doorway and down the concrete ramp into the garage. At the bottom of the ramp the lads ambushed him, a bucket of water was tipped over him and a hose-pipe stuffed up his trouser leg to give him a soaking to end all soakings. He got so wet, that it took some time for his uniform to dry out. The perpetrators had the unenviable experience of getting a dressing down from a supervisor, an ex-messenger himself, noted for his very loud voice and well versed in revenge tactics. The boys went away wondering what he would have done in the same circumstances?

FIRE AND BRIMSTONE

Things changed over the years and the iron rule of the P.H.G. in charge was one. As they started to relax, the boys got bolder trying tricks that previous boys would not have dared to. Such as setting fire to the waste bin under the P.H.G'.s desk, or his newspaper, while he was reading it. Once lead seals were melted into one P.H.G.'s pipe. The same P.H.G. suffered at the hands of one particular boy, who rang through an order for coal with instructions to leave it at the front of the P.H.G.'s house, which was a joke taken too far. Thanks to a tape recording being made of all telephone orders, the culprit was unmasked and it brought an abrupt end to the troubles for this Officer in Charge. Oh how different it was years ago!

THE ODDS AND ENDS IN THE 1960's

The ordinary telegrams came in dull yellow envelopes with Urgent was typed on, if necessary. Life or death telegrams had a green ticket attached with special instructions for delivery. International Telegrams were white with blue lettering and greetings telegrams came in large white envelopes. If a boy couldn't deliver a telegram, having tried a neighbour he would put a T16b yellow card in the letterbox, or under the door if there was not a box, this notified the occupier that a telegram boy had called. Occasionally he had to return to the office with an undelivered telegram and mark it N/A (no answer) and add his badge number. Sometimes this endorsement was used to cover the boys if they could not find the address that was why N/A was often referred to as 'Not Attempted!' Those marked N/A were tried again later in the day. If marked 'Urgent' and the recipient was on the telephone, firstly an attempt was made to pass the message on by 'phone. If the call was successful the telegram would be sent by the next post to give the occupier confirmation of the message. Some delivery places were very popular particularly, the Student Halls of Residence (London Road, Ratcliffe Road & Manor Road Oadby) because there were often pretty girls around. Registered Expresses for Bentley Engineering was a delivery to die for. There was a member of the Corps of Commissionaires on duty in the entrance lobby. He would not allow a boy to get anywhere near the receptionist, an 'absolute cracker' who the commissionaire thought, needed protecting from amorous boys. If the commissionaire had been called away from his post just before the messenger arrived the lucky boy could run up the stairs to the first floor eager to fulfil his duty. Even though the receptionist was behind her desk on the far side of the area, her perfume was all around and if she gave out one of her sexy smiles whilst leaning forward, it was enough to make the boy go weak at the knees. If meeting the overprotective commissionaire on the way out a "Thanks mate. I've delivered it," would leave him seething while the boy would return to the office with a spring in his step and a 'rampant' imagination!

The commissionaires of Corah's Hosiery factory in Leicester were very particular about their areas and any messenger daring to enter in a sloppy fashion whether by foot or machine was treated to a withering look and sharp reminder that he was a disgrace to the Queen's uniform. Which branch of the services these commissionaires served in, could only be guessed at, but everyone thought it must be the brigade of guards!

CHAPTER 11
1970's ON THE MOVE

In 1970 the telegram service (run by the G.P.O.) celebrated its 100th anniversary. There is no record of a telegram being received from the Queen to mark the occasion! It had risen and fallen like a tidal wave since its inception, evolving from boys on foot, to cycles, then to motorcycles and finally mopeds, throughout most of its life competing and eventually capitulating to the rival telephone service. Starting with a handful of boys in the 1870's rising eventually to a peak in the pre First World War days of over sixty, and then ending with just a few boys. Many thousands of Leicester people have experienced the sight of a telegram boy advancing towards them holding that dreaded little dull yellow coloured envelope, usually fearing the worst. Sometimes the recipient was pleasantly surprised to receive good news, perhaps a win on the football pools, news of an inheritance or a new birth. In 1970 approximately eight million telegrams were sent throughout the United Kingdom, this was almost the same number as at its beginning a hundred years earlier in 1870. As the telegram service entered its last full decade of existence, the Post Office suffered its first National Strike in 1971. This lasted from 20th January to 8th March. Telegraph staff at Bishop Street Office refused to take any messages except Life & Death telegrams, which were delivered by unpaid volunteers. Counter staff also refused to accept telegram messages from the public.

STILL SPARKING

As with their predecessors the motorcyclists still tried various 'Circus Tricks' or 'Stunt Riding.' One of the old favourites was speeding round Horsefair Street corner into Granby Street scraping the leg shields along the ground, sending a shower of sparks into the air marking their progress round the corner. This was frightening to passers by and those waiting to cross over to Woolworths Corner it was especially so on a busy Saturday afternoon. For the boys to put themselves at risk without an audience was a non-starter. On one occasion several boys, having done this during a Saturday lunchtime, had the bad luck to be spotted by a police motorcyclist, who duly followed them back, lights flashing, to Blackwells Court. The boys quickly dismounted hurrying into the office expecting the worst. The police officer had an earnest conversation with the Booking Out Officer after which he produced his notebook and asked for the boy's names. At this point the two men looked at each other and burst out laughing. Luckily the police officer who was an ex-messenger, and one who's reputation when a lad was suspect, thought a verbal warning following the fright was all that was needed. Sighs of relief after he had gone (fortified with a cup of tea) must have been heard at the Clock Tower!!

DAY RELEASE

By 1970 there was a total of eighteen boys comprising of eight on telegraph delivery, six on Indoor Messenger duties and four educational reserves to cover college day release. An extra indoor duty was added on 13/7/1970. The boys rotated between indoor and outdoor duties, unless they preferred to stay on one type, then they were allowed to swap rotations, to keep on a similar duty. Messengers had to attend Charles Keene College for a six-week period, which was a change from the old form of day release of one day per week. It was thought that one day a week at college was not productive for either the

Post Office or the student. So a new system of block release was brought into operation. The telegram boys and several Post Office telephonists once visited Bradgate Park as part of their course. During that term a twenty-eight -age booklet was produced by the students for the college about the history of the City of Leicester.

END OF AN ERA

In September 1971 another first happened, the Telegraph Department was moved from Bishop Street Head Office Building to the newly constructed Parcel Concentration Office (P.C.O.) at 200, Charles Street (originally named Northampton Square) it was linked to the Campbell Street Sorting Office by a bridge at 1st & 2nd floor levels. This move was significant as since 1870 the Telegraph Branch had always been located in the same area of Granby Street/Bishop Street in three different buildings. The one link to them all is the name of the alley at the left hand side of the building known to all telegram boys as 'Blackwells Court'. On old maps Post Office Place or Lane appears but not Blackwells Court and no one knows where the name came from, but it is thought there was a plaque on the left hand side-wall, showing the name in the 1920's.

The move to 200, Charles Street was part of a plan to relocate the Head Office and associated services, with the Head Office Counter occupying the ground floor and the services connected with it on the 1st floor, this part of the plan however never happened due to re-allocation of the available space within the tower block to the telephone service. The numbers of telegrams sent were still decreasing, whereas greetings telegrams remained popular. In the new building the Instrument room, writing room and delivery room were all on the ground floor, unlike Bishop Street and its predecessors in Granby Street. The pneumatic tube used to send telegrams from the Instrument room to the delivery room was no longer needed. The boys were now under much closer observation from Instrument room and writing room staff, along with all manner of letter, parcel and administration supervisors, who used the passage outside the telegraph delivery room. The Overseer (later P.E.C.) in the writing room who was directly responsible for the boys, was Arthur Martin and later Fred Benford both ex-messengers. At this time there were also indoor messengers situated at Telephone House (66, London Road) and Lee Circle. Mail also had to be transferred between Essoldo House, (Granby Street,) Wyvern Buildings, (Station Street,) Bishop Street Head Office, Free Lane Telephone Exchange and Ravensbridge Drive Telephone Stores, all on a cycle. Visits to Free Lane were most enjoyable for the boys, who often took their meal relief in the canteen there in preference to their own office, enabling them to admire many of the pretty telephonists based there.

NEW OFFICE - TELEGRAPH STAFF

When the Instrument Room was re-located to 200, Charles Street, fitting everything into the new work area was no longer a problem. Despite the new floor area being a fraction of the size of the top floor of Bishop Street the telegraph traffic had considerably reduced to the point where the staff now consisted of; one Assistant supervisor, twenty telegraphists which included five on wireless records work and one with supervising allowance. Two part time Female Telegraphists shared one duty between them.
There had been no new outside recruits for several years. The

only new telegraphists were those who had re-located from other offices. Vacant posts arising through retirement etc. were not being filled. One change that occurred in the early days at Charles Street was the introduction of a rule, which stated, 'where there are motor cycle duties in attendance, no push bike will travel more than one mile outside the radius of the City Centre.' This followed an incident where a boy was almost suspended after refusing to go to Mowmacre Hill, Birstall and Thurmaston on a cycle. After union intervention including telephone calls to Union Head Quarters the new rule was introduced, a rare victory for the boys had been achieved.

SCHOOL LEAVING AGE RAISED

In 1972 the school leaving age was raised to sixteen. Due to this, the establishment, which until this time consisted of nineteen boys was reduced by four because of the withdrawal of the further education release scheme.

SPORTING PROWESS

Despite the various teams formed by Telegram Boys throughout the years playing Football and Cricket there is only one known instance of anyone becoming a professional sportsman. Terry (Kevin) Stretton left the Post Office to become a professional Cricketer. He was a fast bowler with Leicestershire County Cricket Club from 1972 to 1975.

DRIVING ALLOWANCES

Motorcyclists received a daily driving allowance after the first two hours of riding. Driving allowance was paid for riding both motorcycles and mopeds up till the service ceased in 1982. The allowances paid for motorcycle riding from 1950 to 1973 are to be found on page 215 in the appendices.

LAST LINKS

In 1975 Roy Harper Assistant Supervisor in charge of the instrument room transferred to the Telephone Managers Office, Jean Gamble replaced him. Roy was the last ex-boy messenger to become a Telegraphist left in the Telegraph Department with his departure an era came to an end.

DIALLING DISASTERS

In the 1970's little had changed for a new boy. The first days he was used as a 'Gofer' fetching this, that and the other from the shops in town. He was used in the city centre delivering on foot, as there were always telegrams for delivery in this area. Cycles were needed for collecting and delivering mail from the telephone offices in various locations around the City, the motorbikes and mopeds were used for telegram deliveries on the outskirts and rural areas. Initiations had not really changed since the 40's 50's and 60's pigeon's milk was still requested from the innocents. Buckets of water were still thrown over toilet doors and various items fed through the air holes into personal lockers. There were times when a new boy could return from a run and be told there had been a phone call for him, and would he ring back. Like a fool he dialled the number and would ask to speak to Mr C. Lion only to find he had rung Twycross Zoo. If a letter of complaint followed, the caller was never named, the practical jokers just waited for the next victim! Internal calls were another source of amusement when boys were left to their own devices. The boys could see the parcel loading dock from the delivery office window and the P.H.G. or Supervisor working there was fair game. One of the boys would ring him and ask for some information, or send him from one end of the loading dock to the other looking for a non existent parcel, asking the unsuspecting supervisor questions relating to what he was doing immediately before the call, which when the 'penny dropped' would turn his face like thunder! Once, when the boys found an International Telephone Dialling Book, they decided to dial numbers at random, connecting with someone in Australia during the middle of their night. Getting out of bed to answer the telephone is not conducive to good conversation especially when it was realised that it was a hoax call. It became quite a game for the boys until the day the bill arrived at the accounts branch and was passed to the telegraph writing room, then all hell let loose. The matter was eventually dropped as the culprits could not be identified but that expensive trick was never tried again.

MOPED TRAINING

When a boy reached sixteen he would be given several days training on a Puch 50 c.c. Maxi Moped with a Midland Postal Region Instructor. Usually two boys were trained at the same time. One of the training manoeuvres was to undertake hill starts in a place well known to the messengers, the very steep and cambered Granby Avenue. Many boys trying this for the first time opened the throttle too wide and the moped leapt into the air, depositing the boy embarrassingly on his rump in the road.
The bikes were powered by a 2-stroke engine, which ran on a petrol/oil mixture of 2-1. By this time the fuel pumps had been removed from Campbell Street Sorting Office yard and fuel could only be obtained from a private garage in Saxby Street. After filling the fuel tank of the bike the serial number and the

amount of fuel were logged on a special form and a copy handed to the boy by the garage staff, this form was given to the P.H.G. as soon as the boy returned to the office. These mopeds had a back pedal brake, which could be lethal in the wet.

THE ROUTINE

When telegrams were ready for collection by the boys they were placed in a box outside the instrument room window and a bell was rung. The delivery room was opposite and on hearing the bell the P.H.G. would send a boy to collect the telegrams, which were sorted into the five areas of the City by the P.H.G. North including Mowmacre, Birstall and Thurmaston. South including Eyres Monsell, Aylestone, Oadby and Wigston. East including Highfields, Evington, Thurnby Lodge and Netherhall and the West included Glenfield and New Parks. These were the main areas but there were others, the South East - Stoneygate and the South West Westcotes and Braunstone. When there were sufficient telegrams for one area the P.H.G. would book out the next boy in line. After using the large wall map to put the telegrams into delivery order, the messenger would get kitted out in a white helmet with a drop down visor, the helmet had the words Post Office in red on the front. At a later date helmets were unavailable from the Post Office Supplies Department and a local motor cycle accessory store supplied them, that is why some boys could be seen wearing gold coloured helmets on delivery. Over his jacket he placed his belt and pouch. Brown gloves, short black overcoat (if it was cold) and finally leggings were worn if it was wet. Some of the boys bought their own black peaks to fix onto their helmets in place of the visor as the helmet had fixing buttons on the front and sides. On days when the weather was dry but cool, a brown leather dispatch rider's jerkin was the order of the day. This has always been the telegram boys' favourite item of clothing since they were first issued in the 1950's. Departure from the office had mixed feelings your mood probably depended on the state of the weather, ranging from a glorious sunny day (and disposition) to cold, wet or windy (or all three) and a truculent mood to match. The front pocket of the delivery pouch had to contain different cards to leave if the telegram could not be delivered. Most important was a well-thumbed copy of the Leicester City Street Guide. Long ago were the days when streets of the City stayed the same. Since the late 1940's there was building going on all over the place and houses being built in the grounds of many of the large houses from Queen Victoria's reign. Returning from the run his docket was placed at the bottom of the pile, when it reached the top he was sent out again. If telegram traffic was slow it could be an hour before a boy would go out again so together the boys would often play cards, darts or read newspapers and magazines. Others went out in a group to a nearby cob shop or down Granby Street to the city centre shops.

There were seven bike duties and one reserve, three motorcycles and five mopeds were in use. The early duties came on at 08.30 a.m. and then at intervals up to the last duty which started at 10.15 a.m. The last duty finished at 6.51 p.m. which was much earlier than previous years because of the fall in the number of telegrams for delivery. Boys rotated between the outdoor bike duties, and the indoor duties working in the mailrooms at post office and telephone locations. One duty was based at Bishop Street Office, to collect and deliver the internal mail and transfer it to 200, Charles Street. In the tower block at 200, Charles Street three boys worked out of the Telephone Registry on the 11th floor. Two boys on cycles went round the City to the telephone depots, which were Free Lane Telephone Exchange, Wharf Street Telephone Exchange, Leicester House

(Lee Circle) Cardinal International Exchange (Humberstone Road) De Montfort Exchange (Wellington Street) and Telephone House at 66, London Road. Boys on the late afternoon run to Telephone House, had to call in at W.H.Smith's bookstall on London Road Station to collect newspapers for delivery to the registry. The papers were for the Library on the 12th floor. The boys on these duties started at 07.45 a.m. and finished at 4.21 p.m. Monday to Friday. The last duty of the day involved date stamping all the outgoing post and then despatching it. There were frequent visitors from the typist's pool, which was next door, and the stores were located on the other side of the Registry. The Conference Room was very popular, the huge table was used for games of table tennis until the boys were caught and banned. The rest room was also very popular, until following an incident the boys were forbidden from using it. A table was thrown through the open window, fortunately landing on the roof of the canteen, which was at the fourth floor level, and not the Parcel Office Yard below where people were working, which could have had disastrous results.

There was a vending machine on the 11th floor with a supply of cobs and crisps and also a drinks machine. The meals served in the T.M.O. restaurant were subsidised, so meal tickets were issued to the boys. Watching all the girls coming and going was a better option than using the Postman's canteen in Campbell Street Sorting Office.

Another memorable feature of the Tower Block were the lifts. When first installed they took your breath away, as did the girls who worked there! The lift originally took about nineteen seconds to travel from the lower basement to the top floor, twenty-one floors in record time. Following complaints from visitors and older members of staff, the rate of ascent and decent was slowed down, much to the disappointment of the younger element working in the building, this would not have been out of place at Alton Towers!

SATURDAY NIGHT - SUNDAY MORNING

Saturday on telegrams was a mixed blessing. Unless a boy was a fan of football or rugby he would not mind working because it meant a day off during the week. The day off rotated through the week e.g. Monday week 1, Tuesday week 2 etc. One boy was off each day and two on Saturdays, which seemed odd this being the busiest day of the week (weddings etc.) Although telegram numbers in general were down throughout the week, greetings telegrams were increasing, which was the reason the telegram service survived as long as it did. Greetings telegrams were several times larger than standard telegrams and were pushed inside the messengers' coats to keep them clean and dry because the motor cycle panniers provided to keep them in had long since been removed and the special bags (a small version of the Postman's delivery bag) were just a distant memory. When a boy first went out he could look very overweight! Fully loaded he left the delivery room, walked down the corridor, past the locker room and out into the yard, where the bikes were kept, making sure he did not lose any of the greetings telegrams wedged inside his coat. When he arrived at a wedding reception he was usually made very welcome, food and drink were offered and if he refused a drink because he was driving, sometimes a tip would be hurriedly produced by the Best Man unless he was 'worse for wear' from drink then the boy went often away empty handed.

THE GOLDEN ENVELOPE

Receiving a telegram from Her Majesty Queen Elizabeth II was very special and treated by all involved very carefully. Greetings telegrams were sent from Buckingham Palace to couples who were celebrating their Diamond Wedding anniversary or men and women who had reached their Hundredth Birthday. Applications were made to Her Majesty's Private Secretary, with details and proof of the forthcoming event by friends or family of the intended recipients. The instrument room received the telegram with any special instructions. The boy who delivered it took great care not to damage the telegram when placing it inside his coat. It was a great relief to him when it was successfully handed over and he just hoped a photographer would not be there to capture the event. No boy wanted his mother to make a fuss over his picture appearing in the local newspaper. After the telegram in its golden envelope was safely delivered the Palace would be informed.

WHERE IS IT?

Saturday was half day closing for county sub post offices and so boys were sent to villages they did not usually see. Travelling to Tugby on a moped was no mean feat. Boys would consult the maps available and think, where is it? The maps for the City area were good, but the wilds of Leicestershire were something else. There was a large-scale map of the county in the Television License Record Office (T.V.L.R.O.) which at least pointed a boy in the right direction. The gated roads were a problem, it could be really hard work getting on and off, opening and closing gates, it soon took the fun out of visiting remote addresses. Although Saturdays were busy there was a relaxed atmosphere, all the offices were empty, the Parcel Office closed and after the dinnertime collections had finished, the boys had the place to themselves. As the restaurant was closed someone going out on a run would take orders for fish and chips stopping to collect them on the way back to the office. To work off the chips the parcel yard was used for a 'kick a bout' with a football, it was amazing that none of the many windows were broken.

Even breakdowns were looked on less harshly at weekends. Saturday afternoons and all day Sunday were on overtime for the mechanic on call.

LAZING ON A SUNDAY AFTERNOON

Postman Drivers from the Sorting Office covered Sunday morning duty on overtime and a messenger covered the afternoon period on overtime. This was a nice shift to cover, it was easy work, not having to go out many times and on extra pay. The Messenger worked under supervision from the Instrument Room. This voluntary duty could be boring for a boy on his own, so some had another messenger to keep him company (unpaid of course) who would repay the favour when it was the other way round.

ONE BOY'S MEMORIES OF THE 1970's

Every boy has memories of day-to-day events, which all ex - messengers can share long after they have happened. Some involved girls and after work activities, others got into and out of scrapes that could have cost them their career with the G.P.O. For me, mine were perhaps not as colourful as other boys' memories but they still remain vivid after many years. I remember feeling very proud taking a whole batch of congratulatory telegrams to the County Cricket Ground on the day in 1975 when Leicestershire won the County Championship. The opportunity to meet a world famous star does not come very often. By mistake I walked into (Sir) Cliff Richard's dressing room at the De Montfort Hall whilst trying to deliver a telegram. Coming face to face with the star was not something I expected, I felt my colour come up, mumbled a few incoherent words and made a hasty exit! Another tricky situation was, when returning rather late from a run in the north of the city, I used the excuse of getting lost. The booking out officer found this hard to believe as I lived in that area, I had actually spent the time at Blackbird Road stadium watching Leicester Lions Speedway Team in a pre-season practice session.

FREE TICKET TO WATCH

Boys were still on occasions asked to volunteer to attend football matches at Filbert Street, therefore giving the boy access to see most of the match as well as being paid overtime. There was very little work to do until the end of the match. The important part of the job was to take the copy from the reporters back to the local newspaper's offices.

REGIONAL RIVALRY

Only once to our knowledge did the Leicester boys challenge another Midland office to a game of cricket, it was played against Northampton on Western Park. The result has not been remembered nor recorded.

Other events around this time were the football matches against other Midland Region Telegram Boys. These were arranged by the P.H.G. Mick Watts and as in previous years were against teams from Coventry, Derby and Nottingham. They are remembered more for kicking the opposing team players, rather than the ball! As in past years, Derby telegram boys were Leicester's deadliest rivals. The score was immaterial, more important was hacking the shins of the opponents. Fixtures were made with return legs, which did not always come off, depending on the severity of the injuries and management wishing to avoid further bloodshed. If a boy from the opposing team had received a hacking, there was always someone who said "Wait till you come to our place, we will get you." Nothing changed over the years! An infamous match from the 1950's, which went down in history was played against Derby Telegram Boys. The match took place on a very cold and frosty afternoon at Rushey Fields Leicester. Tempers were stretched to the limit as the Leicester boys were being hacked about, when they gave their opponents similar treatment the referee penalised them and seemingly ignored Derby's infringements of the rules. The match was brought to a sudden end when the Leicester boys without voicing their opinions showed their utter contempt for the referee's decisions by gathering in the centre circle and urinating, yes urinating (in unison) on the ball. The ensuing minutes were full of threats and recriminations that lasted for many months afterwards. The Derby boys were ushered onto their coach and driven away having to forgo the after match socialising, which had been laid on at Gladstone Buildings. This was one match where the score was unimportant. The end result was a 'moral' victory for the Leicester boys', which was savoured for a long time. What is not recorded is, 'who picked the ball up!'

OFF DUTY / UNDER AGE

As in previous years the boys often went out together in a group, going to the pictures was one of their favourite pastimes. Because the boys were of all shapes and sizes getting into an X-rated film was quite an achievement. The six footers found they had no problem, but some of the smaller boys kept their fingers crossed until they were safely inside. Getting into an X-rated film was the all-important thing, actually seeing the film was often a bit of an anti-climax.

TWO WHEELS ON MY WAGON

The boys lived for riding motorcycles both on and off duty. Many of them had their own motorcycles so if possible during the week and at weekends a group of them would meet and ride somewhere together just because they enjoyed motorcycling. When out on a group bike ride one boy managed to fall off his motorcycle at exactly the same bend in a road at Billesdon, once on the outward part of the journey, then repeated on the other side of the road as they travelled back. This same boy even fell off outside the Accident and Emergency Department of the Leicester Royal Infirmary choosing the perfect place to fall! They occasionally set out to go to the coast but no one remembers whether they ever got there. On one such trip to the coast, a boy clipped the kerb and finished up in a ditch with his pillion passenger on top of him. The rider got no further than the Accident & Emergency Ward of Kings Lynn General Hospital. After the accident, the driver had cuts, bruises and concussion, the pillion passenger who only had minor injuries was able to placate the police by claiming they had hit a brick in the road. Later the repair bill came for the bike and much later still two demands for payment from the hospital for the treatment they had both received, just to 'rub salt into the wound!'

LAST RUN

In the 1970's telegrams were getting fewer so the last runs of the day were made up of late received telegrams. These were often spread out over a large area, and a boy had to take the rough with the smooth. To save having to come back to the office some boys would use their own motorcycles, which was of course totally illegal. By going to the basement and taking his own bike instead of the Post Office one, he could go up the ramp and out of the Fox Street gate. This exit was on the far side of the parcel office and could not be seen from the delivery office window enabling the boy to slip out unnoticed. After delivering the telegrams he was able to go straight home. No one was ever caught, or came unstuck doing it, which was just as well.

THE DEMISE OF THE MOTORCYCLE

At the age of seventeen a boy graduated from moped to motorcycle duties after receiving training and passing a further test. The motorcycles used were B.S.A. Bantams 125 c.c. machines which had been in use since early 1950. Birmingham Small Arms Company (B.S.A.) went into liquidation in 1972 and no further motorcycles were produced after 1973. For some time afterwards bikes were cannibalised to obtain spare parts to keep others on the road. At the same time alternative British firms that produced bikes with small engines went out of production. The only option open to the Post Office was to increase the use of mopeds. The long suffering mechanics already had their hands full with the motorbikes and added to this was the problem of the reliability of mopeds which were not as sturdy as motor bikes. All bikes with faults were logged off by the rider. The logbook for the faulty vehicle was filled in, detailing the perceived fault, serial number, vehicle registration and the name of the person logging it off. The logbook with the keys was placed into a special box so the machine could not be used until repaired. It was heartbreaking after logging off a favourite motorcycle to go into the workshop and see it stripped of all usable parts with just the frame left. With each motorbike that was stripped the inevitable day advanced when only mopeds were left to ride.

ACCIDENTS AND BREAKDOWNS

Following an accident or a breakdown, the 150 C.F. van used by the garage was despatched to the scene. If it was a breakdown and the driver sent was a mechanic he would try to repair the machine and get the boy on his way. If he was not a mechanic, or the bike could not be repaired on site he would take both boy and machine back to the garage. Most of the accidents only resulted in damage to the machine rather than the rider, but nevertheless over the years a handful of boys did end up in hospital some with serious injuries but thankfully there were no fatalities. Mopeds were constantly 'crash tested,' mishaps being blamed on wet leaves, black ice or diesel spillage from lorries and buses etc. The truth was sometimes more to do with the rider, going too fast, too close or even just not paying attention. One boy was so accident-prone and always in some kind of trouble that it helped to take the 'spotlight' off the other boys. Even now long after the events the mention of his name in conversation brings many a retired supervisor out in a cold sweat. After an accident no matter what a boys injuries might be, he always felt worse at the thought of filling in the 'accident on duty form.' If it was not his fault, (never was!) it was straight forward, however if he was somewhere he shouldn't have been, or doing something forbidden, the world of fantasy often came into play. Locations were swapped, and time massaged if possible. Most annoying, were the witnesses, if they saw it was a telegram boy, he was doing at least 100 miles per hour, on the wrong side of the road and of course if this was related to a police officer, it was added, "he needs locking up!" They were the things you dreaded, but not as much as waiting for the accident panel's decision (blameworthy or not blameworthy) to come back to you. The waiting could put years on a boy!!

Having an accident could sometimes be excused, but to run out of petrol was unforgivable, no one gave any sympathy, the rule was clear, check the tank on take over of the machine. Generally rules were made to be bent or broken but this one was the golden rule you did not break. No mechanic let a boy who was so irresponsible go unpunished, and his colleagues certainly never gave him chance to forget it.

MOVING UP?

Senior boys advanced to adult duties at the age of eighteen. Moving up to Postman duties, which entailed very early starts and shift work was for some too much of a shock and many resignations followed, others carried on and stayed for years often finishing up as P.H.G.s or Supervisors.

1975 NEW TITLE

1975 and another change of title was instituted for messengers, out went Postman (C) to be replaced by the Young Postman Grade.

THE PRICE GOES UP - AGAIN!

In September 1975 the price of telegrams went sky high with the effect that telegrams sent nationally in the following quarter plummeted by 40%. Between October and December 1975 890,000 telegrams were sent, the previous year (same quarter) it had been 1,490,000.

EXTRA EARNINGS

Under the age of eighteen there were few opportunities for overtime, occasionally a boy would work his day off or perform the odd Sunday duty. During the busy Christmas period boys were asked to work overtime in the Sorting Office usually on letter facing with the drivers. The age rules laid down by government for boys and girls under the age of eighteen restricted the extra hours they could work. Not many of the boys wanted to work extra hours, even if on overtime.

WHEN 'VROOM' CHANGED TO 'PHUT PHUT'

By the summer of 1976 all the spares had been used so finally ending the era of the B.S.A. motorcycle. Over the quarter century of their existence, the distinct sound of the B.S.A. Bantam stayed in the memory of the hundreds of boys who rode them, if only the performance had matched the sound, it would have been sheer bliss!! From now on only mopeds were used for the delivery of telegrams, much to the disappointment of the boys on delivery at the time. Occasionally there was such a shortage of mopeds on the road, the boys were sent to the Sorting Office and telegrams went out by van. Boys were employed on tipping bags, bundle cutting and other mundane tasks, which they hated.

LAST CHANGES BEFORE THE END

In July 1977 the Post Office began recruiting Young Postmen, (their new title since 1975,) for sorting and postal delivery duties only. Towards the end of 1978 with the telegram traffic still falling to less than 100 telegrams received per day, most of the remaining Telegraphists were either offered redundancy or transferred to another grade e.g. Postal Assistant. On 30/11/1978 the Assistant Supervisor transferred to Postal Assistant grade, this left ten Telegraphists and one temporary Assistant Supervisor in charge. Five Telegraphists were needed to retain the Assistant Supervisors post and as by 28/1/1979 only three remained the post was abolished.

TELEGRAMS IN VANS?

Sometime in 1979 an Assistant Inspector (ex-messenger) was placed on special duties by the Chief Inspector and given the onerous task of assessing whether or not it would be cheaper to use vans, with Postmen, to deliver Telegrams and no longer use boys on mopeds. The final cost figure was almost equal and as there was no clear advantage in removing the mopeds, the boys stayed on for a little longer. The person given the assignment was relieved knowing it was not his report which would sever the last link with boys delivering telegrams.

ANOTHER DOOR CLOSES

In May 1979 the Telegram delivery boys' were made a separate unit carrying out telegram delivery work exclusively. There were only seven duties and one leave reserve by this time. At a later date British Telecom replaced the seven indoor messenger boys with their own adult staff. These boys joined the other Young Postman duties on Sorting Office and delivery duties. Another chapter in the boys' work had closed forever.

CHAPTER 12

THE FINAL CURTAIN

The reprieve from the 1979 costing exercise was very short lived, in October 1981 the final nail in the telegraph coffin was driven home. Post Office Telephones split from the Post Office to become a separate unit, as British Telecom P.L.C. The old days of public service without regard to cost, were over.

In May 1981 the new grade of Postal Cadet replaced the Young Postmen grade. These boys did sorting office work and pressure letter deliveries. The deliveries were made up from parts taken off a large delivery to reduce the weight or delivery span or alternately a new development, which had not grown large enough to be made up to a full delivery round. Cadets also attended Youth Training Schemes (Y.T.S.) and diploma courses.

As the existing Telegram boys either resigned or advanced to adult duties they were not replaced and the numbers started to dwindle from seven downwards. By October 1981 there were only three boys left and Postmen drivers were used to assist in the delivery of the telegrams.

The end of the Inland Telegram Service came on October 1st 1982, exactly twelve months after the separation and privatisation of British Telecom. By now most of the population were in possession, or had access to a telephone and telegrams, which were costlier to send were rendered obsolete. For most of their history they had run at a loss for the Post Office but for years they were the only means of conveying urgent messages quickly. In the final year British Telecom lost a staggering twenty one million pounds despite telegrams costing £6.00 for thirty words!!

TELEMESSAGES

British Telecom had one problem to solve before they could finally close down the telegram service. Greetings telegrams and the all important Telegram from Her Majesty The Queen sent from Buckingham Palace congratulating couples who were celebrating their Diamond Wedding Anniversary or for a person reaching 100 years of age had become very popular and a way had to be found to continue this special service. The answer was the Telemessage, it was introduced on the 26/10/1981 by British Telecom, formally part of the Post Office. The Post Office still continued with Inland and Overseas Telegrams, including greetings telegrams, until 1/10/1982 both services running in tandem. From this time only the Telemessage Service was available, which was quite different from the old telegram service. Telegrams were delivered within an hour on average, from being accepted while Telemessages in their bright yellow envelopes, were delivered the following day by a delivery Postman. Telemessages were priced to undercut telegrams they cost £3.00 plus vat (minimum fee) for up to fifty words against the standard telegram fee of £2.00 (fixed fee) plus 16p per word (including the name and address.) Greetings Telegrams cost an extra 50p for the card. There were several standard designs and others by Roland Emmett for special occasions. Telemessages were sent each evening by teleprinter from the Telemessage Centre in London to various sites around the country located in the main Sorting Offices. The message was then stuck onto a card, which had been selected by the sender. Special gold coloured envelopes were used for those sent from Buckingham Palace. The Telemessage P.H.G. sorted them ready for delivery by postal staff the following morning. Confirmation of delivery for

Royal Telemessages ensured there were no disappointments on the appropriate day. This change over from Greetings Telegrams to Telemessages guaranteed messages reaching Weddings, Birthdays and those very special celebrations. The greetings from Her Majesty continued and with it some of the tradition the Telegram Service had built up over the years.

The Chief Inspector gave the task of putting the Telemessage Service in Leicester on line, to the same Assistant Inspector whom he had asked to investigate taking the mopeds off the road in favour of vans. The Assistant Inspector was sent to London to the International Telegraph Centre to learn about the new system. When it was time to check the new system was on line, the British Telecom Supervisor sent to oversee the installation of the teleprinter, was the last Assistant Supervisor in charge of the old Telegraph Instrument Room at Bishop Street. This was not the only coincidence, the Chief Inspector and one of the P.H.G.s receiving the Telemessages were all ex-messengers, thus ensuring the new system was in good hands.

PHOTO 67 MARK GREEHILL ONLY KNOWN PHOTOGRAPH OF A MESSENGER ON A MOPED 1980

POSTSCRIPT

In the conclusion of the story of the Telegram Service in Leicester, we have tried to show the human-interest side of things as well as the factual and historical development over 112 years. Hopefully we have given the reader a picture of what day to day life was like for a Telegram Boy at various stages of his progress through the service during several decades, the good and the bad moments, the ups and the downs and the happy and the sad times. What happened to those 2,000 or so boys who wore the Blue G.P.O. uniform of a boy messenger during the time of the Telegram Service in Leicester? Some went on to greater things within the G.P.O. (Post Office/Royal Mail) Post Office Telephones (British Telecom) the Police, Fire Service or other occupations and achieved great success. An unfortunate few fell on hard times. Several moved to far away places such as Australia, New Zealand, South Africa and Canada. Some boys gave all they had in the Great War and World War II. The one common factor that linked all these boys together was the sense of camaraderie that came from the 'Red Oil' days. The following two stories serve to illustrate the depth of this bond between ex-telegram boys, some may have been deadly rivals but that link from their days together *in the service* is difficult to break even after 70 years!

The time was World War II just after the 'D Day' landings, the place somewhere in Northern France. One ex-messenger was walking along a road when he passed a column of marching soldiers and suddenly recognised a familiar face in the column, he ran across and marched along with them. They immediately started to talk, not about the war or their circumstances but of their time together as "Red Bike Boys'" in Leicester. Reminiscing about old friends and the Head Postman who wrote to his boys in the forces. All too soon they had to part company, each smiling to himself remembering things they had to talk about the next time they would meet. Sadly this was not to be, as one of the soldiers was killed on the 17th July 1944 in Normandy and is buried there. The strength of the camaraderie is shown by the small board, which has been placed at the side of his memorial. Each ex-messenger who visits the graveside to pay his respects adds his name to the board, and the list keeps growing.

Three boys started together as telegram boys in the early 1930's serving for some years at Granby Street and later in the new office in Bishop Street. These boys grew up as good friends and work colleagues and after nearly seventy years still meet regularly and remain firm friends, showing true *'Red Oil'* spirit.

They are not the only ex-messengers who meet to reminisce about old times, some get together on a regular basis in the city, others in the county for a coffee and a chat.

GLOSSARY

S.C.&T. — Sorting Clerk and Telegraphist
Undertakes Sorting writing or telegraph work

S.C.&T. (Tels) — Sorting Clerk and Telegraphist (Telegraphist)
Undertakes Telegraphist work including writing duties

P.H.G. — Postman Higher Grade
Undertakes sorting and writing duties

P.&T.O. — Postal and Telegraph Officer
Undertakes counter, writing or telegraph writing room work

A/I — Assistant Inspector

A/SUPT — Assistant Superintendent
Supervisory work over counter, writing and telegraph duties

CLERK — The rank of Clerk was changed to Overseer after 1905

OVR — Overseer
Supervisory work over counter, writing and telegraph duties

TELEG — Telegraphist
telegraph duties

SKEP Post Office spelling for a skip, a large wicker wheeled container used to sort parcels into or store empty letter or parcel bags. Also used to store letters or packets at peak times prior to sorting e.g. Christmas. A very large version was referred to as a Queen Mary after the Cunard liner.

BAG TIES - made in two lengths, short for tying up letter bags and long for parcel bags. These were made up using pre-cut lengths of sisal string onto which a lead seal was threaded and a knot tied at the end to keep the seal in place. These strings were then made up into lots of twenty-five by plaiting them together ready for use.

THE TELEGRAPH DEPARTMENT

The history of the Telegraph Service in Leicester told in the previous pages, has been written from the viewpoint of those involved in delivering telegrams. This story could not be considered complete without giving some details from the Telegraph Department this is the butter for the bread.

The Instrument Room has always been the 'engine room' of the Telegraph Service, together with the Telegraph Writing Room (T.W.R.) The T.W.R. handled all the administrative work and the Instrument room dealt with the sending and receiving of telegrams.

The General Post Office (G.P.O.) by Act of Parliament took over all private telegraph companies in 1870. At the change over many of their staff joined the G.P.O. as Boy Messengers or Telegraphists. Several of the Telegraphists from this era went on to become Supervisors in the department, whilst many of the boys left the service before they could take up adult duties. The Telegraph Department was a separate unit of the Post Office.

METHODS OF SENDING A TELEGRAM

The original and only method for sending telegrams started with members of the public handing in a telegram form at the Head Office Counter. The hand written message was then sent to the Instrument room for transmitting by morse key. Later they could be sent from a Sub Post Office once the single needle machines came into use. These were replaced by the telephones installed in Sub Post Offices. This method of forwarding the messages to the Instrument Room was also used in some areas to get the telegrams to the delivery point. It did not change greatly until the Post Office nationalised the telephone service. Telegrams sent by telephone subscribers were known as Phonograms, and were dealt with by a growing number of telephonists. In the early days of the service, telegrams were hand written, later the message and envelope were typewritten. In the 1930s teleprinter machines were introduced which printed the message onto a paper tape, which had a gummed backing. The tape was then run across a wheel mounted in a small holder filled with water, and the tape stuck onto the telegram form, the address was typed onto the envelope and the message folded and inserted inside. This cut down the time considerably to get a message ready for delivery. In 1933 the Phonogram section staff along with their Supervisor Miss Minnie Mason were transferred from the Telephone side to the Telegraph Department. Boy Messengers and at a later date Girl Probationers (who wore green overalls as their uniform) collected the messages which were referred to as 'checks' from the teleprinter operators, they then handed them to the telegraphists to type the address on and add the telegram serial number.

TELEGRAPHS THE LATER YEARS

The outbreak of the Second World War in 1939 sharply increased the telegraph and telephone traffic. With the men being called up Temporary Female S.C.&Ts were recruited, some of these stayed on for many years after the end of the war. Immediately following the war the Telegraph Department was very busy. A Telegraph Training School was set up in Telephone House at 66, London Road. By 1949 there were approximately 127 people employed in the Telegraph Department.

MEMORIES OF A 1940's TELEGRAPHIST

During the Second World War there were over 100 staff in the Telegraph Department, these were mainly female as the balance between male and female had changed in the 1930's. Four shifts operated over the twenty-four hours. The night shift was from 11.00 p.m. to 7.00 a.m. with two nights off. Those working between 8.00 p.m. and 6.00 a.m. received a ten minute in the hour time credit for each hour they worked. This reduced the working week for the late and night staff, as the time credit came off the total hours worked in that week, it was a welcome perk to those working unsocial hours. The earliest day shift started at 7.00 a.m. finishing at 3.00 p.m. Other telegraphists started at half hour intervals until 12 noon, finishing the shift at 8.00 p.m. The first persons on the late shift commenced at 1.10 p.m. until 9.00 p.m. the next at 2.20 p.m. until 10.00 p.m. then 3.30 p.m. until 11.00 p.m. and the final late shift 4.40 p.m. until midnight. The late and nightshifts overlapped by one hour. The split shift started at 9.00 a.m. finishing at 1.00 p.m. resuming at 4.00 p.m. and finishing at 8.00 p.m. This was the most unpopular shift of all. All attendances on Sunday were on overtime, paid at one and a half times the hourly pay rate. In attendance were two telegraphists midnight until 8.00 a.m. four 8.00 a.m. until 1.00 p.m. then three 1.00 p.m. until 5.30 p.m. two 5.00 p.m. until 10.00 p.m. and two on the night shift from 10.00 p.m. until 7.00 a.m. Monday morning.

TELEGRAPHIST TRAINING

Training was a sixteen-week course under an Assistant Supervisor, it was principally learning to touch type, which was achieved by placing a board over the keyboard so the keys could not be seen by the trainee, to help get the rhythm flowing the Sailors Hornpipe was played on a record player. Another part of the course was to learn telegraph procedures, after completing the course they started work in the Junior Section.

THE SECTIONS

The Junior was the first tier of the three sections, the others were, Middle and Senior. The atmosphere was very formal, discipline was strict, staff and supervisors addressed one another as, Mr X or Miss Y. Night duty was more relaxed as there were, less staff on duty. Only three minutes late attendance was allowed, any later than this was recorded on a form P18. Other misdemeanours or errors were written in the staff logbook. Controlling the staff at this time were five supervisors.

TIES AND BREAKS

Staff were allowed two fifteen minute tea breaks and a forty minute dinner break. As there was no canteen at this time staff cooked their own dinners in their kitchens, which adjoined both rest rooms, the male and female rest rooms were on different floors. Camaraderie was good and many friendships were formed some of which led to romance and eventually marriage. Shift working made outside interests difficult even Christmas Day was a normal working day for the telegraph staff. There were several social outings to the seaside and dinner dances arranged all funded by the Rain Club. Every day it rained members were expected to pay into the club. There were often disputes on days it rained, as there was always someone who said "It was not raining where I was" and would not pay their dues. Eventually the fund was changed to a weekly collection to avoid any arguments.

LIGHTER MOMENTS AND RELIEF WORK

Although on the receiving end of practical jokes by the telegram boys, with Girl Probationers coming in for particular attention, it was not unknown for the Instrument Room staff to get their own revenge on the boys. As there were only three night duties and no supervisor looking on, it was a less demanding shift and there were occasional bouts of humour. The phone book was searched for similar names, perhaps a Mr Salt and Mr Pepper would be connected to one another and the staff on duty would listen in. The ensuing conversation would sometimes result in a very heated debate and the listening staff would dissolve into hilarious laughter. Relief work at other telegraph offices in the region was undertaken. The type of work in the Telegraph Department was very varied and included messages to and from the King's Flight, which became the Queen's Flight when Princess Elizabeth acceded to the throne. Government and overseas business, the racing press and ships at sea were other special customers. Obtaining payment and the actual transmission of messages to and from ships at sea could be a problem they were the most difficult customers to deal with. First it was necessary to find out if the ship was in harbour or on the high seas. If it was in a harbour the link up was easier to establish. If however the ship was at sea it was sometimes difficult to make contact. The radio link was from an onshore station by radio to the ship, this could take a long time if weather conditions were adverse or the position of the ship was outside the radio stations transmitting area. One important area of work for the T.W.R. was the recording and maintenance of Wireless Licence Records, in the 1950's this work increased with the addition of television licences.

NEW SHIFTS AND WORK

After the war a new pattern of shifts was started and all staff followed this system no matter how long they had been employed. Seniority was only used for holiday signing and was eventually changed several years later to a rotation system. On Sundays the delivery period was 8.00 a.m. to 5.00 p.m. any telegrams left were taken by the messenger to the Sorting Office for delivery by Post Office van. The driver employed to deliver these telegrams and any life or death telegrams, which arrived out of hours, also cleared overflowing pillar-boxes reported by the general public or the police. Of the three sections Junior, Middle and Senior, the Junior Section performed the work previously carried out by Girl Probationers, which involved the distribution of telegrams to the receiving and sending positions. Several ex-boy messengers had been added to this section to create the new rank of Junior Telegraphist. The Middle Section work was accepting Phonograms from Sub Post Offices and telephone subscribers. They also dealt with telegrams handed in at the public counter at Bishop Street Head Office. Circulation of, transmission and receiving of telegrams were also part of their duties. The Senior Section, which included the Acting Assistant Supervisors undertook work on Confirmation Telegrams, Cablegrams, Phonogram enquiries, charging accounts and checking clerk work.

WAYS TO SEND AN INLAND TELEGRAM

In the Leicester area there were three ways to send a telegram. The first method was from a Sub Post Office. The customer wrote the message on the telegram form provided and handed it to a member of staff. The Sub Postmaster checked the wording telephone the telegraph office direct using the national number, 190. The operator took the callers telephone number followed by the destination and message, if requested the caller would be advised as to the cost of the telegram. These telegrams known as phonograms had a serial number and the date stamp added before collection by the charging operator, who then put the cost of the telegram onto a docket, which was forwarded to the Telephone Managers office. The cost would later be added to the subscriber's next telephone bill.

The telegram forms were then routed to the circulation clerk via the conveyor belt, who sorted them into a pigeonhole for either inward or outward traffic.

If the item was inward (local) the addressing position would type out an envelope, place the telegram inside and seal it ready for delivery. At regular intervals the finished check position operator would collect all the telegram forms sent by telephone or teleprinter, check that the codes, signatures and time were correct and if any discrepancies were found a second copy was sent. If any irregularities had been found a green label was attached to the telegram, priority treatment was given and finally the enquiry position would take up the error with the originating office or subscriber. The forms were then filed and kept in the record room for three years.

OVERSEAS TELEGRAMS – CABLEGRAMS

All Cablegrams sent from the Leicester area had their destinations checked and the cost added to the telephone account of the sender by the enquiry position. All the transmitted telegrams were then filed.

AUTOMATION

Automation came in during the 1950's which meant the

teleprinters changed from T.M.S. (Through manual switches) to T.A.S. (Through automatic switching) each Telegraphist now had an independent telephone headset, making the switchboard operator redundant. The new teleprinters had a dial attached so each operator could contact the distant office direct. For outgoing telegrams each position had a switchboard, a circulation book and a teleprinter, which made the circulation clerk redundant. For incoming telegrams three teleprinters were stacked on top of each other so the operator could make all three operations without moving position.

Business users, for an annual fee could have a two word telegraphic address, a business code and the destination address. The addressee could either have the message read out over the telephone and a confirrnation copy sent by post the next day or, have the item delivered by a telegram boy.

The last telegrams were sent to the Telegraph Delivery Room at 8.00 p.m. any received after the cut off time addressed to telephone subscribers were 'phoned through to them up until 11.00 p.m. A driver from Campbell Street Sorting Office collected any telegrams on hand at midnight and returned to the Sorting Office with them. These were then sent out for delivery in the morning. Telegrams received after 8.00 p.m. for areas outside the City delivery area were telephoned to the nearest post office the next morning. City delivery area telegrams received after midnight were held until the Telegraph Delivery Office opened at 8.00 a.m.

Life or Death Telegrams received after 8.00 p.m. were given special treatment, a Postman Driver was sent from the Sorting Office if available otherwise a Police Officer would be called upon to deliver it.

MR. COLIN BURBAGE O.B.E. OstJ

SPECIAL FEATURE 1
FROM BOTTOM TO TOP

Only one man in the history of Leicester Post Office has the achievement of working his way up from a Telegram Boy (Boy Messenger) to Chairman of a Post Office Regional Board.

Mr. Colin Burbage O.B.E. OstJ joined the Post Office in Leicester as a Boy Messenger on 3rd August 1944. In 1946 he was appointed Sorting Clerk & Telegraphist (S.C.&T) serving as a Telegraphist until 1951. From 1951 until 1959 he was a Postal & Telegraph Officer, promoted to Instructor at the Post Office Training School at Wolverhampton from 1959 to 1961. He gained promotion to Overseer at Leamington Spa where he spent four years until another promotion to Assistant Postal Controller Class II (A.P.C.II) at the Midland Region Head Quarters in Birmingham. In 1969 he was promoted to A.P.C.I in which capacity he served until 1971. A further promotion to Head Postmaster at Bromley in Kent lasted until 1976, then he was Head Postmaster at Exeter from 1976 to 1979 and Bristol from 1979 to 1980. A further promotion followed as Postmaster.

Controller Eastern Central District Office and Foreign Section London. His final promotion was in 1986 lasting until 1997 as Chairman of the Post Office Board for Wales & the Marches. Apart from National service his varied and illustrious career spanned nearly 53 years but Colin would be the first person to refute the word 'illustrious' as he has always remained proud to be recognised and thought of as a 'Red Bike Boy' that had *'done well.'*

SPECIAL FEATURE 2

LEICESTER, FROM BOY TO BOSS

Gaining promotion to the top job in a Head Post Office is hard, but to work through the ranks at the same office is an achievement without equal.

David Sidney Hinde accomplished this by working his way up from Telegram Boy (Boy Messenger) to Head Postmaster in Leicester Head Post Office. He was born on 7th January 1889 and commenced work for the Post Office as a Boy Messenger on 4th August 1903, becoming established on 11th October that year. He became an Assistant Postman in 1906 then in 1908 having achieved sufficient marks in the Civil Service Examination to progress to the S.C.&T. Grade (Sorting Clerk & Telegraphist) he transferred to Crewe as there were no vacancies at Leicester.

He returned to Leicester in 1911 as a S.C.&T. He was promoted to the rank of Overseer in 1927, progressing to

Assistant Superintendent in 1934, Superintendent in 1935 and in 1937 he was promoted to Assistant Postmaster.

From 1942 he was nominally in charge of the office acting as Postmaster in the absence of Mr. John Periam who was away on war work. David Hinde was promoted substantially as Head Postmaster of Leicester in 1945 where he remained until his retirement on 31st March 1949. He died on 17th December 1960 aged 71.

During his time as Postmaster David's younger brother Norman Leslie Hinde was promoted to Superintendent (Postal) he held this post from 1946 - 1949.

Norman started as a Telegram Boy (Boy Messenger) in Leicester on the 13th August 1913. To have two brothers reach jobs of this importance at the same time was unique.

DAVID
SIDNEY
HINDE

NORMAN
LESLIE
HINDE

ALDERMAN WILLIAM HENRY SMITH J.P.

SPECIAL FEATURE 3

FROM BOY MESSENGER TO LORD MAYOR

Many Boy Messengers have gone on to various occupations in later life. Several became Leicester City Ward Councillors and two were made Alderman, one of them Frederick George Gumbrill having a sheltered housing building named after him, Gumbrill House. The other, William Henry Smith achieved even greater fame becoming Lord Mayor of Leicester, the only former Telegram Boy to hold that position.

W.H. Smith was born on 26th July 1890 and began work as a Boy Messenger (Telegram Boy) in 1904 - he was established on 31st August that year. He became Postman in 1907. Later in 1920 he progressed to the S.C.&T. Grade (Sorting Clerk & Telegraphist) on the postal side.

He became a member of the U.P.W. (Union of Postal Workers) and held various offices both at local and national level over 40 years.

He was first elected to the City Council in November 1924 and was President of the Leicester & District Trades Council in 1926. He retired from the Council in 1970.

He was appointed a J.P. (Justice of the Peace) in 1933 and High Bailiff of Leicester for 1942/1943.

W.H. Smith was elected as the 489th Lord Mayor of Leicester in 1946/1947, at this time he was a P.&T.O. (Postal & Telegraph Officer) at the Post Office.

He married Nora in 1930 and they had one son.

In 1951 he retired from the Post Office and died 12th December 1976 aged 86.

**SPECIAL FEATURE 4
IMPERIAL SERVICE MEDAL (I.S.M.)
1902 – 1969**

This picture shows Mr Reginald Frederick Yarnell the last Assistant Superintendent Telegraphs being presented with his Imperial Service Medal (I.S.M.) on his retirement from the Post Office in 1962. The I.S.M. was awarded to all qualifying civil servants from 1902 after completing twentyfive years unblemished service. Until 1969 G.P.O. staff were civil servants but ceased to be when the Post Office changed to a Corporation. Any staff who were in employment on vesting day 1st October 1969 were eligible to receive the I.S.M. if qualified to do so. One of the favourite sayings when one of the 'Old Soldiers' received their medal which brought a smile to those at the presentation was, 'Awarded for twenty-five years of undetected crime.'

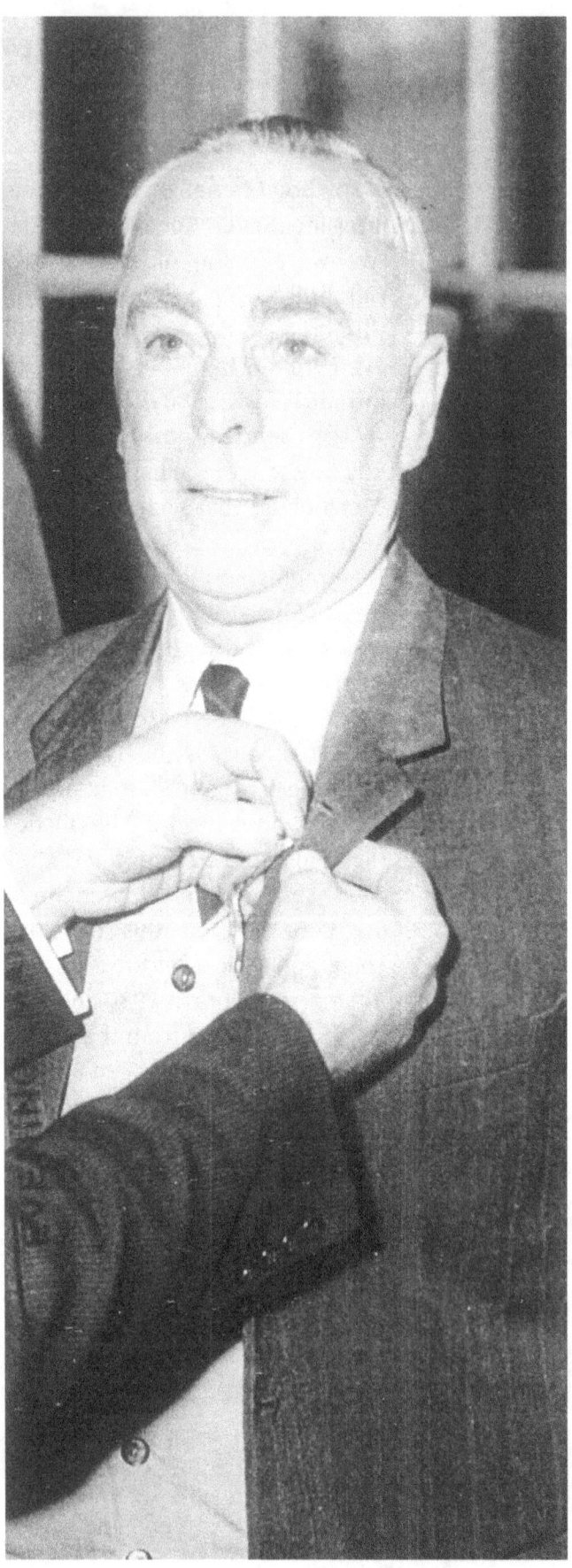

SPECIAL FEATURE 5
LONG SERVICE AT LEICESTER
1909 – 1961

There were many ex-messengers who completed more than thirty years service with the Post Office or its successors. Some went on to record more than fifty years. Even though the normal retiring age was sixty, in later years it was relaxed to allow some to continue until they were sixty-five.

The longest serving of all the messengers was Harry Bowis Bond with over fifty-one years to his credit. Harry was born on 14th March 1896 starting as a Boy Messenger on 4th September 1909 later becoming a Sorting & Telegraph Clerk (S.C.&T.) using morse code to transmit the telegrams.

He served his country in the First World War where his hearing was badly effected by a shell bursting a few yards from him in July 1916. When he returned to the Post Office after war service his hearing problems meant he could not follow the normal promotion path. Employment was found for him on special duties as he was an able typist. Later he met and married a telegraphist and they had two sons. He eventually became a Postal & Telegraph Officer and retired on 14th March 1961.

He died on 4th March 1980 aged 83.

SPECIAL FEATURE 5
LONG SERVICE OF LEICESTER
EX – MESSENGERS

Since 1870 there have been many ex-messengers who completed over thirty years service. After reviewing the available records only those with forty-seven years and above are named. Two transferred to other offices to complete their service and the offices are shown. Despite the moans and groans heard over the years it must have been a worthwhile job to stay so long!

H.B. BOND	1909 – 1961	Over 51 years service.
W.H. FENDELL	1932 – 1983	Over 50 years service
K. FISHER	1936 – 1987	Over 50 years service
N.J. STEWARD	1946 - 1997	Over 50 years service
J.A. BRUTNALL	1941 – 1992	Over 50 years service
S. STEVENSON	1943 – 1994	Over 50 years service
J.E. BENTLEY	1929 – 1950	Leicester &
	1950 – 1979	Oakham Over 50 years service
K. HARPHAM	1933 - 1983	Over 49 years service
J.A. CALWOOD	1909 -1945	Leicester &
	1945 – 1959	Market Harborough Over 49 years service
G.T. GREEN	1950 – 1999	Over 49 years service
D.J. JOHNSON	1936 – 1986	Over 49 years service
D.R. BEANE	1941 - 1990	Over 49 years service
A.R. WILLIAMSON	1953 - 2002	Over 49 years service
G. ASTON	1906 – 1955	Over 48 years service
H. COLLINS	1946 – 1994	Over 48 years service
W.A. JOHNSON	1934 - 1982	Over 48 years service
F.S. DRAYCOTT	1932 - 1980	Over 48 years service
W. TAILBY	1930 - 1978	Over 48 years service
J.D. MURPHY	1927 – 1975	Over 47 years service
W.C. HAYWARD	1927 -1974	Over 47 years service
C.GODDARD	1871 – 1918	Over 47 years service
A.W. CHAMPION	1870 – 1917	Over 47 years service
J.L.OSBORN	1917 - 1964	Over 47 years service
S.R.TAYLOR	1884 – 1931	Over 47 years service

SPECIAL FEATURE 6
REUNIONS

The Telegram Service in Leicester ran from 5th February 1870 (when the General Post Office took over all private Telegraph Companies) until 1st October 1982 (when British Telecom closed it down in favour of the Telemessage Service). It had been in existence for 112 years and around 2,000 boys had passed through the ranks as Telegraph Messenger, Boy Messenger, Junior Postman, Postman 'C' (composite), Young Postman and finally Postal Cadet. All these names applied to Telegram Boys throughout the years. As boys either left the service early, retired from the Post Office or Telephone side contact was often lost between long time friends from their messenger days. It was decided to hold a reunion of ex messengers to give people a chance to meet up again and reminisce about the old days and past friends.

The first reunion is believed to have been held in 1972 at Telephone House (66, London Road) which was where the Post Office Sports and Social Club held their meetings. Further events were held at the same venue in 1976 and 1977.

Unfortunately there was a long gap until the next reunion was organised in 1992. This was held in the lounge of Campbell Street Sorting Office. Because of the long interval the organisers were sad to learn that a number of ex-colleagues had passed away. A book was handed round so that all names and addresses could be kept for future gatherings.

The next reunion could no longer be held at a Post Office venue due to changes in policy, so it was held at the Victory Public

House on Aylestone Road, Leicester in 1998. By this time the book from the last event had disappeared from the Sorting Office so contact with many people was impossible.

The next reunion was held at the Tigers Rugby Football Ground on Aylestone Road during May 2000 it was decided to construct a Data Base for future events. At present about 300 known ex-messengers are on the list with contact details, but with the ages ranging up to those celebrating over 90 years and health restricting travel not all were able to attend. With the passing of the years the number of surviving ex-messengers will decrease, but we are always pleased to learn the whereabouts of missing members whether they are living in this country or overseas. Who knows we may be able to put you in touch with an old friend through our contact list, please get in touch!

'RED BIKE BOYS' BADGES!

Many of the 'Red Bike Boys' asked if we could produce something they could wear to show the link to their days in the service. A lapel badge was produced and is available from either of the contacts on page 200.

Left   Michael Petty 25 The Fairway, Blaby, Leicester. LE8 4EN

Right   Andy Marlow 15 Thatcher Close, Beaumont Leys, Leicester. LE4 0WE

APPENDICES

Pages 201 – 243

SPECIAL LISTS Pages 226 – 243

These cover only the known Telegram Boys in the Leicester Head Postmaster's delivery area. The dates start in 1864 with a messenger who worked for a private telegraph company and transferred over when it was nationalised in 1870. The list ends in 1982 at the end of the service under Royal Mail.

Abbreviations have been used for offices outside Leicester Head Office, when a boy started elsewhere in the United Kingdom and later transferred into the Leicester office.

These abbreviations are explained on p243.

CHRONOLOGY TELEGRAPHS (1870 - 1982)

1870 — General Post Office take over Private TelegraphCompanies Following Act of Parliament.

New Granby Street Office — 1887
(Telegraphs Entrance in Bishop Street)

1892 — Extension of Town Boundaries

Boys employed at Sub Post Offices — 1894

1896 — Extension of Free Delivery Area

Introduction of first bicycles — 1901

1908 — Grade of Boy Messenger replaces Telegraph Messenger

Telegram Peak - 82 Million sent in Great Britain — 1912

1920 — End of Adult Night Messenger Telegraph Office not open during night

Boys withdrawn from Sub Post Offices — 1922

1935 — Move from Granby Street Head Post Office to Bishop Street Head Post Office

Reduction in cost of telegrams Greetings Telegrams introduced Increase in Traffic — 1935

1939 -1945 — Increase in Traffic and staff due to World War II

Abolition of Boy Messenger Grade (now Junior Postman or Postman (c) = Composite) — 1947

1948 Examinations — Abolition of Boy Messenger

BOY MESSENGERS GENERAL EXAMINATION MARK & GRADES TABLES

SUBJECTS		1915	1922	May 1934	Nov 1934	1940	1943
English		400	400	200	200	200	200
Arithmatic		300	X	X	X	X	X
Calculations		X	300	150	150	150	150
Handwriting		200	200	200	?	?	50
History		200	{300}	75	?	?	X
Geography		200		75	?	?	X
Spelling		100	X	X	X	X	X
Drawing		X	100	X	X	X	X
Total marks available		1400	1300	700	650	500	400
Clerical assistant	Pass mark	950+	X	X	X	X	X
learner		700+	X	X	X	X	X
N.C.&T. from Nov 1921		X	700+	400+	350+	275+	220+
Postman		470+	470+	240+	210+	160+	130+

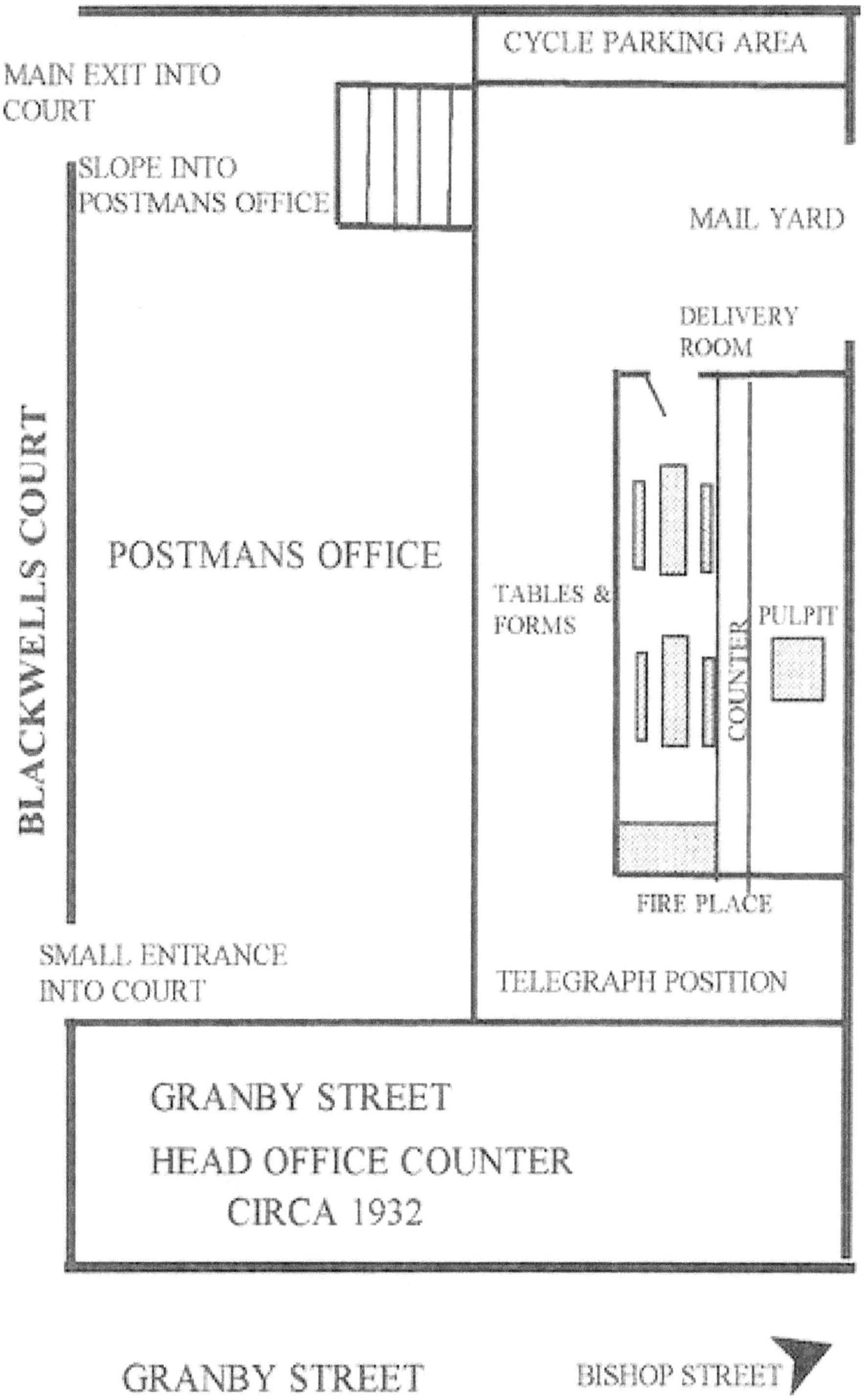

GRANBY STREET HEAD OFFICE COUNTER CIRCA 1932

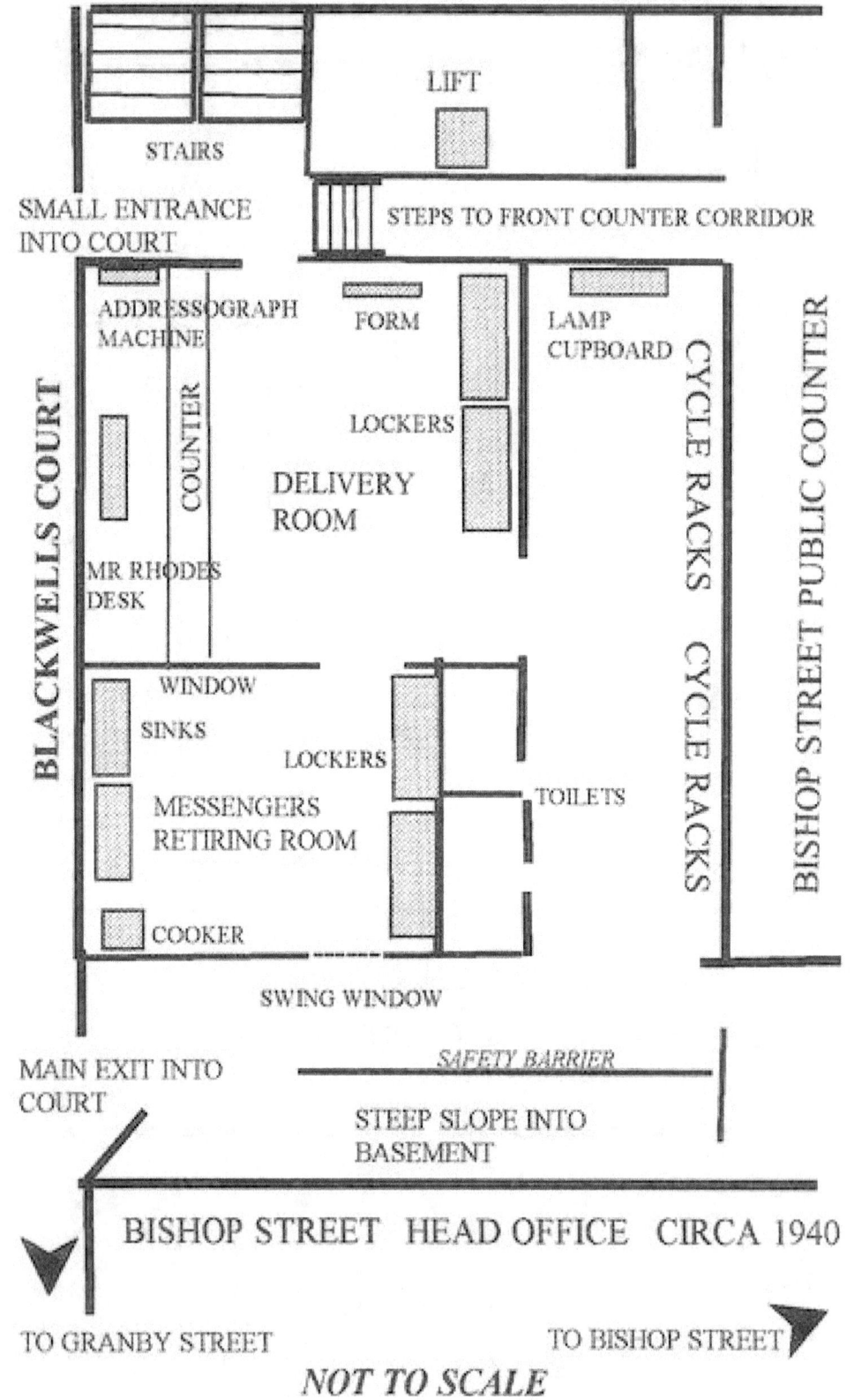

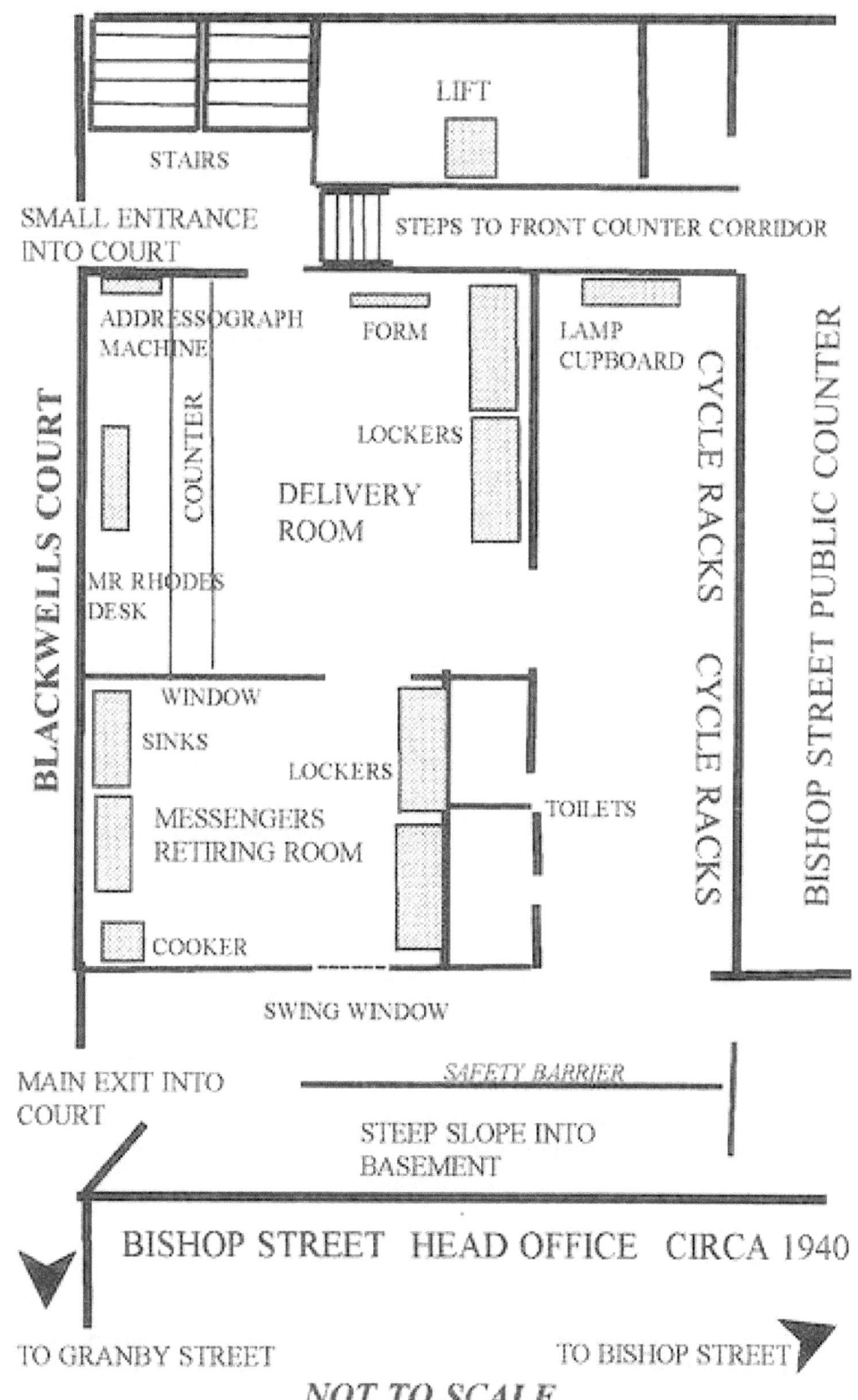

Reproduction of the application form for employment as a Boy Messenger circa 1933.

T4W (Revd. 84686/33.)

       PROVINCES   Form A.
APPLICATION FOR EMPLOYMENT AS BOY MESSENGER.
CONDITIONS OF EMPLOYMENT.

Age.- Candidates must be under 14½ years of age, and must produce satisfactory evidence of their age. No candidate will be employed until he is legally exempt from further full-time attendance at school, i.e.,. normally at the end of the term in which he attains the age of 14.

Educational Standard-.--Candidates must have reached the standard of
attainment normally expected of a boy of good average ability on leaving School
Physical Qualifications-.--Candidates must be not less than 4 ft. 8 in. in height, without boots, and must satisfy the Post Office Medical Staff as to their physical fitness.
Nationality-,--Every candidate must be a natural-born British subject, and the child of a person who is (or was at the time of death) a British subject. Residence.--Boy Messengers are required to reside within a reasonable
distance of the Office, either with their parents or guardians, or with some responsible person approved by them. They will, in most cases, be called upon to perform temporary duty before being regularly appointed, and will be required to perform Sunday duty, when necessary.
Hours of Duty-.--A Boy Messenger's duty does not commence, as a rule, before 8 a.m., or finish later than 8 p.m., but at the larger offices it may commence as early as 6 a.m., or finish at 9 p.m. ; the attendance (apart from Sunday duty, for which extra pay is given) is 48 hours a week.
Wages-- At ...Leicester....the present wages are 7/- under 15 years of age; 8/-, 10/-, 12/-, 15/-, a week at 15,16;17 and 18 years respectively and 18/- at 19 years and over.
Uniform.-- Uniform (including boots, if the boy is employed on outdoor duties for not less than 8 hours per week) is supplied.
Privileges--Boy Messengers are allowed 12 working days' holiday annually. When they first enter the service they receive free medical attendance from the Post Office Medical

Officer and two-thirds pay during properly certified sick absence up to a limit of three months in any twelve months. At 16 years of age a Boy Messenger becomes liable to compulsory insurance under the National Insurance Acts (Health, Pensions and Unemployment) and thenceforward the insurance contributions due from him are deducted weekly from his wages, unless he produces Certificates of Exemption. When he becomes, insured he ceases to be entitled to free medical attendance from the Post Office and he should choose a doctor from the local panel. When he is eligible for sickness benefit under the National Health Insurance Act (i.e., normally at the age of 16½), or would have been eligible but for Certificate of Exemption, a deduction corresponding to the benefit will be made from his sick pay. When a Civil Service Certificate is obtained, a Boy Messenger ceases to be insurable except for contributory pensions, and sick pay without deduction is again allowed, and also free medical attendance after he ceases to be eligible for attendance from his panel doctor. If he elects, and is accepted, for employment in the Engineering or Stores Dept., he is liable for full insurance.

_s8-Attendance at Educational Classes_s0-.--Until the question of their selection for permanent retention in the Post Office has been decided, that is, roughly during the first two years of their employment, Boy Messengers are required to attend suitable classes at local continuation schools, if available, for not less than four hours a week during the class session, their fees, up to a maximum of five shillings per annum, being paid by the Post Office. All time devoted to school attendance is additional to the normal hours of official duty.

_s8-Prospects_s0-.--Boys who give every satisfaction, and can satisfy the Civil Service Commissioners as to their character and as to their physical and educational fitness, will be retained permanently in the service of the Post Office.

At the Offices at which educational classes covering the examination syllabus are available, the boys to be selected for permanent retention are chosen by means of a General Competitive Examination which is held every half-year for the boys reaching 16 years of age during that half-year. The syllabus comprises Handwriting, English, Calculations, History and Geography. Further particulars may be obtained from the Head Postmaster.

Candidates who take the highest places in the General Examination and obtain a sufficiently high percentage of marks are considered, so far as vacancies allow, for appointment as

Sorting Clerk and Telegraphist. At Offices at which the Indoor Staff is "divided" for Postal and Telegraph duties respectively, these candidates are also considered, so far as vacancies allow, for appointments as Sorting Clerk and Telegraphist (Postal) during the twelve months following the half-year in which they attain 18 years of age.

For those boys who qualify for retention but do not obtain such posts, appointments as Postmen are reserved; after attaining the age of 18 those boys become eligible to take part in Limited Competitions for appointment as Sorting Clerks and Telegraphists on the Postal side of Divided Offices. Particulars of these Competitions can be obtained from the Head Postmaster.

At the Offices where no classes covering the General Examination syllabus are available the boys are required to pass a qalifying examination at the end of the half-year in which they reach the age of 16, and the majority of the boys who pass this examination eventually become Postmen. Boys at such offices may, if they so desire, take part in the General Examination and if they obtain a sufficiently high percentage of marks they will be considered, so far as: vacancies allow, for appointments as Sorting Clerk and Telegraphist. Suitable Boy Messengers at smaller offices may be granted special nominations for appointments as Sorting Clerk and Telegraphist provided their education is regarded as approximating to the Secondary School standard. Further particulars regarding these situations can be obtained from the Head Postmaster.

Boys who qualify for retention are also given the option of employment in the Engineering Department and are considered for such employment so far as openings are available. In certain towns facilities exist for a preliminary course of training in engineering work.

Boy Messengers who voluntarily express a desire to enter the Navy or Army may, if their parents or guardians approve, be retained as Messengers until they are old enough to enlist, provided they do so by the time they are 19 years of age. A proportion of the total entries of Seaman Class Boys are reserved for Boy Messengers, who will be afforded every opportunity to qualify for the Wireless Telegraphy and Signalling Branches of the Royal Navy. The age limits are 15-16½, but an extension to 16¾ will be allowed in exceptional cases on the recommendation of the Postmaster-General. Suitable Boy Messengers of good education between the ages of 16 and 17 are eligible for nomination for the Competitive Examinations, for the situation of Aircraft Apprentice, Royal Air Force, a position offering good prospects to boys with a mechanical bent of mind; further particulars can be obtained from the Head Postmaster. Boy Messengers who join the Forces will be given an opportunity of returning to the Post Office with a view to appointment as Postmen when their service with the Forces expires, provided that they have had not less than 3 years' adult service and that their character and health are satisfactory.

Boy Messengers have no claim to pension, gratuity or compensation for loss of Office, and their services are liable to be dispensed with at any time if they fail to give satisfaction or if they prove unsuitable in any respect for further employment; but Postmen and officers in other established positions open to Boy Messengers are entitled to the benefits of the Superannuation Acts enjoyed by established Civil Servants generally.

BOY MESSENGERS GENERAL EXAMINATION

The Civil Service Commission was inaugurated in 1855 and covered all Civil Service Departments including the General Post Office until 1969. Examinations for messengers started in 1870 when the private telegraph companies were taken over by the G.P.O. Examinations were split into 2 sections; LONDON and the PROVINCES these were held twice a year in May / November and later changed to June / December. Records held for these examinations date from 1912 and end in 1948 when the examinations were discontinued. The Pass Mark awarded determined what Grade could be achieved.

In May 1915 the total number of possible points totalled 1400. The subjects taken were ; SPELLING = 100 points, HISTORY = 200, GEOGRAPHY = 200, HANDWRITING = 200, ARITHMETIC = 300 and ENGLISH 400.
Candidates with eligible pass marks were graded into the following posts: top mark 950 + Clerical Assistant, 700 + Learner, 470 = Postman.
The pass rates and jobs remained the same until November 1921 when S.C.&T. (Sorting Clerk & Telegraphist) replaced Clerical Assistant and the post of Learner was abolished. Passes were then graded as, 700 = S.C.&T. 470 = Postman. From November 1922 the marks available were reduced to 1300, these were made up as follows: DRAWING = 100 marks, HANDWRITING = 200, CALCULATIONS = 300, HISTORY / GEOGRAPHY = 300 (shared between them,) ENGLISH = 400.
In May 1934 the marks total was again revised to 700. This now consisted of; HANDWRITING = 200, ENGLISH = 200, CALCULATIONS = 150, HISTORY = 75 GEOGRAPHY = 75. Passes were graded as; 400 = S.C.&T. and 240 = Postman.

In 1943 the marks available were further reduced to 400, this was made up as follows: ENGLISH = 200, CALCULATIONS = 150 and HANDWRITING = 50. Passes were then graded as, 220 = S.C.&T. and 130 = POSTMAN.

BOY MESSENGERS GENERAL EXAMINATION
MARK & GRADES TABLES

SUBJECTS	1915	1922	May 1934	Nov 1934	1940	1943
ENGLISH	400	400	200	200	200	200
ARITHMATIC	300	X	X	X	X	X
CALCULATIONS	X	300	150	150	150	150
HANDWRITING	200	200	200	?	?	50
HISTORY	200		75	?	?	X
GEOGRAPHY	200	{300}	75	?	?	X
SPELLING	100	X	X	X	X	X
DRAWING	X	100	X	X	X	X
TOTAL MARKS Available	1400	1300	700	650	500	400
CLERICAL ASSISTANT	950+	X	X	X	X	X
LEARNER	700+	X	X	X	X	X
S.C.&T. From Nov 1921	X	700+	400+	350+	275+	220+
POSTMAN	470+	470+	240+	210+	160+	130+

n.b. from clerical assistant to postman (Pass mark) vertical

TELEGRAPH MESSENGER'S WAGES 1870 – 1982

The chart opposite shows the various pay rises awarded to Telegraph Messengers over the years. From 1870 boys had to wait 46 years for the next pay rise, the 1916 rise changed the system. Docket Messengers ceased leaving all messengers on a fixed wage. It was a wait of 6 years for the next pay rise, followed by a further 12 years to the next increase. This shows the stability of prices in those times, workers may not have been paid large sums of money but they did know from week to week what it could buy. In the 1940's and 50's pay rises were more frequent, during the 1960's annual pay rises came into force as the cost of living started to rise. In the 1970's costs went through the roof and the pay had to keep pace and a twice yearly pay rise became normal.

 Over the years all staff including messengers had another burden placed on them, incremental scales. This was one problem of a job that was under the banner of the Civil Service. Most staff had four steps on the incremental scale, higher ranks had five. These increments were paid on the person's birthday each year until the maximum rate for the grade was reached. If a member of staff were to get into trouble, one punishment could be to lose an increment or in very serious cases two increments, so for a whole year the person being punished could work for less pay than someone the same age.

 To quote one ex-messenger, then a Chief Inspector, " You know lad I started on incremental scales, and I will still be on them when I retire!"

TELEGRAPH MESSENGER'S WAGES 1870 – 1982

L.S.D.		DECIMAL CURRENCY	
1870	5/-	1/1/1971	£8.15
1916	6/-	1/1/1972	£8.84
1922	7/-	1/4/1973	£10.19
1/11/1934	11/-	1/1/1974	£13.47
1/10/1938	12/6d	26/7/1974	£15.02
1/2/1944	13/6d	1/1/1975	£20.32
1/6/1946	28/-	14/6/1975	£21.67
1/10/1947	47/-	1/1/1976	£26.44
4/6/1949	49/-	1/1/1978	£30.92
1/1/1951	53/-	1/1/1979	£33.38
1/1/1953	62/-	1/7/1979	£35.54
1/7/1954	65/-	1/1/1980	£36.78
1/7/1955	70/-	1/4/1980	£43.56
1/7/1956	80/-	1/4/1981	£47.36
1/7/1957	84/-	1/11/1981	£48.02
1/1/1961	87/6d	1/4/1982	£51.38
1/4/1962	91/-		
1/1/1964	108/6d		
1/1/1965	113/-		
1/1/1966	117/-		
1/7/1967	125/-		
1/7/1968	130/-		
1/7/1969	134/6d		
1/1/1970	148/-		

FACTS & FIGURES £ S D

The following is the "new halfpenny" conversion table recommended by the Decimal Currency Board and accepted by the Government. In this table only sixpence, one shilling, ten shillings and £1 have the exact equivalent; all other prices up to one shilling are rounded up or down. Five are rounded up and five down and the overall effect is that buyers' and sellers' gains even out.

£ s. d.	=	£p.	(Rounding)
1d.	=	½ p.	(+ 0.2d.)
2d.	=	1p.	(+ 0.4d.)
3d.	=	1p.	(- 0.6d.)
4d.	=	1½ p.	(- 0.4d.)
5d.	=	2.p.	(- 0.2d.)
6d.	=	2½ p.	
7d.	=	3.p.	(+ 0.2d.)
8d.	=	3½ p.	(+ 0.4d.)
9d.	=	4p.	(+ 0.6d.)
10d.	=	4p.	(- 0.4d.)
11d.	=	4½ p.	(- 0.2d.)
1s.0d.	=	5p.	
10s.0d.	=	50p.	
£1. 0s. 0d.	=	100p.	

DRIVING ALLOWANCES

A daily allowance was paid for riding a motorcycle. It started after the first two hours of a duty. The rate shown is the daily rate by the number of days. A comparison of rates between 1950 and 1973 is shown below; there are no details available for the 1960's. The number of motorcycle duties at the start in 1950 was eight from Monday to Saturday and two on a Sunday.

Number of M/C duties	19/6/1950
8 Monday – Saturday	6 days = 6/-
2 Sunday	Sunday 4 Hours = 1/-
	9/4/1951
10 Monday – Saturday	6 days = 9/-
2 Sunday	Sunday 4 Hours = 1/6d
	16/9/1956
7 Monday – Friday	5 days = 7/6d
10 Saturday	Saturday = 1/6d
4 Sunday	Sunday 4 Hours = 1/6d
	14/9/1958
7 Monday – Friday	5 days = 1/9d
10 Saturday	Saturday = 1/9d
4 Sunday	Sunday 4 Hours = 1/9d

Saturdays in the 1950's and 60's were very busy but by the 1970's traffic had dropped a great deal.

	12/4/1970
2 Monday – Friday	5 days = 13/9d
6 Monday – Saturday	6 days = 16/6d
4 Sunday	Sunday 4 Hours = 2/9d
	9/1/1972
2 Monday – Friday	5 days = 69p
6 Monday – Saturday	6 days = 82.8p
4 Sunday	Sunday 4 hours = 13.8p
	8/1/1973
2 Monday – Friday	5 days = £0.83p
6 Monday – Saturday	6 days = £1.00p
4 Sunday	Sunday 4 Hours = £0.16p

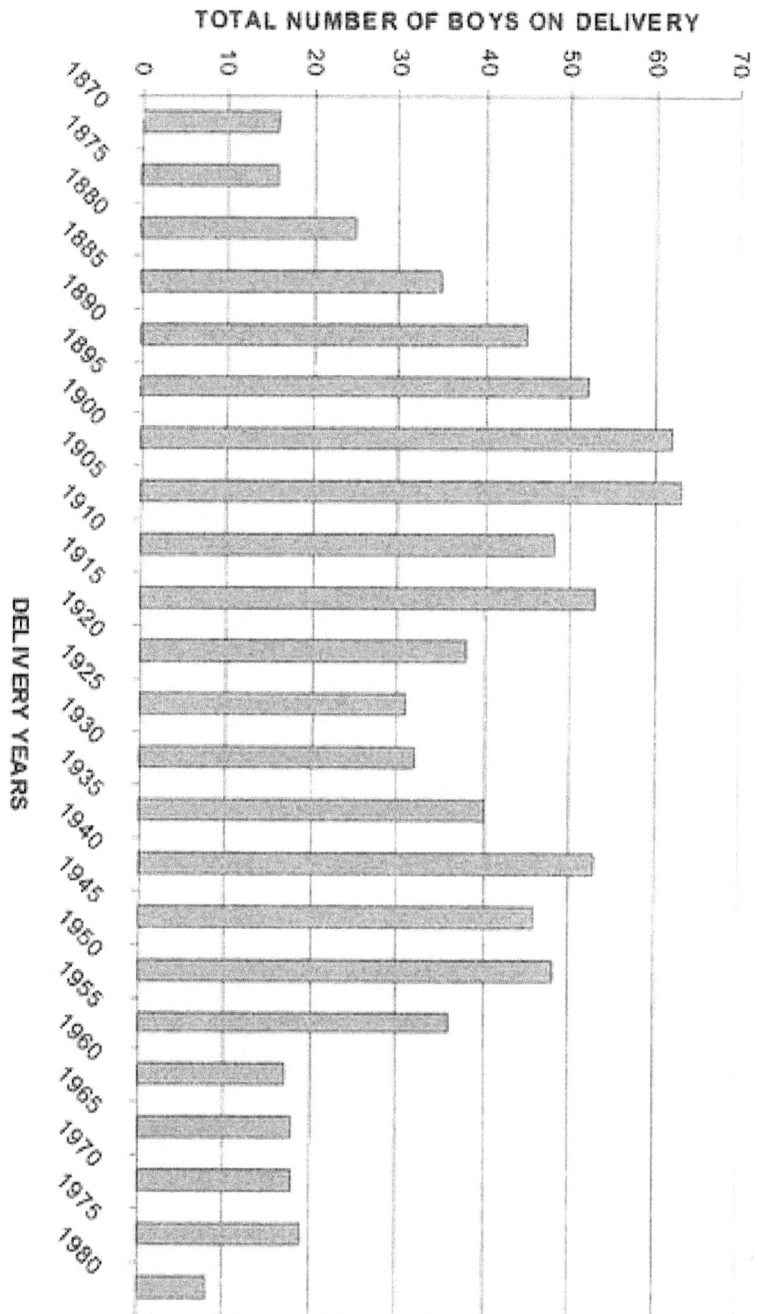

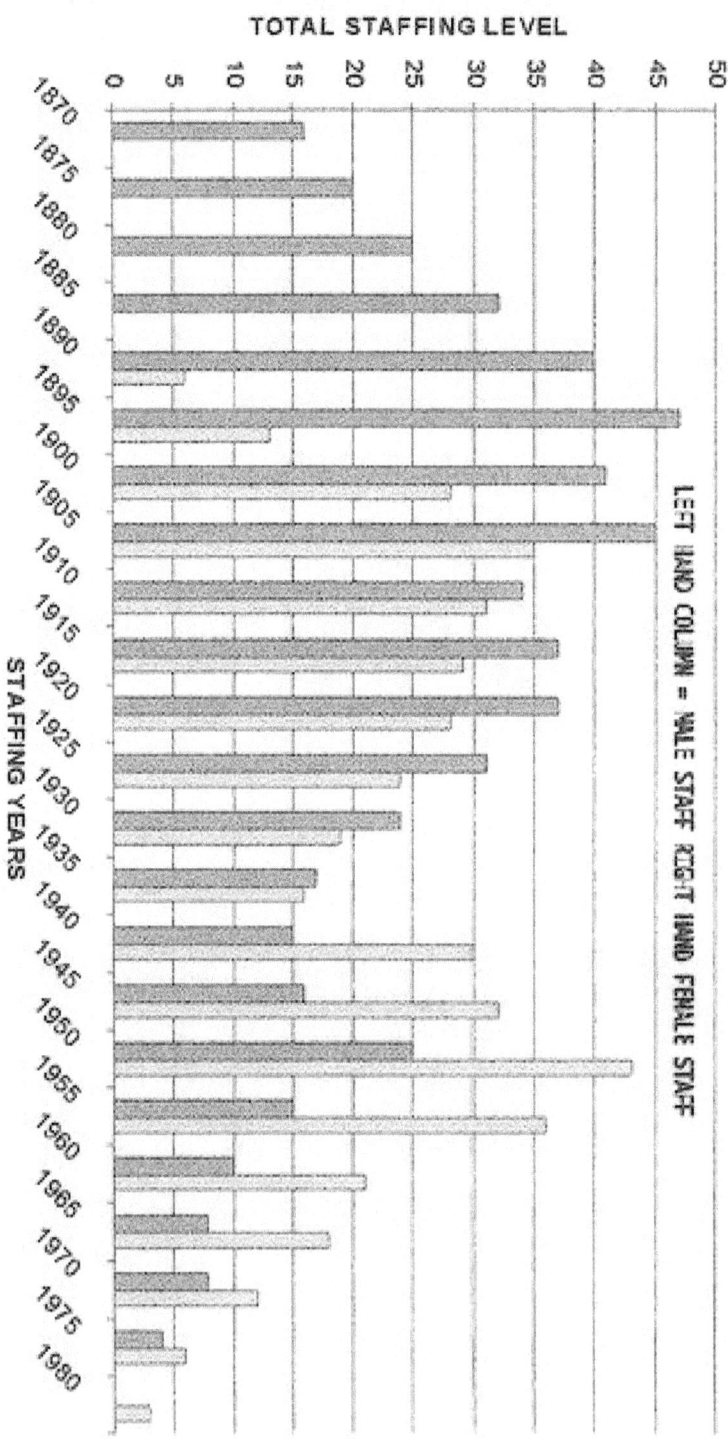

LEICESTER
SUPERINTENDENT TELEGRAPHS
1870 - 1956   ONE IN POST

1870 - 1883 T.C. Morris
1883 - 1887 J.H. Gibbins
1887 - 1894 J.M. Dayson
1895 - 1897 R. Featherston
1898 - 1900 W.W. Bolton
1901 - 1908 F.G. Richardson

1908 Post downgraded to
Assistant Superintendent Telegraphs

1908 - 1917 A.W. Champion
1917 - 1919 D. Ross

Restored to Superintendent in 1919

1919 - 1923 D. Ross
1923 - 1935 E.W. Crafter

1935 Post downgraded to
Assistant Superintendent Telegraphs

1935 - 1936 J. H. Judson
1937 - 1942 M.J. Darch

Restored to Superintendent in 1942

1942 - 1944   M.J. Darch
1944 - 1947   H.W. Neal

1947 Post downgraded to
Assistant Superintendent Telegraphs

1947- 1956 R. F. Yarnell

1956 Re - graded to Assistant Superintendent
(Telegraphs merged with Postal Grades)

1956 - 1962 R. F. Yarnell

R. Featherston   W.W. Bolton
1895 - 1897   1898 - 1900

LEICESTER

ASSISTANT SUPERINTENDENT TELEGRAPHS

1891 - 1898   ONE IN POST

1891 - 1898 J. Goddard

1898 - 1919   TWO IN POST

1898 - 1908 A.W. Champion
1898 - 1912 J. Griffiths
1908 - 1914 R. H. Lippitt
1913 - 1918 G. Wiggington
1914 - 1915 J.W. Thrall
1917 - 1919 D. Ross

1919 - 1947   ONE IN POST

1919 - 1923 E.W. Crafter
1923 - 1933   A.W. Walker
1935 - 1936   J. H. Judson
1937 - 1942   M.J. Darch
1942 - 1944 H.W. Neal
1944- 1947 R. F. Yarnell

Supernumerary Post

(Vice R.F. Yarnell H.M. Forces)

1944 - 1947 W.T. Smith

CLERK / OVERSEER LEICESTER TELEGRAPHS

1870 - 1887	ONE IN POST
1887 - 1891	TWO IN POST
1891 - 1899	THREE IN POST
1899 - 1902	FOUR IN POST
1902 - 1919	SIX IN POST
1870 - 1891	J. Goddard
1887 - 1895	J. Frisby
1891 - 1893	C. Lucas
1891 - 1908	R. H. Lippitt
1894 - 1898	A.W. Champion
1895 - 1898	J. Griffiths
1898 - 1913	G. Wiggington
1898 - 1919	F. Hewson
1899 - 1918	C. Goddard
1902 - 1910	G.H. Voss
1902 - 1925	A. Flint
1910 - 1925	H.W.C. Morris
1913 - 1914	J.W. Thrall

1914 - 1933 W.H. Williams
1919 - 1927   W. Sturman
1919 - 1923 A.W. Walker
1925 - 1928 W. Bateman
1928 - 1935 J.H. Judson
1933 - 1942 H.W. Neal
1935 - 1946   C. Chapman
1942 - 1944 R.F.Yarnell
1942 - 1944 W.T. Smith
1942 - 1947 J.N. Whan
1943 - 1955 G. Aston
1943 - 1958 G.H. Naylor
1944 - 1960 H.Harris

From 1870 until 1905 the person in charge of the Instrument Room was graded as Clerk (Telegraphs.) From 1905 the grade changed from Clerk (Telegraphs) to Overseer (Telegraphs).
Supervisor's posts were increased to provide Supervision for the Telegraph Writing Room Duties. The number of posts increased in relation to the staff, reaching six at its peak and then eventually decreasing to two.

LEICESTER TELEGRAPHS

From 1881 - 1956 ONLY ONE POST IN CHARGE OF TELEGRAPH MESSENGERS

INSPECTOR OF BOY MESSENGERS

1881 - 1885   J. Paulson
1885 - 1887   J. Stone
1888 - 1895   W. Neale
1895 - 1912   W.E. Norris
1912 - 1926   T.C. Marshall

ASSISTANT INSPECTOR OF BOY MESSENGERS

1926 - 1931   S. Vanes
1931 - 1947   F. Rhodes #
1947 - 1956   H.S.W. Peel

The Officer in Charge of Boy Messengers was originally graded as Inspector, it then was downgraded in 1926 to Assistant Inspector. After 1931 it was further downgraded to Head Postman but was restored to Assistant Inspector in 1938.
Mr Frank Rhodes held the rank of Head Postman and then Assistant Inspector and held the unique distinction of serving for 16 years in charge of the boys. He was still remembered long after he had retired as 'Dusty Rhodes.'

Acting ASSISTANT INSPECTOR OF BOY MESSENGERS

CONTINUED

1896 - 1900   J. Cufflin

1901 - 1904   J.K. Harrison

1904 - 1912   T.C. Marshall

1904 - 1905   T.P. Watts

1905 - 1924   R.M. Chalmers +

1913 - 1926   S. Vanes +

1924 - 1931   F. Rhodes + #

1926 - 1938   F.C. Wing +

1931 - 1938   J. Lumb +

1938 - 1943   J.W. Stocks +

1943 - 1947   L.G. Worts +

Two Booking Out Officers assisted the Inspector in Charge. From 1883 to 1904 Postmen with an allowance and the title of Acting Assistant Inspector performed the duty. Between 1904 and 1947 the rank was Head Postman with an allowance. In 1947 the Postman Higher Grade (P.H.G.) took over these duties but without the allowance.

Mr Frank Rhodes held the rank of Head Postman and then Assistant Inspector and had the unique distinction of serving for 16 years in charge of the boys. He was still remembered long after he had retired as 'Dusty Rhodes.'

ASSISTANT SUPERVISORS LEICESTER TELEGRAPHS

(Female)

1898 - 1933   Miss E.M. Oakey
1902 - 1910   Miss E.A. Leak
1910 - 1921   Miss H.M. Sweetman
1921 - 1936   Miss F.G. Bentley
1933 - 1943   Miss M. Mason
In 1933 Miss Mason transferred from Phonogram
Section G.P.O. Telephones with her staff

1941 - 1944   Miss I.E. Gardiner
1942 - 1951   Miss M.E. Maclean
1943 - 1953   Mrs A.F. Pickett
1943 - 1953   Miss J. Riley
1943 - 1960   Miss W.D. Freeman
1944 - 1949   Miss V. Watts
1953 - 1955   Miss N. Glossop

SUPERVISOR TELEGRAPHS (Male)

1946 - 1953   Mr Choice Chapman

ASSISTANT SUPERVISORS TELEGRAPHS (Male)

1946 - 1964   Mr Harold Ball
1965 - 1975   Mr Roy Harper

ASSISTANT SUPERVISORS TELEGRAPHS (Female)
1975 - 1978   Miss Jean M. Gamble / Mrs Jean M. Greenwood

J	Goddard	EITC	1864
A.W.	Champion		1870
C	Goddard		1871
C.H.	Orgill		1874
W	Smith		1875
C.E.	Pegg		1878
A	Flint		1878
J.A.	Moore		1879
W J	Wigginton		1880
F	Hewson		1880
T.L.	Lythall		1881
C.F.	Crane		1881
G	Hughes		1881
B.L.	Weston		1882
A	Furborough		1882
F.W.	Edwards		1882
G	Bates		1883
J.T	Allbrighton		1883
E	Worley		1883
L.G.	Lightfoot	T17	1883
S.R.	Taylor		1884
J	Langham		1884
G	Pollard		1884
T.J.W.	Woods		1885
W.G.	Norfolk		1886
A	Reed		1886
C.C.	Gurr		1886
P.J.W.	Norfolk		1886
J.T.	Simpson		1886
R.T.	Wormell		1887
F.G.	Wilson		1887
A.H.	James		1888
M.F.V.	Hughes		1888
J.T.	Shilton		1888
E	Orton		1889
E.V.	Bown		1889
A.E.	Lamsdale		1889
A.L.	Yates		1889
F.W.	Spicer		1890
W.E.	Simpson		1890
W	Haigh		1890
H.J.C.	Sutton		1890
H	Dickman		1891
A.A.	Watson		1891
H	Briers		1891
W.E.	Chetwyn		1891
W.W.	King		1891

J	Norton	BN	1891
J.E.	Baker	T14	1891
J	Parker		1891
W	Baker		1892
J	Boulter		1892
E.E.	Wright		1892
J	Baker		1892
B.G.	Reid		1892
J.H.	Mason		1892
J.L.	Foster		1892
E	Pardoe		1892
L.F.	Sutton	T33	1892
S	Underwood	T5	1892
J.L.	Rogers	T15	1892
A	Simpson	T4	1893
H.E.	Peace	T51	1893
T.A.	Wright	T8	1893
G.H.	Haigh		1893
E	Carter	T1	1893
D	Knight		1893
S	Stead		1893
P.H.	Pratt	T3	1893
F	Brainbridge	T49	1893
A.E.	Nice		1893
F	Brown	T40	1893
G.F.	Walker		1893
A	Muir	T11	1893

A.J	Smith	T30	1893
W.H.	Smith		1893
W.F.	Kilburn	T21	1893
P.H.	Cooper		1893
J.L.	Muston	T35	1893
E.G.	Soar	T32	1893
J.	Hancock		1893
B	O'Shea		1893
F.S.	Benskin	T37	1893
J	Cobley		1893
E	Bray	T36	1893
H	Chaplin	T6	1893
W	Pratt	T25/T54	1894
E.A.	Gardiner	T56	1894
W.E.	Bishop	T43	1894
A	Hawkins		1894
F	Davis	T27	1894
J.A.	Bryan	T31	1894
C.W.	Moore	T55	1894
E.A.	Howe		1894
L.A.C.	Craddock		1894
E.H.	Cooper		1894
A..	Grimsley	T12	1894
G.E.	Sullivan	T19	1894
L	Furborough	T24	1894
W.A.	Humberstone	T50	1894
G.V.	Driver	T28	1894
A.E.	Bird		1894
W.A.	Chawner	T10	1894
F	Smith	T23	1894
J	Swingler	T16	1894
J	Craythorn	T17	1894
F.A.	Kettle	T34	1894
V.C.	Cooper	T38	1894
T.W.	Coleman	T9	1895
H.M.	Hainsworth	T47	1895
J.G.	Denithorne	T2	1895
C.A.	Hill	T53	1895
W	Hensman	T45	1895
W	Allsopp	T41	1895
F	Wright		1895
A.J.	Langran	T39	1895
W.L	Smith	T13	1895

J.W.	Sharman	T56	1895
E	Tidd	T7	1895
W	Harrison	T48	1895
F	Clarke	T29	1895
E	Dowell	T54	1895
E.J.	Holden	T42	1895
E.H.	Clarke	T26	1895
C.F.	Hall	T52	1895
A.J.	Kendrick	T57	1895
F.J.J.	Swingler	T46	1895
W	Broom	T20	1895
H.J.	Tarratt	T44	1895
A.J.	Geary	T22	1895
W	Garner	T18	1895
F	Weston	T39	1895
J	Tarry	T36	1895
E	Whitmore	T33	1895
A	Grimes	T23	1896
C	Smith	T30	1896
R	Stephenson	T11	1896
C.F.	Dean	T24	1896
F.H.	Dilkes	T41	1896
E	Atkins	T50	1896
J	Nichols	T6	1896
H.C.	Wells	T12	1896
R.W.	Spicer	T24	1896
H.E.	Hunt	T28	1896
W	Weston	T21	1896
H	Marsden	T15	1896
J.H.	Hancock	T4	1896
E.G.	Voss	T52	1896

J.W.	Davis	T9	1896
F.A.	Taylor	T53	1896
S.T.	Chambers	T40	1896
H.G.	Lawrence	T5	1896
A.A.	Langley	T42	1896
J	Langton	T6	1896
J.F.	Griffin	T8	1896
E.F.	Horne	T1	1896
G.E.	Stanyon	T49	1896
W.M.	Thompson	T5	1896
E.H.	Marvin	T14	1896
J	Swingler	T47	1896
T.E.	Atter	T12	1896
A	Allen	T57	1896
A.E.	Holland	T53	1896
A	Teeboon	T50	1896
W G	Sharp	T48	1896
T.W.	Stanhope	T46	1896
F	Clarke	T38	1896
W	Moore	T17	1897
G.H.	Gilbert	T35	1897
H	Green	T14	1897
F.A.	Hunt	T3	1897
E	Scattergood	T44	1897
W.J.	Hyde	T32	1897
E	Squires	T57	1897
H	Greaves	T26	1897
S	Adams	T25	1897
C.W.	Clarke	T56	1897
E	Eabry	T43	1897
G.E.	Knight	T11	1897
W.A.	Pickford	T10	1897
S.J.	Hawkes	T27	1897
A.J.	Keeling	T31	1897
L.H.	Underwood	T19	1897
C.W.	Hyde	T49	1897
G.O.	Alton	T37	1897
H.A.	Pearson	T49	1897
W.I.	Collett	T41	1897
J.A.W.	Freeman	T31	1897
W	Vincent	T25	1897
R.W.	Bloomfield	T2	1897
H	Buckingham	T6	1897
T.B.	Hunt	T15	1897
A.E.	Aston	T44	1897

A.E.	Arnold	T20	1897
P.E.	Webber	T4	1897
H.G.	Bodycot	T17	1897
V.S.	Harris	T51	1897
H.W.	Barratt	T48	1897
W	Tongue	T6	1897
H	Britten	T37	1898
R	Wearn	T38	1898
J	Allen	T13	1898
P.J.	Mousley	T42	1898
S.J	Sheldon	T34	1898
R	Page	T47	1898
H	Brown	T3	1898
J.B.	Wood	T55	1898
W	Beck	T33	1898
H	Warburton	T26	1898
H	Gilbert	T16	1898
W.H.	Brewin	T1	1898
G.R.	Burt	T9	1898
G.C.	Hillsdon	T35	1898
G	Morbey	T56	1898
T.H.	Walker	T14	1898
A.E.	Kemp	T22	1898
G	Lappage	T27	1898
S	Blackwell	T36	1898
W.H.	Moss	T6	1898
W.R.	Rippin	T15	1898
A.C.	Embry	T50	1898
F	McCabe	T52	1898

W.T.	Collings	T31	1898
J	Tugby	T30	1898
F.E.	Williamson	T16	1898
M.J.	Egan	T5	1898
F.E.	Burton	T10	1898
S	Sharpe	T62	1898
T	Kirkland	T7	1898
W.H.	Purdy	T29	1898
H	Benson	T28	1898
P.S.	Greaves	T54	1898
W.T.	Smith	T49	1898
P	Dalby	T53	1898
H.O.	Smith	T38	1898
S.C.	Mayall	T61	1898
A	Weston	T64	1899
R	Shenton	T60	1899
W.J.	Keevill	T63	1899
E.M.	Wright	T65	1899
B	Smith	T66	1899
F	Chamberlain	T67	1899
J	Hall	T69	1899
W	Davis	T15	1899
T.K.	Banks	T68	1899
J	Palmer	T27	1899
C.E.	Scrivens	T13	1899
W	Porter	T47	1899
H	Bryan	T25	1899
T.A.	Hartley	T34	1899
S.E.	George	T35	1899
T	Chetwyn	T51	1899
G.H.	Jones	T2/T5	1899
E	Barrett	T52	1899
S.G.	Godfrey	T51	1899
J	Hutchins	T17	1899
A.F	Allsopp	T63	1899
A.C.	Yates	T37	1899
C.H.	Gray	T18	1899
L	Clayton	T13	1899
J	Lawrence	T1/T64	1899
A	Wright	T19	1899
J	Fitchett	T30	1899
C	Brown	T57	1899
E	Riley	T39	1899
A.J.	Harris	T3/T50	1899
E.C.	Cordery	T2/T35	1899

H.W.	Clarke	T33	1899
W	Garratt	T25	1899
T	Cooper	T63	1899
W.A.	Piggott	T36	1899
H	Staples	T8	1899
T	Limbert	T62	1899
H.G.	Burdett	T40	1899
F.J.	Townsend	T6	1899
W.H.	Gardiner	T22	1899
H.B.F.	Dewis	T44	1899
T	Noble		1899
A.A.	Bates	T49	1900
J.T.	Pugmore	T32	1900
J.A.	Smith	T39	1900
A.R.	Bown	T45	1900
E.E.	Davis	T31	1900
J.E.	Facer	T44	1900
J	Sylvester	T37	1900
S	Beal	T16	1900
W T	Smith	T4/T36	1900
G A	Bass	T3	1900
J B	Oram	T30	1900
F W	Bloxham	T1	1900
E L	Askham	T28	1900
W	Collins	T13	1900
H	Hill	T17	1900
T	Arnold	T64	1900
T W	Bonsell	T24	1900
F H	Ludlam	T21	1900

F I	Whiston	T31	1900
A M	Digby	T19	1900
A E	Marsh	T16	1900
A	Dunkley	T5	1900
A	Wiggins	T11	1900
S E	Smith	T43	1900
E	Millard	T56	1900
E A	Perkins	T52	1900
W H L	Buckby	T5/T9	1900
J A	Davis	T3/T33	1900
A	Watt	T35	1900
H H	French	T4	1900
T E	Heatley	T3/T7	1900
W	Brookes	T41	1900
B	Gulliver	T55	1900
C T	Foster	T48	1900
H W	Starkie	T56	1900
G	Brear	T26	1900
T C	Shenton	T11	1900
G	Curtis	A	1900
J	Dickinson	T47	1900
B W	Clifford	T50	1900
T E	Dilkes		1900
J H	Burdett		1900
F	Osborn	T26	1901
V	Cox	T20	1901
E	Jacques	T5	1901
H	Gibbs	T10	1901
W	Hutchinson	T42	1901
H G	Williams	T60	1901
G H	Taylor	T2	1901
H P	Martin	T49	1901
E T	Franklin	T51	1901
P	Waterfield	T71/T18	1901
T	Clayton	T72	1901
F.C.	Lewin	SY/T74	1901
H.S.	Riley	SY/T75	1901
T.W.	Tomlinson	T73	1901
A	Smith	T34	1901
A	Gardner	T15	1901
P F	Edwards	T39	1901
A E	Kitchen	B/T76	1901
F	Kitchen	B/T77	1901
C A	Davis	T38	1901
R M	English	T23	1901

C F	Bolingbroke	T53	1901
W	Hunt	T48	1901
R	Batt	T5	1901
R	Johnson	T61	1901
W G	Hallam	T17	1902
A E	Mason	T63	1902
H W	Moore	T24	1902
J H	Kerrigan	T2	1902
A E	Townsend	T30	1902
A G	Southern	T54	1902
R	Blankley	T12	1902
A	Allen	T36	1902
J A	Garratt	T27	1902
?	Heath	T50	1902
A	Noon	T1	1902
W I	Tyers	T71	1902
W R	Fitchett	T35	1902
H	Greasley	T25	1902
B	Powers	T22	1902
E	Johnson	T40	1902
J T	Dale	T57	1902
H	Pickard	T43	1902
F W	Dickerson	T7	1902
W	Cave	T45	1902
C	Miller	T39	1902
H	Roe	T44	1902
H	Parker	T6	1902
H B	Robinson	WK/T46	1902
B H	Beckworth	WK/T33	1902

W J	Bradford	T13	1902
P F	Smith	T31	1902
G F	Benskin	T8	1902
A	Burrows	T64	1902
F	Skarth	T9	1902
A E	Warburton	T21	1902
G W	White	T4	1902
H	Smith	T32	1902
W J	Howkins	T31	1902
A	Clark	T37	1902
W A	Wood		1902
S O	Walker		1902
A	Brotherhood	GR	1902
W	Greenwood		1902
J.F.	Neale		1903
G A	Biggs		1903
D S	Hinde		1903
D	Smith		1903
J T	Bartlett		1903
J H	Whittington		1903
A	Johnson		1904
S W	Hubbard		1904
W H	Smith		1904
A S	Goddard		1904
J A	Schdey		1904
W	Parker		1904
C E	Hornby		1904
H W	Randall		1904
B G	Jordan		1904
A G	Taylor		1904
H H	Booth		1904
F W	Ward		1904
J W	Deacon		1904
A S	Faulkner		1904
S	Dilks		1905
C H	Cook	SY	1905
R J	Broome		1905
H W	Stone		1905
W S	Short		1905
F A	Jones		1906
T J	Blower		1906
W	Antill		1906
A E	Smith		1906
E A	Chambers		1906
W H	Holles		1906
P J	Holwell		1906

A	Sawbridge	1906
L H	Timson	1906
G	Aston	1906
F	Kenney	1907
H W	Cramp	1907
B H	Allett	1907
E E	Calow	1907
W A	Weston	1907
F	Cockbill	1907
A J J	Farmer	1907
H	Miller	1908
E J G	White	1908
H	Nixon	1908
H	Hubbard	1908
H C	Wood	1908
S T	Webster	1908
C	Ask	1908
W	Watts	1908
G R	Staley	1908
J C F	Hodgson	1908
D	Vanes	1908
F	Chetwyn	1908
G E	Coale	1909
J A	Calwood	1909
P A	Hubbard	1909
W	Broughton	1909
C A	Brett	1909
C	Major	1909

G C	Hardy		1909
W T R	Munton		1909
A	Foreman		1909
T A	Spradbury		1909
H B	Bond		1909
A	Day		1909
C	Chapman		1909
W E	Richardson		1909
A E	Shielsole		1910
J C	Roberts		1910
G	Gamble		1910
H	Wheldon		1910
F G	Gulliver		1910
W O	Gell		1910
H A	Wilford		1910
J.R.	Oxbrough	GY	1910
C.L.	Barnes		1910
R V	Wright		1910
F P	Clarke		1910
G S	Button		1910
H A	Knock		1910
J W	Ford		1910
J A	Bennifer		1910
W R	Whiteman		1911
E	Neville		1911
C F	Spence	N	1911
H	Hill		1911
A L	Broome		1911
H V	Richardson		1911
T B	Hubbard		1911
J	Marvell		1911
W A	Halliday		1911
J	Clarke		1911
A G	Atkins		1911
G W	Mottashed		1911
R V	Knight		1911
E E	Redfern		1911
J W	Smith		1912
F H	Perry		1912
H B	Reading		1912
E	Thompson		1912
L H	Dickman		1912
F H	Thorp		1912
T A	Gammage		1912
H	Wilson		1912

J R	Ball		1912
H	Jones		1912
J	Lumb		1912
A H	Wells		1912
G H	Naylor		1912
G E	Standley		1912
J	Bland		1912
A	Thirlby	C	1912
C	Whitehouse		1912
W	Garner		1912
P	Mason		1913
L V	Brewster		1913
N A	Brewin		1913
J G	Cooke		1913
L N	Smith		1913
N L	Hinde		1913
R	Entwhistle		1913
A H	Clapham		1913
M A	Riddiford		1913
J	Simpson		1913
H W	Perrin		1913
S E	Weston		1913
T	Baker	SY	1913
W H	Rixen		1913
H	North		1913
W F	Moore		1913
H B	Coltman		1913
A	Chalmers		1913
J G	Betton	SW	1913

W E	Pratt		1913
G H	Loomes		1913
H V	Groomes		1913
A	Hubbard		1913
L C	Heath		1914
F B	Martin		1914
T C	Marshall Jnr		1914
J W	Flude		1914
S T	Littlewood	GY	1914
A	Branson		1914
G H	Greenwood		1914
W	Bowditch		1914
C A	Dalby		1914
H	Harris		1914
A	Atkins		1914
H H	Stoneham		1914
R P	Lawrence		1915
E	Jackson		1915
W J	Lomas		1915
G H	Calow		1915
A E	Garbett		1915
W F	Calwood		1915
S J	Broughton		1915
F	Cross		1915
W H	Thorp		1916
J A	Atkins		1916
G	Galpin		1916
R F	Yarnell		1916
G E	Dilley		1916
F E	Edwards		1916
F R	Duffey		1916
C A	Jones		1916
A E	Lock		1916
J	Hughes		1916
A	Gillett		1916
C T B	Deacon		1916
B A	Bevan		1916
H E	Garner		1916
A	Gutteridge		1917
S	Gibbs		1917
E H	Lawrence		1917
V W	Caulfield		1917
S	Clarke		1917
R	Burrows		1917
E H	Holyoake	T7	1917

H S	Lant		1917
G H	Breese	LN/LE	1917
J L	Osborn		1917
A	Deacon		1918
S T	Billings		1918
F M	Hickman		1918
H W W	Hallam		1918
H	Bland		1918
A T	Archer		1918
F W E	Hales	T34	1918
F	Blackburn		1918
E W	Faulkner		1918
C	Garner		1918
G	Joyce		1918
T S	Hardy		1918
L A	Wakefield	T4	1918
L R	Botterill		1918
A A	Holyoake	T24	1918
L	Ironmonger		1918
E	Baines		1918
C A	Tams		1918
F E H	Williamson		1918
C L	Palmer		1918
C W	Morris	GY	1918
G H	Cleobury	A	1919
A A	Ledwick		1919
S	Cragg		1919
L B	Collings		1919
L	Hill	T25	1919

F T	Hopkins		1919
F	Duggan	T18	1919
G E	Briers	WK	1919
A S	Cooke	T47	1919
E A A	Jarvis		1919
F J	Brown	T29	1919
W S	Bingham		1919
H A	Reeve		1919
N C	Perkins		1919
W T	Olphin	T22	1919
H F	Wheater		1919
C V	Simpson	T13	1919
R W	Major		1919
H	Cheaney		1920
F L	Howkins		1920
G S	Holmes	SY	1920
C H	Kennell		1920
H A	Dixon		1920
R W	French		1920
B	Blower		1920
E	Hubbard	CM/LE	1920
A E	Pemberton		1920
E H	Milsom		1920
D P	Mitchell		1920
A T	Hill		1921
L	Herbert		1921
J W	Woods	T14	1921
B F	Phillips	T9	1921
J W A	Tyers	SW	1921
J T	Moseley		1921
C J	Mobbs	T42	1921
E	Staples	T11	1921
C H	Waite	T44	1921
J	Warner	T2	1921
C H	Clapham	T27	1922
J	Tebbutt	T5	1922
S E	Howkins		1922
J W	Barker	T4	1922
C A B	Sargent	T51	1922
C E	Cameron	T10	1922
A F	Knight	T15	1922
L C L	Parkinson	T37	1922
A L	Hickson	T33	1922
L	Coleman	T31	1922
S G	Beadman	C	1922
S	Garratt	T17	1922

W A	Smalley	T20	1922
R S	Marshall	T35	1922
J C	Butler		1923
H F	Perry		1923
P	Collins		1923
W A	Williamson		1923
C F	Greenwood	T1	1923
G R	Kennedy		1923
A B	Maxfield		1923
F E	Gage		1923
E R	Burgess		1923
F J	Tilley	T30	1923
W J H	Burditt		1923
H A	Eagle		1924
O W	Sawbridge		1924
H L	Evatt		1924
G E	Osborn		1924
W G	Mellor		1924
G E	Woodcock		1924
R L	Laywood	C	1924
J W	Jarvis	T24	1924
H W F	Cotterill		1925
G	Parkin		1925
C L	Gunthorpe		1925
A W	Cooper		1925
F J	Arnold		1925
P	Lowe		1925
C W	Smith		1925

Initials	Surname	Code	Year
E	Johnson		1925
S M	Cooke		1926
W M	Mason		1926
W R	Plummer	A	1926
H W	Seville	SW/T38	1926
F	Anstee		1926
T G	Kirkland		1926
G E L	Adams		1926
A J	Martin		1927
H G	Grainger		1927
R A	Tilley	T15	1927
W C	Hayward		1927
C J	Dunkley		1927
J D	Murphy		1927
F W B	Barratt	C	1927
J H	Facer		1927
D A	Seare		1927
G A	Turner		1927
K J	Cope		1927
J M	Bennett		1927
M B	Lees		1927
F H	Masters		1927
L J	Fisher		1928
J F	Wilkins		1928
S R	Mann		1928
D	Tookey		1928
K	Bugby		1928
K H	Harrison		1928
S C	Greenwood		1928
L	Frost		1928
J W	Childs		1928
G	Cave		1928
L H	Phillips	T24	1928
E R	Ward		1929
R P	Stevens		1929
J E	Bentley		1929
A G	Jeffs		1929
R	Miller		1929
H K	Marshall		1929
H	Smith	C	1929
N E	Rudkin		1929
C W	Mitchell		1929
A	Saville		1930
S J	Dilks		1930
N T	Blakemore		1930

C F	Lester		1930
G R	Grimshaw		1930
E J	Battle		1930
W A	Simpson		1930
G W	James		1930
G R	Eagle		1930
D S	Oliver		1930
S	McNally		1930
W	Tailby	T20	1930
E A	Sibson		1931
W S	Sandom	T6	1931
J J	Jobburn	C	1931
F S	Draycott	T37	1932
G H	Collins	T8	1932
W H	Fendell	T17	1932
F W	Willis	T3	1932
N H	Parramore	T30	1932
R E	Twigg	T31	1932
A J	Martin	T27	1932
R H	Gamble		1932
F G	Benford	T26	1932
C H	Price	T22	1932
B M	Flavill	T12	1933
F E	Finch	T28	1933
R G	Webber	T11	1933
S	Jones	T29	1933
K	Harpham	T16	1933
J W J	Edge	T7	1933
W A	Johnson	T4	1934

F W	Hames	T18	1934
D R J	Purser	T1	1934
R G	Pearson	T9	1934
N T S	Hawkins	T21	1934
T D M	Reeves	T15	1934
J P	Hennessey	T10	1934
D A	Adcock	T13	1935
N A	Adcock	T23	1935
D S	Broughton		1935
R J	Trevithick	T5	1935
D K	Pearson		1935
H	Langton	T14	1935
K L	Zanker		1935
C F S	Wells	T20	1935
K T	Hunt	T12	1935
E A W	Evans	A	1935
D I	Pallett	T6	1935
N J	Stone	T33	1935
W T	Underwood	T34	1935
L S C	Newcombe	T25	1936
L E	Hextall	T18	1936
K C	Dyer	T23	1936
J W	Ainsworth	T8	1936
C G	Aston	T37	1936
D J	Johnson	T30	1936
D	Tuckwood	T4	1936
E	Kinsey	C	1936
R V E	Jbeane	T27	1936
R D	Bonner	T8	1936
K	Fisher	T9	1936
K G	Hill		1937
H	Ball	T16	1937
D	Hurst	T35	1937
B A	Pepper	T26	1937
W G	Holyoak	T22	1937
R	Swinfield		1937
A	Middleton		1937
T P	Fitchett	T39	1937
E B	Beach	T38	1937
G R W	Newcombe		1937
R R	Bamber	C	1937
R A	Hill		1937
F W	Bull	T16	1938
G D	Walters		1938

E G E	Turner	T29	1938
D W W	Baker		1938
W H	Crump		1938
C R	Scotney	T25	1938
S F	Turland	T7	1938
D H	Grant	T4	1938
A R	Inchley	T21	1938
J A	Chamberlain	T1	1938
E F H	Burdett		1938
J E	Catlin	T42	1939
R G	Draycott		1939
A E	Critchlow		1939
S C	Judson	T38	1939
B R	Abbott	T10	1939
I A	Moore	T23	1939
E	Shaw	C	1939
W K	North	T6	1939
H J	Fox	T19	1939
E B	Hawkins		1939
T F A	Woollerton		1939
W F L	Richardson	T20	1939
N P	Mann		1939
P H	Dawson	T34	1939
R L	Page		1939
R E H	Richardson		1940
A	Morris		1940
F R	Grant		1940
C E	Starr		1940
L	Websell	C	1940
N H	Cooper		1940

J A	Seymour		1940
G G	Tebbutt		1940
S F	Wells		1940
K	Lowe	C	1940
A L	Forryan	T39	1940
G	Worley		1940
C	Bradley		1940
J W	Heath	A	1940
K A	Gough		1940
F W	Rogers	T27	1940
D A	Hudson	T17	1940
E L	Critchlow		1941
J B	Green	T37	1941
H S	Sharp		1941
H J	Chesney		1941
A E	Neville		1941
J K S	Mensley		1941
H J A	Baker		1941
F A	Platts		1941
R E	Monk		1941
R	Cross		1941
G H	Fisher		1941
J A	Brutnall		1941
R	Bentley		1941
C R	Billings		1941
D R	Beane	T20	1941
R G	Willott		1941
N V	Merrikin		1942
J N	Hewes		1942
R A	Kirton		1942
G E	Sharpe		1942
J W	Coombes		1942
M	Sylvester	T11	1942
J	Branston		1942
R W	Murgatroyd		1942
D G	Leedham		1942
L W	Guest	C	1942
D F	King	W	1942
N	Proctor		1942
C G	Wright		1942
D G W	Brayfield		1942
A S	Cobb		1942
R F	Johnson	T17	1942
K	Herrick	C	1942

A S	Skinner		1943
G S	Lyon		1943
K	Taylor		1943
J A	Fuller	W	1943
C	Greaves		1943
F A	Taylor		1943
K J	Martin		1943
B W	Richardson		1943
L R	Goodwin		1943
D A	Gow		1943
N C	Blount		1943
W G	Naylor	SY	1943
B A	Newton		1943
G N W	Walker	T4	1943
L P	Cullen		1943
J M	Buckler	T13	1943
N V	Broome		1943
N T	Tanner		1943
B R	Pickering		1943
D	Waring		1943
P S	Meacham		1943
S	Stevenson		1943
D	Jones		1943
A M	Oram	W	1943
R	Plumb	C	1943
L	Pawley		1943
J D E	Brittain		1944
D R P	Goggins	T16	1944
J A	Mason		1944
J M	Hill	A	1944

R	Barrs		1944
N H	Freeman		1944
R R	Roberts		1944
J R	Crawford		1944
J E	Crick		1944
J L	White		1944
N	Ayres		1944
E R	Swann	SY	1944
D K G	Swinfield		1944
C	Burbage	T3	1944
J E	Fish		1944
M E	Hammond		1944
W J	Facer	T29	1944
R	Harper	T39	1944
J L	Young	T49	1944
G	Hawes	CS/BM	1944
T	Desborough		1945
P T	Stretton		1945
E	Johnson		1945
N	Hughes	T38	1945
L G D	Somers		1945
A T	Tester		1945
H	Greenwood		1945
G T G	Bennett		1945
R J	Fraine		1945
D	Groom		1945
J A	Cox		1945
M D	Carter		1945
S	Cobbett		1945
R E	Ingram		1945
P	Collins		1945
K P	Brighty		1945
R	Richardson	C	1945
P J	Whatton		1946
D	Ward		1946
V J	Archer	A	1946
R	Malaghan		1946
T	Hickman		1946
H	Collins		1946
R W	Howard		1946
A R	Twigger		1946
C S	Baker		1946
R W	Merryfield		1946
N J	Steward		1946
L J	Tilley	T45	1946

J A	Crouch		1946
M A	Crookes	C.T568	1946
M G	Bailey	A	1946
F J	Dawkins		1946
R	Lock		1947
T	Geeson		1947
J S	Dumelow		1947
B E	Tanner	T17	1947
M H	Harriott	W	1947
B J	Holyoak		1947
J	Sweetman	T934	1947
K W	Deacon		1947
D J	Bunting	T16	1947
T J	Coleman		1947
G J	Lewitt	T44	1947
F T H	Clipson	C	1947
N E H	Kinnard		1947
A R	Kilby	T3	1947
K J	Gamble		1947
M J	Hallick		1948
M	Taylor	T924	1948
J	Denham		1948
D W	Glover		1948
C D	Taylor		1948
P B	Whitcombe		1948
J H	Raine		1948
W C	Garner		1948
D G	White		1948
P R J	Stuart		1948

G E	Barrett		1948
D A J	Pemberton		1948
D W	Naylor		1948
J D	Webster		1948
A	Capewell		1948
K	Burdett	T15	1948
P D	Beighton		1948
J E	Reeve		1948
J A	Raynor	T13	1948
G R	Morris		1948
A	Lester		1948
R	Monk		1948
G H P	Bennett	C	1948
B K	Fowkes	C	1948
H	Hutchcraft		1949
T K	Eagle		1949
D L	Ward		1949
D C	Vaux	T901	1949
G	Brooks		1949
D	Phillips		1949
P J	Smith		1949
G	Norris		1949
R A	Hill		1949
A	Walker		1949
S	Kennell		1949
D	Sharpe		1949
P	Quinn		1949
J C	Wilson		1949
N	Hault		1949
T J	Berry		1949
A A	Thompson		1949
C H	Burton		1949
K J	Lock		1949
A E	Potter		1949
J	Taylor		1949
B J	Monk	T23	1949
R W	Bratt	T942	1949
J H	Richards		1950
D	Wesley		1950
B E	Abbott		1950
R G	York		1950
W	King		1950
T S	Ward		1950
P H	Mayoh		1950
B	Major		1950

D	Fisher		1950
P W	Brewin		1950
A A	Adams		1950
G T	Green	T952	1950
J	Brennan	T28	1950
F O	Richardson	T909	1950
J A	Betts	T925	1950
J B	Pickering		1950
S A	Beane		1950
A	Smith	A	1950
D	Clarke		1951
J W	Allen	T15	1951
C	Barratt		1951
P.	Westerman		1951
D W	Coulson		1951
J	Brown	W	1951
D W	Baker	T911	1951
M G	Taylor	T942	1951
J H	Woodward	C	1951
P M	Reynolds		1951
J M	Mason		1951
J A	Stephens		1951
S	Knowles		1951
P D W	Johnson	C	1951
D B	Green		1951
B A	Tilley	T921	1951
B A	Smith		1951
R	Lauper	T916	1951
T K	Bullous		1951

M J	Heawood		1951
T M	Spriggs		1951
H	Liquorish		1952
J M	Belcher		1952
J E	Bell		1952
J P R	Pollard		1952
K	Irving	T22	1952
B R	Pepper		1952
P B	Kirk	T953	1952
J	Blackwell	T901	1952
J D A	Rosen		1952
R	Chandler	T31	1952
D	Ensor		1952
A F G	Allcroft		1952
B L	Simms		1952
M J	Wragg	T955	1952
R F	Prince		1952
R	Mellor		1952
B	Souter	T943	1952
B L A	Clarke		1952
N A	Goodman	T957	1952
A	Thornton	T951	1952
R	Wright		1952
R E	Dickens		1952
S C	Parsons	T941	1952
D	Dingwall		1952
E P	Dauven		1953
D A	Lever		1953
D B	Johnson		1953
G	Blakesley		1953
A R	Williamson	T952	1953
M H	Tidmarsh		1953
R V	Hackett	T933	1953
K F	Powell	T934	1953
A	Robey	C	1953
E R	Dagley		1953
J A	Lapworth		1953
D	Barratt		1953
A	Shore		1954
J L	Farrar		1954
R A P	Melia		1954
J T	Robinson		1954
A R	Smith		1954
D T	Mason		1954
R I	Smallwood		1954

J	Warner		1954
G	Whatley	T923	1955
D J	Seaton		1955
N	Kent		1955
E	Cartmell		1955
G W	Bradshaw		1955
D A L	Lewin		1955
T E	Bevan		1955
B L	Love		1955
L	Ward		1955
M I S	MacDonald		1955
N W	Pick		1956
B C	Taylor		1956
M R	Petty	T901	1956
J A	Heatherley	T933	1956
J	Cable		1956
F A E	Seal		1956
J D	Davies	T903	1956
G G	Hefford		1956
B E	McGowan		1956
W	Liquorish	T940	1956
D J	Bent		1957
M T	Wood		1957
J F	Dean		1957
J A	Bevans		1957
P W	Hunt		1957
D J	Ayre		1957
J	Chinnery		1957
A	Burdett		1958

B L	Blower		1958
R G	Bown		1958
J C	Porter		1959
B L	MacDonald		1959
M J	Riley	T942	1959
D A K	Calow		1959
R W	Chafer		1959
R C	Broughton		1959
R N	Dilley		1960
T D	Ward		1960
R J	Posnett		1960
R K	Chambers	T903	1960
D P	Hendy		1960
M B	Poole		1960
R P	Newton		1960
C J	Simpson		1961
F J	Antliff		1961
R F	Bentley		1961
P R	Pegg		1961
M J	Swinfield		1961
J R	Norton		1962
K	Tiplady	T950	1962
T E	Tyrrell		1962
J J	Boulton		1962
D L	Harvey		1962
C E	Calow		1962
M H	Page		1962
P	King		1962
J	Coombes		1962
D	Carleton		1963
M R	Woollerton		1963
N J	Veal		1963
N	Wilton		1963
M R	Wade		1964
J S	Davies		1964
R E	Geary		1964
D F	Smith		1964
M J	Watts		1964
M.R.	Axtall		1964
M	Quilter		1964
M A	Faulkner		1964
D K	London		1964
G A	Hunt		1964
S J	Cooke		1964
R J	Harris		1964

G F	Price		1965
R K	Braines		1965
D J	Pearson		1965
R A	Read		1965
K J	Wilkes		1965
S	Fraser		1965
P V	Duffy		1965
I T	Hunt		1965
E K R	Georg		1965
B R	Lynch		1965
G R	Markillie		1965
P J	Marvin		1965
P G	Nethercott		1966
T J	Brown		1966
R J	Shaw		1966
N H V	Sinfield		1966
J R	Clarke		1966
D	Booth		1966
R A	Egan		1967
C V	Taylor		1967
D J	Rimington	P1033	1967
D	Gallagher		1967
T K	Stretton		1968
P A	Muggleton		1968
C P	Maddocks		1968
R A	Orrill		1968
A J	Longland		1968
I	Hafford		1968
D R	Turner		1969

B	Massey		1969
C E	Bradshaw		1969
P K	Taylor		1969
T G	Mulroy		1969
D L	Lyon		1969
R A	Rimington		1969
R S	White		1969
D F	McLean		1969
R	Prentice		1969
S N	Swann		1969
A F	Srawley		1969
R A	Carter		1969
D H	Bailey	P617	1969
J M	Hay		1970
S	Barnes		1970
A S	Frankland		1970
N D	Bailey		1970
M J	Bates		1970
D A	Ward		1970
S	James		1971
A	Curry		1971
D A	Rojahn		1971
H B	Johnson		1971
K J	Pawley		1971
D J	Arno		1971
P R	Linthwaite		1971
N	Darbyshir		1971
C T W	Baker		1972
W F	Heelan		1972
M J	Stretton		1972
S	Singh		1972
S J	Shipley		1972
G P	Clarke		1972
P K V	Majithia		1972
T R	Bailey		1972
R M	Jagot		1972
M J	Webb		1972
I S	Morton		1973
M A	Grant		1973
P R	Bamford		1973
B N	Turner		1974
R E	Ward		1974
A	Maidment		1974
C	Hood		1974

K A	Hurst		1974
S R	Peel		1974
J S	Matharu		1974
A E H	Walton		1974
A J	Marlow	P41	1974
N	Pittard		1974
W R	Staddon		1974
M	Bright		1974
J E	Dillman		1974
G	Pittard		1974
F W	Setchell		1974
J	Austin		1975
H R	McMillan		1975
P P	Spencer	P971	1975
M J	Harris		1975
T	King		1975
M	Payne		1975
M J	Webster	RY/LE	1975
K B	French		1975
P	Chapman		1975
C S	Shotton		1976
C J	Barrett		1976
P J	Gaunt		1976
S J	Rigley		1976
S	Ali *		1976
M	Akhlaq *		1976
S G	Boston		1976
S P	Iwasiw		1976
D A	Ryan		1976
R	Ridley		1976

A	Mustafa		1976
T P	Davies		1976
S J	Bosden		1977
M A	Soo		1977
K R F	Watson		1977
L M	Hopkins		1977
W A	Pope		1977
S C	Knight		1977
I M	Deacon		1977
M J	Ewert		1977
M A	Sharpe		1977
A P	Cross		1977
D P	Davis		1978
S J	Coley		1978
R W	Bacze		1978
P B	Bolton		1978
P R	Fixter		1978
M A	Greenhill		1978
M G	Holland		1978
W S	Basey		1978
D L M	Ayriss		1978
M A	Jacques		1979
S J	Clifford		1979
A P	Clarkson		1979
S J	Price		1979
K A	Dauven		1980
S T	Walker		1980
P J	Bass		1980
A D	Cooke		1980
A F	Hemmings		1980
S K	Ingram		1980
D A	Withers		1980
I J	Pawley		1980
D	Seare		1981
M J	Snow		1981

ABBREVIATIONS USED IN LISTS

A	Ashby De La Zouch
B	Belgrave Leicester
BN	Billesdon
C	Coalville
CM	Camborne Cornwall
CSBM	Casual Boy Messenger
E.I.T.C.	Electric International Telegraph Company
GR	Groby
GY	Gaddesby

L	Lincoln
N	Narborough
RY	Rugby
SW	South Wigston
SY	Syston
W	Wigston
WK	Whitwick
N.B	* Name changed

BOY MESSENGERS PERFORMING RIFLE DRILL AT THE MAGAZINE IN THE NEWARKES C1900

PHOTO 1

ARTHUR
SIDNEY
GODDARD
POSTMAN
BOY
MESSENGER
1904 - 1908

PHOTO 2

ARTHUR
HENRY
CLAPHAM
ASSISTANT
INSPECTOR
1952 - 1959
BOY
MESSENGER
1913 - 1917

PHOTO 3

HARRY WHELDON
CHIEF INSPECTOR
1935 - 1955
BOY MESSENGER
1910 - 1912

PHOTO 4

WILLIAM ERNEST
RICHARDSON
INSPECTOR
1955 - 1956
BOY MESSENGER
1909 - 1913

PHOTO 5

PHOTO 6

THOMAS CHARLES MARSHALL
LONGEST SERVING ASSISTANT INSPECTOR OF BOY MESSENGERS
1904 - 1926
HIS SON IS BELOW

THOMAS CHARLES MARSHALL JUNIOR
ASSISTANT INSPECTOR 1941
ACTING INSPECTOR
1942 - 1945
BOY MESSENGER
1914 - 1918
HIS BROTHER ROWLAND STEEL MARSHALL
ASSISTANT INSPECTOR
1947 - 1953
BOY MESSENGER
1922 - 1927
BOTH BROTHERS DIED IN SERVICE AT THE AGE OF 45

PHOTO 7

JOSEPH REGINALD BALL
POSTAL & TELEGRAPH OFFICER (P.&T.O.)
BOY MESSENGER
1912 - 1915
RETIRED ILL HEALTH 1940
RETURNED FOR WWII
LIVED UNTIL AGE 90

PHOTO 8

LESLIE ALBERT WAKEFIELD
POSTAL & TELEGRAPH OFFICER (P.&T.O.)
BOY MESSENGER
1918 - 1920

PHOTO 9

STANLEY GARRATT
POSTMAN
BOY MESSENGER
1922 - 1927

PHOTO 10

CECIL FRANK
GREENWOOD
ASSISTANT HEAD
POSTMASTER
1968
BOY MESSENGER
1923- 1927
BOTH THESE MEN
WERE STILL GOOD
FRIENDS IN 2002
BOTH IN THEIR
94th YEAR.

PHOTO 11

**WILLIAM ARTHUR
SMALLEY
CHIEF INSPECTOR
1956 - 1968
BOY MESSENGER
1922 - 1927**

PHOTO 12

**HENRY ARTHUR
EAGLE
INSPECTOR
1956 - 1968
BOY MESSENGER
1924 - 1928**

PHOTO 13

REGINALD ARTHUR TILLEY
BOY MESSENGER 1927 - 1931
THIS PHOTOGRAPH SHOWS THE UNIFORM OF
THIS PERIOD WITH SHOULDER EPAULETS,
PILL BOX HAT, 'T' NUMBER BADGE ON THE
HAT AND UNIFORM JACKET. ALSO ON THE
JACKET IS THE BADGE FOR A MEMBER OF THE
UNION OF POSTAL WORKERS.

PHOTO 14

STEPHEN MCNALLY
HEAD POSTMASTER
WARRINGTON
1971 - 1976
BOY MESSENGER
1930 - 1935

PHOTO 15

GEORGE CAVE
ASSISTANT HEAD
POSTMASTER
1971 - 1974
AT HIS
RETIREMENT
PRESENTATION.
BOY MESSENGER
1928 - 1933

PHOTO 16

PHOTO 17 GRAFFITI ON THE WALL OUTSIDE CLARENDON PARK T.S.O. Between 1894 - 1922

GEORGE HORACE GREENWOOD & HIS BROTHER CECIL FRANK GREENWOOD

BOTH BROTHERS FINISHED AT THE TOP OF THE CIVIL SERVICE EXAMINATION FOR BOY MESSENGERS IN THE UNITED KINGDOM, GEORGE IN 1916 and CECIL IN 1925

PHOTO 18

WALTER HENRY FENDELL
POSTMAN
BOY MESSENGER
1932 - 1936

PHOTO 19

Photo Below
NORMAN JAMES STONE
POSTMAN
BOY MESSENGER
1935 - 1939

PHOTO 20

Above Photo
STANLEY JONES
P.E.B.
1971 - 1979
BOY MESSENGER
1933 - 1938

PHOTO 21

LEFT TO RIGHT in Blackwells Court 1934 J.LUMB O.I.C. Boy Messengers G.R.EAGLE W.TAILBY R.G.WEBBER N.H.PARRAMORE E.A.SIBSON F.E.FINCH B.M.FLAVILL S.McNALLY W.S.SANDOM (with the WHEELER SWIMMING CUP) S.JONES G.W.JAMES N.T.BLAKEMORE W.A.SIMPSON R.G.PEARSON F.S.DRAYCOTT

PHOTO 22

DONALD STEWART BROUGHTON BOY MESSENGER
1935 - 1939 (double crossbar cycle)

PHOTO 23

BERNARD MURRAY FLAVILL, BOY MESSENGER
1933 - 1935 (single crossbar cycle)

PHOTO 24

DONALD STEWART BROUGHTON BOY MESSENGER
1935 - 1939 (double crossbar cycle)

PHOTO 23

BERNARD MURRAY FLAVILL, BOY MESSENGER
1933 - 1935 (single crossbar cycle)

PHOTO 24

HORSE BY POST - Mr. Frank Rhodes, Head Postman, Officer in Charge of Boy Messengers, handing a delivery note to Stuart Sandom the senior Boy Messenger outside Leicester G.P.O. on the day in 1935 when a horse went by Express Post for the first time. This was also to publicise a film being shown at the Trocadero Cinema where the horse was delivered to. Photograph by courtesy of the Leicester Mercury.

PHOTO 25

PHOTO 26
ON THE LEFT
C1936
W.T.UNDERWOOD
D.S.BROUGHTON
D.R.J.PURSER

PHOTO 27
ON THE RIGHT
JOHN EDWARD
CATLIN
P.E.C. 1976 - 1985
BOY MESSENGER
1939 - 1943

LEICESTER
POST OFFICE
MESSENGERS F.C.
1938
From left to right,
D.TUCKWOOD
C.R.SCOTNEY
K.G.HILL
H.BALL
L.E.HEXTALL
K.T.HUNT
R.J.TREVITHICK
D.HURST
K.L.ZANKER
N.J.STONE
C.F.S.WELLS

PHOTO 28

SUPERVISORS C1937 From left to right
MONTAGUE JOHN DARCH Assistant Superintendent Telegraphs
HARRY WHELDON Chief Inspector JAMES LUMB 'Jimmy' Head Postman
FRANK RHODES 'Dusty' Head Postman In charge of Telegraph Delivery
FREDERICK CHARLES WING 'Tom' Head Postman

PHOTO 29

COPY OF A DRAWING HELD BY THE POST OFFICE ARCHIVES OF A TYPICAL LARGE TELEGRAPH DELIVERY ROOM C1935

PHOTO 30

BOY MESSENGERS C 1944
FRONT ROW   BRIN NEWTON   FRANK JOHNSON   DOUG GOGGINS
BACK ROW   MICK SYLVESTER   SAM STEVENSON

PHOTO 31

PHOTO 32

**UPPER PHOTO
LEFT TO RIGHT
COLIN BURBAGE
JOHN ROBERT
CRAWFORD
JOHN LESTER
YOUNG
WILLIAM JAMES
FACER
BOY MESSENGERS
C1947**

**LOWER PHOTO
LEONARD JOHN
TILLEY
P.E.B.
1982 - 1991
BOY MESSENGER
1946 - 1950**

PHOTO 33

TELEGRAPH UNITED FOOT BALL TEAM 1946 - 1947
BACK ROW
N. HUGHES H. GREENWOOD L.J. TILLEY W.J. FACER P. COLLINS D.K.G. SWINFIELD
FRONT ROW A.T. TESTER J.A. COX J.E. CRICK R. MALAGHAN C. BURBAGE
T.J. COLEMAN FAR RIGHT OF PICTURE N.J. STEWARD

PHOTO 34

CYCLE RELIABILITY TRIALS PHOTO TAKEN 1947 BY LOCAL NEWSPAPER AT START OF TRIAL.
L.J. TILLEY J.R. CRAWFORD A.T. TESTER R.W. HOWARD K.W. DEACON P.J. WHATTON
E. NEVILLE Assistant Inspector A.R. TWIGGER J.S. DUMELOW J.A. COX J.A. CROUCH.

PHOTO 36

CYCLE RELIABILITY TRIALS PHOTO TAKEN 1947 BY LOCAL NEWSPAPER AT START OF TRIAL
L.J. TILLEY J.R. CRAWFORD A.T. TESTER R.W. HOWARD K.W. DEACON P.J. WHATTON
E. NEVILLE Assistant Inspector A.R. TWIGGER J.S. DUMELOW J.A. COX J.A. CROUCH.

PHOTO 36

1949 CHRISTMAS PARTY Left to Right Full faces only named J. BRENNAN A. CAPEWELL H. COLLINS R.W. BRATT B.J. MONK T.J. COLEMAN J.A. BETTS J. HOLYOAK P.B. WHITCOMBE Postmaster A.E. HALL D. FISHER Mrs HALL P.D. BEIGHTON T.S. WARD K. BURDETT D.L. WARD J. TAYLOR A. WALKER P.H.G B.M. FLAVILL G. BROOKS C.D. TAYLOR Miss A. MARRIOTT

PHOTO 37

PHOTO 38   TELEGRAPH UNITED FOOTBALL TEAM 1949 - 1950
Back Row C.H. BURTON T.J. COLEMAN D. FISHER D. PHILLIPS
P.B. WHITCOMBE L.J. TILLEY
Front J.A. RAYNOR T.J. BERRY R.W. BRATT K. BURDETT A. WALKER

TELEGRAPH UNITED CRICKET TEAM 1949
Back Row P.B. WHITCOMBE C.H. BURTON J. SWEETMAN K. BURDETT
T.J. COLEMAN Middle Row B.J. MONK D. FISHER G.J. LEWITT K.J. LOCK
Front D.W. NAYLOR L.J. TILLEY D.L. WARD

PHOTO 39

PHOTO 40 TELEGRAPH UNITED FOOTBALL TEAM 1950 - 1951
Back Row T.J. BERRY T.J. COLEMAN C.H. BURTON P.W. BREWIN
K. BURDETT P.B. WHITCOMBE
Front B.J. MONK D. PHILLIPS R.W. BRATT R.A. HILL W. KING

BRIAN (B. J.) MONK & RAY (R.W.) BRATT in 1950

PHOTO 41

Pictured below is
TONY (J.A.) STEPHENS
a messenger who received a book from the R.S.P.C.A. for rescuing a cat stuck at the top of a tree in Town Hall Square in 1951

PHOTO 42

PHOTO 43

In June 1950 the G.P.O. Introduced five green B.S.A. Bantam 125 c.c. Motorcycles in Leicester for telegram delivery.
PETER (P.D.) BEIGHTON is pictured above on one of the bikes.

PHOTO 44

Top Picture 1954
St Joseph's Church
Nev (N.A.) Goodman
delivering a telegram
to the Bride & Groom.

Picture on the right
Gordon (G) Blakesley
and
Roy (R.V.) Hackett
c1954 at the bottom of
Blackwells Court.

PHOTO 45

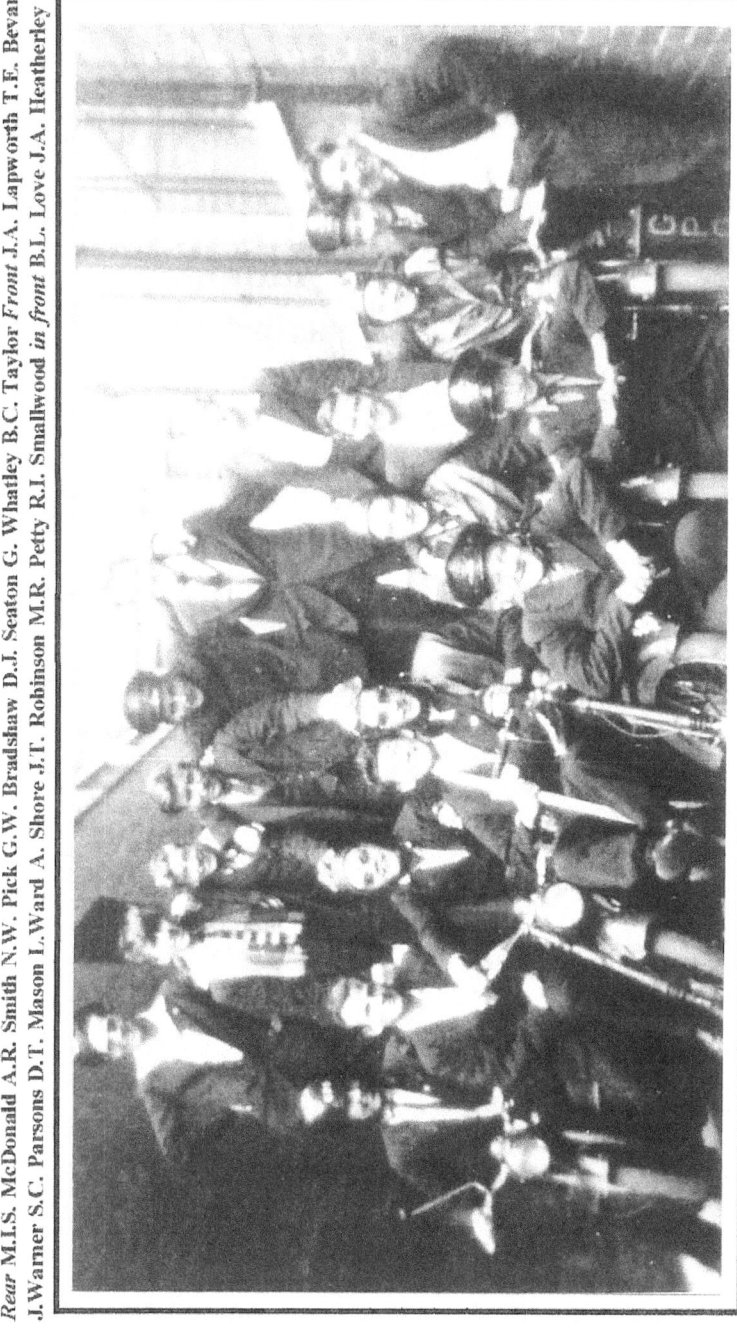

Rear M.I.S. McDonald A.R. Smith N.W. Pick G.W. Bradshaw D.J. Seaton G. Whatley B.C. Taylor *Front* J.A. Lapworth T.E. Bevan J. Warner S.C. Parsons D.T. Mason I. Ward A. Shore J.T. Robinson M.R. Petty R.I. Smallwood *in front* B.L. Love J.A. Heatherley

PHOTO 46

PHOTO 47 C 1957 J.A. HEATHERLEY T.E. BEVAN J. CABLE D.T. MASON N.W. PICK W. LIQUORISH

Bottom Picture C 1957 **HARRY JEFFREY (P.H.G.) and P.W. HUNT** watching **M.R. PETTY** on the motorcycle

PHOTO 48

SATURDAY AFTERNOON STUNT RIDING IN BLACKWELLS COURT C 1957
Standing up TREV (T.E.) BEVAN
Riding the Motorcycle 'BILL' (D.T.) MASON

Blackwells Court 1957 *Left to Right* Frank Seal Dave Lewin Mick Wood Bill Mason Bill Liquorish Trev Bevan Danny Desborough (P.H.G.) Dave Bent Joe Heatherley Jimmy Dean Mike Petty

PHOTO 50

Blackwells Court 1957 *Back Row* J. Cable J.A. Heatherley D.A.L. Lewin
Middle Row D.T. Mason T.E. Bevan
Front Row N.W. Pick M.R. Petty F.A.E. Seal *In Front* M.T. Wood D.J. Bent W. Liquorish

PHOTO 51

A Leicester Evening Mail picture of Frank (F.A.E.) Seal and Bill (W) Liquorish at the entrance to Blackwells Court 1958

PHOTO 52

ON THE LEFT
DAVID PHILIP
HENDY
P.H.G.
MESSENGER
1960 - 1963

PHOTO 53

ON THE RIGHT
FREDERICK
JOHN ANTLIFF
POSTMAN
MESSENGER
1961 - 1963

PHOTO 54

PHOTO 55

C 1961 - 1962

FROM LEFT TO RIGHT TELEGRAPH MESSENGERS P.R. PEGG R.K. CHAMBERS C.J. SIMPSON F.J. ANTLIFF R.F. BENTLEY AT THE REAR OF THE GROUP J.R. NORTON

ON THE RIGHT CHRISTOPHER JOHN SIMPSON POSTMAN MESSENGER 1961 - 1962

PHOTO 56

PHOTO 57

**ON THE LEFT
CHRISTOPHER
JOHN SIMPSON
POSTMAN
MESSENGER
1961 - 1962**

**ON THE RIGHT
ROGER NOEL
DILLEY
MESSENGER
1960 - 1962
POSTMAN
ROGER CYRIL
BROUGHTON
MESSENGER
1959 - 1962
P.E.D.
DAVID PHILIP
HENDY
MESSENGER
1960 - 1963 P.H.G.**

PHOTO 58

PHOTO 59   The Telegraph Instrument room on the first floor of the General Post Office at the corner of Granby Street and Bishop Street, in the late 1920's. Each operator had a key and a sounder contained in a hooded box to confine the sound.

The Telegraph Instrument room on the top floor of the General Post Office in Bishop Street, in the late 1940's.

PHOTO 60

PHOTO 61   The Post Master General Mr. E. Short talking with operatives in the Leicester telegraph department, 1967.
Left to right: Mrs. R. Walters, Mr. E. Short, Mr. J. H. Williams Assistant Head Postmaster, Mr. R. Harper, Mrs. T. Jesson.

A copy of a greetings telegram for weddings sent on 22/12/1956. Provided by the bride Mrs S.D. Kukk

PHOTO 62

PHOTO 63 1972 Reunion at Telephone House 66, London Road
Front row L to R:
Terry Coleman Brian Monk Alan Kilby Dennis Ward Ray Bratt
Back row L to R: Clive Burton, Fred Willis Alan Capewell
Stuart Kennell

1977 Reunion at Telephone House 66, London Road
Front row L to R:
Henry Hubbard John Allen Horace Seville Jack Hughes

PHOTO 64

PHOTO 65

1977 Reunion Telephone House 66, London Road
Front row L to R: S. Garratt J.W. Allen N.A. Goodman
R. Wright *Unknown* J.A. Raynor F.G. Benford
Back row: K.T. Hunt R.D. Bonner M.R. Petty F. Anstee
H. Hubbard R.W. Bratt S. Kennell A. Walker
A. Capewell A.R. Kilby J.C. Wilson R.W. Howard

1992 Reunion Campbell Street Sorting Office
Front row L to R: A.J. Martin J.B. Green C.H. Price
Back row: J.L. Fisher J.D. Murphy C.F. Greenwood H.W. Seville

PHOTO 66

www.ingramcontent.com/pod-product-compliance
Lightning Source LLC
Chambersburg PA
CBHW082014220426
43671CB00014B/2581